D1564918

AUGSBURG SERMONS

SERMONS ON
EPISTLE TEXTS FROM
THE NEW LECTIONARY
AND CALENDAR

AUGSBURG
SERMONS

EPISTLES
SERIES B

AUGSBURG PUBLISHING HOUSE
MINNEAPOLIS, MINNESOTA

AUGSBURG SERMONS—EPISTLES—SERIES B

Manufactured in the United States of America

Contents

Introduction

FIRST SUNDAY IN ADVENT
Isa. 63:16b-17; 64:1-8   Mark 13:33-37
Always?—1 Cor. 1:3-9   Timothy G. Johnson   15

SECOND SUNDAY IN ADVENT
Isa. 40:1-11   Mark 1:1-8
What Kind of People Should We Be?—
2 Peter 3:8-14   Merle G. Franke   19

THIRD SUNDAY IN ADVENT
Isa. 61:1-3, 10-11   John 1:6-8, 19-28
Doing What Doesn't Come Naturally—
1 Thess. 5:16-24   Paul W. F. Harms   24

FOURTH SUNDAY IN ADVENT
2 Sam. 7:(1-7) 8-11, 16   Luke 1:26-38
God Gets the Bottom Line—Rom. 16:25-27   Roy M. Hendrickson   28

THE NATIVITY OF OUR LORD—Christmas Day
Isa. 52:7-10   John 1:1-14
Christmas Beyond Christmas—Hebrews 1:1-9   Fred E. Ringham, Jr.   32

FIRST SUNDAY AFTER CHRISTMAS
Isa. 45:22-25   Luke 2:25-40
God's Chosen Ones—Col. 3:12-17   F. Dean Lueking   35

6

THE BAPTISM OF OUR LORD—First Sunday after the Epiphany
Isa. 42:1-7   Mark 1:4-11
For One; For All—Acts 10:34-38   Lilette E. Johnston   40

SECOND SUNDAY AFTER THE EPIPHANY
1 Sam. 3:1-10   John 1:43-51
A Christian View of the Body—1 Cor. 6:12-20   Robert W. Stackel   44

THIRD SUNDAY AFTER THE EPIPHANY
Jonah 3:1-5, 10   Mark 1:14-20
What in the World Do Those Words Mean?—
1 Cor. 7:29-31   Alfred Buls   49

FOURTH SUNDAY AFTER THE EPIPHANY
Deut. 18:15-20   Mark 1:21-28
Knowledge Governed by Love—1 Cor. 8:1-13   A. Joseph Everson   54

FIFTH SUNDAY AFTER THE EPIPHANY
Job 7:1-7   Mark 1:29-39
Bound to Be Free/Bound to Be Bound—
1 Cor. 9:16-23   Dennis A. Anderson   58

SIXTH SUNDAY AFTER THE EPIPHANY
2 Kings 5:1-14   Mark 1:40-45
Run for Your Life—1 Cor. 9:24-27   W. A. Poovey   61

SEVENTH SUNDAY AFTER THE EPIPHANY
Isa. 43:18-25   Mark 2:1-12
God's Overwhelming Yes—2 Cor. 1:18-22   Rod Kvamme   65

THE TRANSFIGURATION OF OUR LORD—Last Sunday after the Epiphany
2 Kings 2:1-12a   Mark 9:2-9
Unveiling the Truth—2 Cor. 3:12—4:2   Morris J. Niedenthal   68

FIRST SUNDAY IN LENT
Gen. 22:1-18   Mark 1:12-15
His Love Does It All—Rom. 8:31-39   Herbert E. Hohenstein   72

SECOND SUNDAY IN LENT
Gen. 28:10-17 (18-20)   Mark 8:31-38
The Cross Is the Gift God Gives His Friends—
Rom. 5:1-11   William R. White   75

THIRD SUNDAY IN LENT
Exod. 20:1-17   John 2:13-22
Our Surprising God—1 Cor. 1:22-25   Paul L. Harrington   79

FOURTH SUNDAY IN LENT
Num. 21:4-9   John 3:14-21
The Past and God's Presence in Your Future—
Eph. 2:4-10   Glenn Schoonover   84

FIFTH SUNDAY IN LENT
Jer. 31:31-34   John 12:20-33
Power to Endure—Heb. 5:7-9   Vernon R. Schreiber   88

SUNDAY OF THE PASSION—Palm Sunday
Zech. 9:9-10   Mark 15:1-39
Do We Weep or Do We Rejoice?—Phil. 2:5-11 Theodore J. Vinger   93

MAUNDY THURSDAY
Exod. 24:3-11   Mark 14:12-26
E Pluribus Unum—1 Cor. 10:16-17 (18-21)   LaVern K. Grosc   95

GOOD FRIDAY
Isa. 52:13—53:12   John 19:17-30
Our Great High Priest—Heb. 4:14—5:10   James G. Manz   99

THE RESURRECTION OF OUR LORD—Easter Day
Isa. 25:6-9   Mark 16:1-8
On a Clear Day You Can See Forever—
1 Cor. 15:19-28   Reuben D. Groehler   104

SECOND SUNDAY OF EASTER
Acts 3:13-15, 17-26   John 20:19-31
The Debt That's Never Paid—1 John 5:1-6   Harold C. Skillrud   111

THIRD SUNDAY OF EASTER
Acts 4:8-12   Luke 24:36-49
The Resurrection of Christ Makes Our Fellowship Possible—
1 John 1:1—2:2   Arne Kristo   116

FOURTH SUNDAY OF EASTER
Acts 4:23-33   John 10:11-18
Who Am I?—1 John 3:1-2   Homer Larsen   120

8

FIFTH SUNDAY OF EASTER
Acts 8:26-40   John 15:1-8
One Truth in a Supermarket of Ideas—
1 John 3:18-24   George W. Carlson 124

SIXTH SUNDAY OF EASTER
Acts 11:19-30   John 15:9-17
From Beware to Embrace—1 John 4:1-11   Victor L. Brandt 128

THE ASCENSION OF OUR LORD
Acts 1:1-11   Luke 24:44-53
Absence Makes the Faith Grow Stronger—
Eph. 1:16-23   Gustav Kopka, Jr. 132

SEVENTH SUNDAY OF EASTER
Acts 1:15-26   John 17:11b-19
Live in Love and God Lives in You—
1 John 4:13-21   Howard A. Lenhardt 137

THE DAY OF PENTECOST
Ezek. 37:1-14   John 7:37-39a
Pentecost Today—Acts 2:1-21   W. J. Fields 141

THE HOLY TRINITY—First Sunday after Pentecost
Deut. 6:4-9   John 3:1-17
A Living Trust in the Triune God—
2 Cor. 13:11-14   Gerhard L. Belgum 145

SECOND SUNDAY AFTER PENTECOST
Deut. 5:12-15   Mark 2:23-28
God's Pentecost People—2 Cor. 4:5-12   Reynold N. Johnson 149

THIRD SUNDAY AFTER PENTECOST
Gen. 3:9-15   Mark 3:20-35
What We Believe, We Speak!—2 Cor. 4:13-18 Robert G. Heckmann 154

FOURTH SUNDAY AFTER PENTECOST
Ezek. 17:22-24   Mark 4:26-34
What If I Die?—2 Cor. 5:1-10   Milton Ost 158

FIFTH SUNDAY AFTER PENTECOST
Job 38:1-11   Mark 4:35-41
What Is a Christian?—2 Cor. 5:14-21   Roland Martinson 163

SIXTH SUNDAY AFTER PENTECOST
Lam. 3:22-33   Mark 5:21-24a, 35-43
Blessed to Be a Blessing—2 Cor. 8:1-9, 13-14   William S. Waxenberg 167

SEVENTH SUNDAY AFTER PENTECOST
Ezek. 2:1-5   Mark 6:1-6
Overcoming Frustration—2 Cor. 12:7-10   Ralph L. Moellering 171

EIGHTH SUNDAY AFTER PENTECOST
Amos 7:10-15   Mark 6:7-13
A Gospel Panegyric—Eph. 1:3-14   Robert J. Brown 177

NINTH SUNDAY AFTER PENTECOST
Jer. 23:1-6   Mark 6:30-34
Jesus Christ, Hard Hat—Eph. 2:13-22   H. Dixon Slingerland 182

TENTH SUNDAY AFTER PENTECOST
Exod. 24:3-11   John 6:1-15
The Impossible Dream—Eph. 4:1-7, 11-16   Alton F. Wedel 185

ELEVENTH SUNDAY AFTER PENTECOST
Exod. 16:2-15   John 6:24-35
The New Life in Conduct—Eph. 4:17-24   Byron L. Schmid 190

TWELFTH SUNDAY AFTER PENTECOST
1 Kings 19:4-8   John 6:41-51
The Art in Christian Unity—Eph. 4:30—5:2   William E. Lesher 194

THIRTEENTH SUNDAY AFTER PENTECOST
Prov. 9:1-6   John 6:51-58
Buying Up Each Opportunity—Eph. 5:15-20   Lester E. Zeitler 199

FOURTEENTH SUNDAY AFTER PENTECOST
Josh. 24:1-2a   John 6:60-69
Do You Know That I Love You?—Eph. 5:21-31   Christine Miller 205

FIFTEENTH SUNDAY AFTER PENTECOST
Deut. 4:1-2, 6-8   Mark 7:1-8, 14-15, 21-23
The Futile Battle—Eph. 6:10-20   Hubert Beck 209

SIXTEENTH SUNDAY AFTER PENTECOST
Isa. 35:4-7a   Mark 7:31-37
James: Straight-Up Religion—
James 1:17-22 (23-25) 26-27   Jerry L. Schmalenberger 214

10

SEVENTEENTH SUNDAY AFTER PENTECOST
Isa. 50:4-10   Mark 8:27-35
God's Power and Light Company—
James 2:1-5, 8-10, 14-18   Erling C. Thompson 219

EIGHTEENTH SUNDAY AFTER PENTECOST
Jer. 11:18-20   Mark 9:30-37
The Difference True Wisdom Makes—James 3:16—4:6 David Kaiser 222

NINETEENTH SUNDAY AFTER PENTECOST
Num. 11:4-6, 10-16, 24-29   Mark 9:38-50
Jogging with Jesus—James 4:7-12 (13—5:6)   Gene H. Hermeier 227

TWENTIETH SUNDAY AFTER PENTECOST
Gen. 2:18-24   Mark 10:2-6
With Glory and Honor—Heb. 2:9-11 (12-18)   Robert L. Hock 231

TWENTY-FIRST SUNDAY AFTER PENTECOST
Amos 5:6-7, 10-15   Mark 10:17-27 (28-30)
It's Time to Build—Heb. 3:1-6   Omar Stuenkel 235

TWENTY-SECOND SUNDAY AFTER PENTECOST
Isa. 53:10-12   Mark 10:35-45
On Escaping God's Word—Heb. 4:9-16   John R. Thorstensen 239

TWENTY-THIRD SUNDAY AFTER PENTECOST
Jer. 31:7-9   Mark 10:46-52
Run for Your Life!—Heb. 5:1-10   James R. Stephenson 243

TWENTY-FOURTH SUNDAY AFTER PENTECOST
Deut. 6-1:9   Mark 12:28-34 (35-37)
It's Who You Know—Heb. 7:23-28   Roger J. Berg 246

CHRIST THE KING—Last Sunday after Pentecost
Dan. 7:13-14   John 18:33-37
Who Needs a King?—Rev. 1:4b-8   M. Franklin Pudas 249

DAY OF THANKSGIVING
Deut. 8:1-10   Luke 17:11-19
"Thank You, God" Is Not the End of a Conversation—
1 Tim. 2:1-4   Eldon Weisheit 253

Introduction

The Calendar and Lectionary introduced by the Inter-Lutheran Commission on Worship (ILCW) in Advent 1973 has become one of the most popular liturgical tools for contemporary worship and preaching. It is the answer to many requests in Lutheran churches for a revision of the church year and a new lectionary.

The church year calendar has been modified and modernized. The lectionary has been extensively overhauled by drawing on parallel efforts by the Protestant, Episcopal, Presbyterian, and Roman Catholic churches.

The New Church Year Calendar

This new calendar is similar to all previous calendars in that Easter is still the heart of it, and the Gospel still tells the story of Jesus Christ throughout the year.

The revisions in the new calendar are these:

- The *gesima* Sundays, sometimes known as pre-Lent, are now listed as Sundays after Epiphany. The season of Epiphany is therefore lengthened, which makes possible a fuller development of Epiphany themes.

- The Sundays between Easter and Pentecost will be known as the Sundays *of Easter,* rather than *after* Easter.

- The Latin titles for the Sundays of Lent and Easter have been deleted.

- Passion Sunday has been moved from the Fifth Sunday in Lent to the Sixth Sunday (Palm Sunday).

- The Sundays in the Pentecost-Trinity season have been numbered *after Pentecost* instead of *after Trinity.*

- In color terminology, *purple* replaces *violet,* and *red* is suggested for use during Holy Week.

The New Lectionary

The new lectionary presents a three-year cycle of lessons for the church year. The texts designated for the specific year will be chosen alternatively from Series A, Series B, or Series C of this lectionary.

This lectionary follows the traditional pattern of appointing an Old Testament Lesson, an Epistle, and a Gospel for each Sunday. During the Easter season, however, a reading from the Acts of the Apostles replaces the Old Testament Lesson.

The Epistles of Series A

The first three volumes of *Augsburg Sermons* based on the Gospels are now available. Series A is based on Matthew; Series B on Mark; and Series C on Luke. With the appearance of this book, three volumes of *Augsburg Sermons*, Epistles are also available.

Beginning in Advent of 1978, Series B will again provide the texts for worship and preaching. This time, however, the Epistles will be highlighted, and therefore the present volume is offered as a year-long resource for preaching and meditation on the Epistle texts for the next church year.

This book, like its predecessors, is offered in the hope that the sermons, the calendar, and the lectionary will contribute to the renewal of preaching.

ALWAYS?

First Sunday in Advent
1 Corinthians 1:3-9

Charlie Brown said it: "I love humanity, it's people I can't stand!" Charlie, like the rest of us, enjoys playing with words. We twist and turn meanings, or we use words that we don't really mean at all. Exaggerations are an example. "If I've told you once, I've told you a thousand times" (though not really). Or, a favorite of young people, "Everybody's doing it" (everybody?). There are two words that are often overused and misused: never, and always. "I'll never tell" (just give me time). "I'd never do that" (yet). "It can never happen to me." Or, on the other hand, "It's always the same" (though nothing is). "You always do it wrong." And, that favorite in churches, "We've always done it that way" (really?).

Never. Always. They are opposites, yet equally misused. Perhaps it is because we can't see the total picture, or don't try. Our own frames of reference are limited, and often our memories are poor.

What, then, of the statement made by Paul in today's text? "I give thanks to God *always* for you . . . ." Is that also an exaggeration? Is he too misusing that word? It can hardly be true! Think back to that statement by Charlie Brown: "I love humanity, it's people I can't stand." It is easy, or relatively so, to love humanity, the world. It is easy to love that faceless mass, that great, abstract grouping of people. After all, God says we are to love everybody, and so I will. I remember the answer a young freshman in college gave when asked why she was going into social work. "Why, because I just love everybody," she said. That kind of love is sometimes in evidence at Mission Festivals. "Those heathen need our love, that's why we send our money. It's nothing personal, you understand." But that is precisely where the rub comes. It *is* personal. It's either personal or it's nothing. And it is tough when "everybody" gets a face put on it. It is tough when the abstract becomes concrete. When "everybody" becomes those at your place of business, or those over the back fence, or those who sat with you in the pews this morning, then we, like Charlie Brown, have trouble loving everybody, especially those we know!

Paul says again, "I give thanks to God always for you." That can mean only one thing. Paul is thankful to God for the people to whom he is writing, *always!* How could he say that to the

good

Corinthians of his day? And how in the world can we say it to each other?

Apparently on his second missionary journey, Paul spent about eighteen months in the city of Corinth. His efforts at building a fellowship of believers had been relatively successful, with the congregation consisting of Jewish Christians from the synagogue, many poor people, and a few of the wealthy from the Gentiles of Corinth. But as soon as he left, things seemed to go downhill. Most of Paul's letters to the Corinthians deal with problems that had risen in the congregation. A particular one is mentioned in the pericope which immediately follows today's text. Factionalism, division, had reared its ugly head, splitting the congregation. Some members claimed superiority because of who had preached to them or who had baptized them. This is not so difficult to understand when we consider the diverse membership of the group at Corinth, both ethnically and economically. Nor does it seem so difficult when we look at the myriad of denominations, to say nothing of divisions within our own churches. But for Paul, who would write to the Galatians, "There is neither Jew nor Greek, there is neither slave nor free, there is neither male nor female; for you are all one in Christ Jesus," (3:28) it must have been tragedy. To have worked so hard, and then be so disappointed—but still he begins his letter to these people, "I give thanks to God *always* for you."

If our thankfulness is dependent on or determined by the current situation, if it is dependent on each action toward us, if it is dependent on the faithfulness of others, then certainly, we will not be able, always, to be thankful for one another. However, this thankfulness for each other is, strangely enough, not very dependent on how we act toward each other. (Though I must admit that some make it much more difficult than others.)

Paul's thankfulness to God for the Christians at Corinth and our thankfulness for each other had best be dependent on something or someone outside ourselves. And it is! We can begin our own letters of attitude toward each other with Paul's phrase, "I give thanks to God *always* for you," for at least three reasons.

God's Gift to You

It has not been so long ago that I cannot remember observing my grandfather on Christmas Eve. While everyone was tearing at paper, eagerly opening our presents, Grandpa sat with his small packages unopened, looking about with a small grin, seemingly grateful for what the rest of us were getting. (It was to

take too long in my own life before I enjoyed watching others
open their gifts more than opening my own.) Perhaps that is a
bit like Paul and the Corinthians. He was pleased to watch as
they discovered their gift from God. "I give thanks to God
always for you because of the grace of God which was given you
in Christ Jesus" (1 Cor. 1:4). The gift is grace. "Grace to you
and peace from God." Grace is, by definition, a gift. It can be
nothing else. Other gifts we receive can be earned, bought, stolen
—but not grace. What is it? Better, who is it? Jesus, the presence
with us which is undeserved, sometimes even unwanted. But the
gift seeks the recipient. God's gift is himself, his presence. But
there's more. "Grace to you and *peace.*" Those two do not always
go hand in hand. If we believe in God's presence, it can and should
be something of an unsettling experience. What then of peace.
Surely the meaning is deeper, more complex than the absence of
war, the temporary respite from hostilities.

I have heard and read that Lutherans are among the most
susceptible to those who would ring your doorbell or stop you
on the street, questioning your beliefs and giving you the real
goods. In most cases, one of the initial questions has to do with
whether or not you know you're saved. And oft times we stand
there stammering, shrugging our shoulders, and rummaging in
our pockets looking fruitlessly for an answer. That scenario is
the opposite of peace. The assurance that the gift is real comes
with the gift. If grace has been given to us, then peace should
be in us. In the Old Testament Lesson, the prophet asks that
tough question, "in our sins we have been for a long time, and
shall we be saved?" (Isa. 64:5). The question is not to be taken
lightly, but neither is the answer, "Grace and peace to you from
God."

God's Hope for You

As Paul is thankful to God for the Corinthians because of
God's gift to them, so he is always thankful for them because
of God's hope for them. So, too, I am thankful for you, we are
thankful for each other because of God's hope for us.

Now, wishing and hoping are not the same. I can drive to a
wishing well in my Toyota, throw in my pennies, and wish to
drive home in a Rolls Royce. But it's not going to happen. God's
hope for us is not like that. "Now faith is the assurance (sub-
stance) of things hoped for" (Heb. 11:1). God's hope for us is
that faith be brought to life in us. His hope for us is that we
too, like the crowds in today's gospel text (Mark 11:1-10), will
shout, "Blessed is he who comes in the name of the Lord." Unlike

our hopes for each other, which often are without the means of bringing about the reality hoped for, God provides that which is necessary to bring to fruition that which he hopes for us. As Luther puts it in his explanation of the Third Article, "I cannot by my own reason or strength believe in Jesus Christ, my Lord, or come to him. But the Holy Spirit has called me through the gospel, enlightened me with his gifts. . . ." God provides his spirit so that his hope for us, faith, can become reality.

Paul is always thankful, we can be always thankful that God's hope for us becomes realized when, "the testimony to Christ was [is] confirmed among you [us]—so that you are not lacking in any spiritual gift, as you *wait* for the revealing of our Lord Jesus Christ." God's hope for us is that, in faith, we have a worthwhile waiting. Waiting does not negate the time spent doing it! This time of waiting, and how we spend it is, in large measure, dependent on that for which we wait. And that, in traditional Christian language, is the "day of our Lord Jesus Christ," which is our third reason for being thankful to God for each other.

God's Goal for You

There are two promises in v. 8. We will be sustained to the end, and we will be "guiltless in the day of our Lord Jesus Christ." Christianity is not an individualistic religion, though it often is distorted in that direction by a culture which over-emphasizes and exalts the ego in all of us. But like Moses of old, we often need to be sustained by others. When Moses' arms grew weary, they were held up by two others. (This story is told in Exod. 17:8-13.) It's holding up that we need, and the family of God does this, sustaining us when we tire.

It is "to the end" that we are sustained. Thankful for that too? Even that, for we will be "guiltless in the day of our Lord Jesus Christ." That can make the end of our earthly existence more of a transition than a terror. As Jesus is God's gift to us now, so also he continues as our guide through the door of death and fulfills God's promise to be with us, even in the end. We may well wonder why there is any reason to believe that our end will be anything but a box of decayed flesh and old bones. "God is faithful," not because I say he is, but because of his gift to us, grace; his hope for us, faith; his goal for us, new life. It is this faithful God who has called us into fellowship with his Son, and by so doing, called us into fellowship with each other.

I suspect that even after all these words, perhaps because of them, you may not believe we can be thankful for each other.

Certainly our thankfulness for each other is not an "always" kind of thing.

In his novel, *The Fixer*, Bernard Malamud tells the story of a Jew living amidst the heated and irrational anti-Semitism of Czarist Russia. A young Russian boy is killed and the Jewish man is imprisoned on the barest of circumstantial evidence. He seems to be alone in the world till he is visited by the Russian public defender. During the visit, the Jew begins to sense that this man is truly concerned about the case. Realizing that his case is unpopular, and the Russian lawyer has nothing to gain by defending him, the Jew asks the lawyer the reason for his efforts. His answer: "If your life is without value, so is mine. If the law does not protect you, it will not, in the end, protect me. I dare not fail you, I must not fail you."

If God's gift is not for you, it is not for me. If God does not hope for you, he does not hope for me. If God will not be with you to and through the end, he will not be with me. But I have seen the gift in others, I know the hope, and the end is not so ominous. The grace and love of God has been given to you, and thus it has been given to me! And I am thankful, "thankful to God *always* for you because of the grace of God which was given you in Christ Jesus."

TIMOTHY G. JOHNSON
Zion Lutheran Church
Ashley, North Dakota

WHAT KIND OF PEOPLE SHOULD WE BE?
Second Sunday in Advent
2 Peter 3:8-14

What's the Difference?

One of the embarrassing aspects of the Christian church is that too frequently you can't tell the difference between members and nonmembers. The guy down at the office who is not a member of any church gets under the skin of true-blue church people when he says, "So what if you people go to church every Sunday? I stay home and relax or mow the lawn. What's the difference?" Unfortunately, he's too often right. Except that he's too generous with us—if he were one of us, he'd know that most Christians (and certainly most church members) don't worship every

Sunday. Were that the case, at least we could cite *that* as a modest difference between Christians and non-Christians. As it is, we are usually hard-pressed to show any difference at all. *Sometimes*

Oh, I expect you are already mentally cataloging a host of differences. We church members get quite defensive when it is implied that there's little or no difference between us and non-members. Heavens, we're wasting our money (well, not a whole lot of it) and time and effort on this whole thing if there's no detectable difference! But let's explore this for a few minutes. Just how certainly would people be able to detect the fact of your Christian faith or church membership—particularly if you didn't say anything about it? What would happen if people were expected to discern your Christian faith solely by studying your actions? Or by observing the kind of person you are? Now, bear with me a bit longer: suppose you spoke not a word about your belonging to the church or about being Christian. Would people be able to observe the fact of your Christian faith if you said nothing about it? Maybe the guy at the office was right—"What's the difference?"

Too Many Ought-to's?

The Apostle Peter must have done some serious thinking about the difference that should show up between Christians and non-Christians in his day. Perhaps it would have been safer for those early Christians *not* to demonstrate much difference—because it wasn't really safe to be Christians; but they plunged ahead anyway. In today's Epistle we find Peter speaking to his fellow believers about that event called by him the Day of the Lord. Apparently, as most Christians believed then, that day was coming very soon. The point Peter was trying to make, however, was this: In view of all that is soon going to happen, what kind of people should we be? That gets to the bottom line real fast, doesn't it? He's saying, "Look, folks, the most important encounter you'll ever face is about to happen; and in view of that, we had better decide what kind of people we're going to be. We ought to be able to tell the difference between those of us who are and those who aren't."

I find this to be a delightful passage on the subject of the difference between Christians and non-Christians. In its own way it is abrupt and to the point—much like Peter himself. For when all is said and done, and all our theological tapestries have been woven, and all our energies on proving we're right and someone else is wrong—somewhere there's a bottom line. And that bottom line must describe what I must *do*, what I must *be*, if I lay claim to this thing called the Christian faith, or if I claim to be a disciple of Jesus.

No doubt you are aware of the fact that it can be counter-productive to be harping constantly on the kind of people we ought to be. We get far too many ought-to's thrown at us as it is, from the time we are little tots until we are grown adults. So by the time we reach adulthood, we are more than slightly turned off by any attempts people make to build models for our life-style. ("It's for your own good," they say.) "I'm sick and tired of hearing what I *ought to do*" is a complaint—probably justifiably made—by vast numbers of people. And many of these are church people who are made to feel that way by preachers who delight in haranguing people and telling them how rotten they are. I can't estimate how many people suffer through interminable sermons in which preachers scold them for not being what the preachers think those poor folks ought to be. How parishioners put up with it is beyond me.

Having said that, my sermon title and what I am getting into—may sound like just one more of what I've described. So let me offer this early disclaimer: my intention is not to scold, harangue, or otherwise abuse the listening ear or the eager heart—should there be those who expect something uplifting and positive from this sermon. I do not see Peter's words as a put-down. Rather he speaks within the context of the culmination of all things—and he speaks with an eager enthusiasm about it all. He speaks with the joy of knowing that God is in control. He is in control of creation and preservation—he is the Lord of time and history and events—of past, present and future. Then he sums up the relationship of those facts to our individual lives by asserting that in view of all of this, we had better be thinking what sort of people we should be.

I can't see Peter's words as being a scolding or haranguing of us. Remember that he is speaking from the viewpoint that the end of all things is imminent—but that we don't have the time-table. Since we don't know when all of this will take place, he says, doesn't it make sense to be the kind of people we should be? Then we'll have no cause to worry about the final day of the Lord. God is in control, Peter says, and God will control the finality of all things. God will ring down the final curtain; therefore, since we don't know much about this, what kind of people should we be?

Peter Is Too Idealistic

In a way, it's a curious question. Why should we be different from anyone else? Peter might not have been popular in America, because here we're supposed to be pretty much the same—although we aren't. But, you know, as long as we pay our bills and keep our kids off the streets, what's the big deal about being church members or Christians (they're not always synonymous)? Well, one reason is—I would assume—that *because* Christian people are aware of some important information about God and us, our lives ought to reflect that awareness. What *is* that information we are privy to? Peter spells it out—he says that there is some information you should not lose sight of. We have already mentioned some of it: God is in control of his creation—make no mistake about that! But more than that, God is faithful to his promises and to his plans; though *we* may not be faithful to *our* promises, God is faithful, and that is a fact about God that is critically important for us to remember. Furthermore, Peter reminds us, God is patient with us—a fact for which we ought to be continually thankful.

Peter's chief point is a summary, then, of some of these things we know about God. He seems to be saying, "Since this is true about God—that is, he is in control, he will fulfill his promises, he is patient with us, and one of these days he will ring down the curtain on the whole thing—isn't it our responsibility to decide on the kind of people we should be?" Or, what difference should there *be* between us and all those who don't know these things about God? Or who don't care?

And Peter supplies answers. He says (1) "Your lives should be holy and dedicated to God" (2 Peter 3:11b. . . . Good News), and (2) "As you wait for that day do your best to be pure and faultless in God's sight" (v. 3:14b). Well, hold on a minute! Such high and mighty "answers" are simply impossible of attainment. And I'm not convinced that the average church member really desires to fit the description of those two answers anyway! So there we go again, apparently right back in the old business of holding up expectations and standards that do little but frustrate people. The average person reading these lines from Peter's epistle (if the reader is really honest) will react with feelings something like, "I don't even know what it means to be holy and dedicated to God, much less accomplishing it!" So the person again feels guilty about not being able to reach the preacher's expectations (this time Peter being the preacher). And surely if the reader can't handle the first of those two suggestions, well, forget the second. I don't think I *know* anyone who is waiting for that glorious day by being pure and faultless in the sight of God.

A Classic Tension Point

So that brings us to a classic tension point of the Christian life: expectations versus performance. Are the expectations too high and unrealistic for us to attain? If so, what happens as a result of our failure to live up to them? Nice try? Is that all we get? What kind of people should we be? Different. But how? Holy and dedicated to God? Pure and faultless in God's sight? Perhaps so. Since we are always trying to bargain things downward so we can get everything as cheaply as possible, let's keep the expectations for Christians high—even unattainably high! Since we take such delight in hard negotiations, always looking for a discount, for once let's accept something as presented to us. Peter gives us something to aim for; alright, let's take aim on those targets without trying to lower them to a more comfortable position. No discount this time, folks.

By the way, there are many other scriptural standards that are equally high: Jesus saying "Be perfect as your father in heaven is perfect," and Paul saying that we should be imitators of Christ. And many more. We'd have to do a lot of deleting if we were to expunge all the scriptural passages that set high standards for us. So when Peter gives us those two guideposts about being holy and dedicated, and pure and faultless, he's really addressing our tendency to seek the minimum requirement. He's saying, "Here are some things that will make you different from the non-Christian." Try those on the guy down at the office! But chances are he won't understand what holy and dedicated mean any more than most Christians do.

The trouble with the guy down at the office—and most people who want to see some measurable difference between Christians and non-Christians—is that the difference is difficult, if not impossible, to measure. The kind of people we should be cannot be described in terms other than very nebulous qualities. For instance, if the Christian is supposed to be holy and dedicated, that is difficult to prove to a skeptic. That is basically an inner quality, an understanding of the fact that God has chosen us to be his people; that's one definition of holiness: the state of being chosen. When we understand and appropriate that chosenness, that's an important aspect of the kind of people we should be.

So the kind of people we should be—the difference—will probably have to be demonstrated in the way we live.

MERLE G. FRANKE
First English Lutheran Church
Austin, Texas

DOING WHAT DOESN'T COME NATURALLY
Third Sunday in Advent
1 Thessalonians 5:16-24

Rejoice always!
Pray constantly!
Give thanks under all circumstances!
That's a big order any time, an even bigger order at the end of time. Rejoice always, even in 1978? Pray constantly, no interruptions? Give thanks always, always without exception? That's what the language says. That's also what the language means.

No qualifications. "When things get to be peaceful." "When I'm in good health." "When everything is going well in the family." Further, thanking, rejoicing, and praying is our response as we wait for the coming of the Lord. When tensions increase—when times are doubtful—when one has all one can do to keep his life in order—then pray always, rejoice always, give thanks always.

"Isn't that a bit much?"

Seeing What We Said (and Say)

But, this is not the first time we have heard these words. In fact, each time we have received the body and blood of Christ we hear, "It is truly meet, right, and salutary, that we should at all times and in all places give thanks." To that we have said Amen a thousand times.

If over the years we have not regarded these words as an exaggeration, we must believe the cause for rejoicing, for praying, for giving thanks lies somewhere other than in the circumstances. If circumstances were to dictate, we should be right, more than once in not rejoicing, not praying, not giving thanks. But these three actions are rooted in the very will of God in Christ Jesus.

Christ urges us to rejoice. There is never a time when we are not in his presence. If he is always present, then it would be strange if we were not encouraged to rejoice—always. And this rejoicing is a shared, communal activity. Rejoicing alone is difficult.

So it is with praying constantly. We pray because we are certain of him who has asked us to pray constantly. Prayer may be a turning inward, but it is also a turning outward . . . as in the general prayer, "Most heartily we beseech thee so to rule and govern thy Church Universal . . . send laborers into thy harvest . . . grant also health and prosperity to all that are in authority . . . may it please thee also to turn the hearts of our enemies and adversaries that they may cease their enmity . . . all who are in trouble . . . comfort with thy Holy Spirit . . . out of thine unspeakable goodness, grace and mercy defend us from all harm and danger . . . protect us from hail and tempest, failure of harvest . . . cause all needful fruits of the earth to prosper . . . these and whatsoever other things thou wouldst have us ask of thee, O God. . . ."

Prayer is a reaching out to the whole world for the sake of the whole world, for the sake of him who is the center of the world, Jesus Christ our Lord.

So it is with thanking under all circumstances. Is there a time and a place where Christ is absent from us? Whether that be war or peace, success or failure, fame or notoriety? If the answer is no, then give thanks under all circumstances. Since thanks is rooted in Christ rather than circumstances, we should at all times and in all places give thanks. Only a sometime god gets sometime thanks.

All three actions: prayer, rejoicing, giving thanks are reflective of the center, a center of incredible power. All three actions are outgoing, self-giving, reflective of God himself who invites and encourages. All three are the very will of God in Christ Jesus. At first they seem demands, impositions. In fact, they are impositions about as much as a steak is an imposition on a hungry person.

Doing What We Are

The constant prayer, the constant rejoicing, the constant thanksgiving are not so much something we do as it is expressive of a relationship with God, the father of our Lord Jesus Christ. The accent does not lie with us, but on him who requests that we pray, rejoice, give thanks. Our response is like the response of Another. When he was nearing his end, and Advent reminds us that the end will come, he said, "What shall I say, 'Father, save me from this hour?' It was for this cause that I came to this hour." The circumstance was the crucifixion. The rejoicing continued. The prayer continued. The thanksgiving continued. If Christ had looked to the end rather than to his father, his last moments could well have been despair.

The end of things could produce fear, overwhelming self-concern, bitterness, skepticism, cynicism, a keen sense of loss, and a wondering whether it has all been worthwhile. All understandable, all natural, all expected, normal reactions.

Because these responses are common, God urges the uncommon: prayer, rejoicing, thanksgiving.

The common view sees the end as the end, finished, *kaput*. The uncommon sees beyond the end. It recognizes the master of the end of all things as the same Master of the beginning and the middle. This is the Omega God as well as the Alpha God.

If God is indeed the God of the Omega, why then should not the end be lived out in his presence as much as the Alpha? We, therefore, rejoice because he is always present. We pray constantly because he is constantly present. We give thanks under all circumstances because he prayed for all sorts and conditions of men under all sorts and conditions.

Using What We Have

If prayer, rejoicing, and thanksgiving are the order of the day who would want to suppress, stifle, extinguish or grieve the spirit, the source of the power? The spirit is the spirit of Christ, Christ's spirit, the Lord and giver of life, who energizes our rejoicing, praying, thanksgiving.

Praying, rejoicing, thanksgiving may be rare commodities because they tap their energy source irregularly. The energy for praying, thanksgiving, and rejoicing is the Christ. "The spirit of the Lord God is upon me, because the Lord has anointed me to bring good tidings to the afflicted; he has sent me to bind up the broken-hearted, to proclaim liberty to the captive, and the opening of the prison to those who are bound; to proclaim the year of the Lord's favor." That is the food behind our praying, rejoicing, thanksgiving.

The energy is Baptism which made us one with him in his life, his suffering, his crucifixion, his death, and his resurrection. So magnificent is this energy source that John the Baptist can describe Christ as one whose shoe's latchet I am not worthy to unloose.

The energy behind the praying, the rejoicing, the thanksgiving is that of the body and blood of our Lord in the Holy Supper. Words fail us when we try to describe the power that is in the gift that he gives us. It is himself. Not something that he made, but he himself is the gift in this meal, prepared especially for us, for the likes of us, that is to say, sinners.

Can we begin to see more clearly that the only possibility is to pray constantly, rejoice constantly, to give thanks under all circumstances? For no circumstance is untouched by his presence.

With the energy supplied by Christ's spirit, by his presence with us in Baptism and in the Holy Supper, we can be supremely alive. We listen carefully. We examine with great and searching care. We test the spirits. We test the messages that come our way. We examine them scrupulously. We scrutinize them for their genuineness.

No cowering before the dire things to come. We are alert because we know who is coming. The one who is coming is the one who has come, who is to come, who is with us right now. No need to fear such a one! He is welcomed, therefore the alertness. We do not want to miss anything.

Responding to the One Who Responds

If we are to meet him as he wants to be met . . . blameless in body, soul, and spirit, that will indeed call for the continued attention of the God of peace himself, the God of our Lord Jesus Christ. And God continues to attend to us. "Through the resurrection he establishes the death of Christ as the sacrifice of the eternal covenant which he makes with men and which enables the doing of his will" (Alan Richardson).

That's the kind of God who directs and energizes us for these last days and through these last days. He is the one who calls. He will do it. He is faithful. He is trustworthy. The one who calls us maintains us.

Rejoicing always, praying constantly, giving thanks under all circumstances which seemed so impossible, now very clearly is the only way.

PAUL W. F. HARMS
Evangelical Lutheran Theological Seminary
Columbus, Ohio

GOD GETS THE BOTTOM LINE

Fourth Sunday in Advent
Romans 16:25-27

That's the way it has to be if we are really focused on the grace of Jesus Christ. Look at it this way. Grab your checkbook and think what it is that catches your attention? Isn't it the bottom line, your bank balance? Or listen in on a corporate meeting. Woven through the fabric of a high-level executive discussion, as people review, report, and plan, is an underlying concern, "how will it all come out on the bottom line?"

Haven't you experienced the urge to flip the pages of a form letter to see the signature at the end, and then make a response or throw it out, depending on the bottom line? In some way or another, we get caught up in the bottom line in life. It seems to me that this is where the Apostle Paul (and I hold the position that he did write the end of Romans) latched on to a vital part of the Christian faith. It is like saying, "some folks will give that credit line to Ceasar, some to the gods of the Pantheon, some to the latest guru on the streets of Rome, and some to an unknown god over in Athens," but hear me out, "to the only wise God be glory for evermore through Jesus Christ! Amen." I like that. I like that ringing clarity of conviction in a day when many are claiming the bottom credit line in religion. I like it on this Advent Sunday as a mighty testimony to the Lord of all history who holds the future in his hand.

Who will be the latest guru "out there" this Christmas Eve when we pause to celebrate the birth of Jesus Christ in all the Christian churches of the world. Someone will lay claim to a piece of the action and promise a bit of light or reward or success if people will just buy in. That kind of thing is not new. It has been on the religious scene since day one. Man has a way of seeking the bottom line. Oh! Just a piece of glory, just a tiny piece for what I have done to tidy up my part of the turf. And, say, didn't you know that a bit of navelgazing can ease the anxieties of this time of year and give you a running start on the next one? Five easy lessons for $250.00 will do it. Sure, the world has its religion of self, and the flesh, and the "Old Adam," if you are inclined to call it by the name Luther used.

Into the Stuff of Religion

The great doxology of Romans sixteen leaps beyond the dark maneuverings of man and bootstrap religion or flights of the mind. Listen to the gutsy revelation that God gave Paul, and the apostles, and the church, and you hear it like this. "Paul, a servant of Jesus Christ, called to be an apostle, set apart for the gospel of God which he promised beforehand through his prophets in the holy scriptures, the gospel concerning his Son, who was descended from David according to the flesh and designated Son of God in power according to the Spirit of holiness by his resurrection from the dead, Jesus Christ our Lord, through whom we have received grace and apostleship to bring about the obedience of faith for the sake of his name among all the nations, including yourselves who are called to belong to Jesus Christ" (Romans 1:1-6). From that towering testimony to Jesus Christ and the all-embracing purpose of sharing his gospel with all the nations, to the last syllables of Romans, we are privileged to feel the pulse-beat of the gospel that Paul proclaimed. It is no wonder that in this doxology we can encounter a word that beat upon the heart of "God's man" with a persistent beat, for this gospel had set Paul free. So free in the newness of resurrection life, so free in the power of forgiveness, so free in the blood of Christ spilled at the cross, that he glorified in the power of that Name, Jesus. That's why Paul gave God the bottom credit line.

Good News This Christmas

Paul wrestled with the issues of religion, life, the law, sin, faith, righteousness, his own Hebrew background, commitment and life-style, in the book of Romans. Peruse the pages of that letter and you are caught up in the message of grace. I cannot number the times I have been stirred with the spirit of rejoicing as I read the words, "while we were yet helpless, while we were yet sinners, while we were enemies, we were reconciled to God by the death of his Son." The memory of the words learned at a very early age came flooding back, "without any merit or worthiness in me." "I believe that I cannot by my own reason or strength believe in Jesus Christ my Lord or come to him, but the Holy Spirit has called me through the gospel." It is that good news which throbs in the heart of the "mystery kept secret for long ages but is now disclosed."

On Christmas Eve, we have a rather new tradition at the twilight service. At one point in the celebration of song and word, we have a children's time under and around the huge tree. There it stands, in a special beauty of Chrismons and lights, and life-like green. The children come by the dozens to sit with me on the floor and listen to a little story just for them. We look at the symbols, we smile, and laugh, and talk about gifts. Surprise, surprise, I have a big box, all wrapped in colorful paper and they guess what is inside. As I carefully unwrap it, I ask them how big a gift must be to be a really good gift. In a chorus of answers, I only learn that they are eager kids waiting to see what is inside. Last year I gave them each a bookmark with a candy cane, shaped like the letter J, stapled to the back. The face of the bookmark said, "God is love." Before I gave this rather tiny gift to each child, I said, "part of me is in this gift, because this morning I wrote what I feel inside for each of you." That little message was, "I love you—Pastor Roy." That is my gospel, Paul's gospel, the church's gospel, and God's gospel of good news disclosed in Jesus Christ. God got into man's skin, the word became flesh, the mystery was disclosed, and the nations of the world have been given the light, and love, and life that transforms darkness into light.

Isn't that what Paul is saying in this doxology? "According to the command of the eternal God," that news is to be preached to all nations, including us. That is the good news held forth in the world that is very much crunched under the bad stuff. Look into the eyes of busy people on busy streets and check-out counters. Look into the eyes of one suffering the loss of a loved one without hope. See the dull and vacant stares of those who are hungry and lonely and lost. See what humans do to humans that hurt and spoil the gift of life. Now listen to Paul in Romans 10:1, "Brethren, my heart's desire and prayer to God for them is that they may be saved." Paul burned with love and compassion for people. He had been launched by the power of the indwelling Spirit of God into an orbit of selfless sharing of good news that reached from high steeples to the muddy ruts of life. It is no wonder that he and all who believe the gospel are charged with the desire to reach out and minister. But, they do it with the knowledge that the bottom line belongs to God. "To the only wise God be glory for evermore through Jesus Christ!"

Strength to Press On

The word declares an assurance all of us need in the journey of life. "Now to him who is able to strengthen you—." Honestly, I get tired sometimes. Tired of deadlines, tired of demands, tired of answering questions, tired of being pushed into a role that God didn't fling on me in the mantle of my call. God, let me out, give me space, let the stars shine in, give me the breath of newness. And he does. Gently he reminds me of the gospel, the love, the sacrifice for uptight me, the freshness of morning dew, and winter snow, and the water of life in his name. My gospel? Paul's gospel? Your gospel? Yes, God's gospel in Jesus that keeps on coming with the persistence of the watchman on the wall, a lover at the door, a searcher in the night. He keeps on coming and that is strength.

Do you recognize his grace when it comes to you? There it is, a little gem from the verse in a program, when you were five, "God so loved the world." There it is, that summer you were struggling over the relationship with the new boyfriend and the pastor had quoted in a sermon, "I have loved you with an everlasting love." There it is, "Come to me all who labor." And you recall how it melted your fears that night John was mangled in that accident. There it is coming to you and me again in many ways. I will share just one personal experience with you.

To the Only Wise God Be Glory

I stood there, seven years old, a short little runt trying to be big and say goodbye as I peered over the metal foot board of an old bed. Lying there was a very old man, a cripple, whom my folks had cared for. We were moving, so he must move, but not with us because there was no way to care for him. I can't forget that scene because it was the last time I saw the one who had often hobbled across the rooms in our house. How does a seven-year-old say goodbye to an old crippled man who could never play but simply be. I don't know what I whispered that day, but old Chris gave me a blessing and a doxology in such a spirit of godliness that in the years later when I kicked over the traces, and did my own thing, the God of all glory never let it slip away. He lifted his tired, pale, grey head and said, "Roy, if God calls you to the ministry, say yes—goodbye." I slipped away, but not from a memory, for there it is. When can I say but, "to the only wise God be glory for evermore through Jesus Christ." God gets the bottom line and that's what really counts when all is said and done.

How About You?

Has the tug of his Holy Spirit been a part of that gentle reminder of God's love for you? Has that love you know is there moved you in a way that says, I believe! Has the moment come on a Christmas Eve to remember and to confess his name as the only wise God and Savior in your life. You see, dear friend, the doxology of faith springs from the heart that lives by faith in the Lord Jesus Christ. The hope and prayer I have for you is that the final word in your life is that "God gets the bottom line" as Lord and Savior. To him be glory forever. Amen.

ROY M. HENDRICKSON
Trinity Lutheran Church
Albert Lea, Minnesota

CHRISTMAS BEYOND CHRISTMAS

The Nativity of Our Lord—Christmas Day
Hebrews 1:1-9

We are all familiar with the Christmas story as it appears in St. Luke's Gospel. We repeat it every year on Christmas Eve—about the decree from Caesar Augustus and about Joseph and Mary and the manger cradle and the Christ child and the shepherds and the angels. Not only is the story the same each year, but so is the way we celebrate it: with carols and Christmas trees and gifts, with the church all decorated and with candlelight. It's all so familiar that the whole meaning of Christmas has been tied to the holiday itself, and we all become heirs of the fourteenth century writer: "At Christmas, play and make good cheer; for Christmas comes but once a year." Afterwards we go back into real life like Cinderella at midnight returning to her grubby kitchen. Yet, if the story has meaning, then it's for all the year. Perhaps our problem is that we have not gone sufficiently beyond the mere recounting of events. The writer of Hebrews gives us an interpretation of the events that finds its meaning beyond Christmas.

He Is Fulfillment

The account begins: "In many and various ways God spoke of old to our fathers by the prophets; but in these last days he has spoken to us by a Son." Christmas is not a solitary isolated event that we celebrate in a vacuum. It has its background in the history of God's people, Israel. God has spoken before in many and various ways in order that his purpose would not be thwarted by our indifferent hearing. He had spoken through the deliverance of his people from Egypt, through drought and disease, through harsh rulers and cruel invaders, and through the prophets who saw God clearly at work in history. But now God's chosen Word, his ultimate Word, is spoken not in the thunderous tones of a prophet's voice, but, "There came a night," in the words of

Paul Scherer, "in Bethlehem when God walked down the stairs of heaven with a baby in his arms."

Certainly there are other people and other ways through which God has spoken; but the Word in all its fullness is in Jesus Christ. That closes doors we would rather leave open, and confronts us with a choice we'd rather not have to make. When we avoid making that choice, however, the half-gods, the demi-gods, take over the causes we serve with passionate loyalty—the sects and the semi-faiths that dot our religious landscape. Even for those of us mature enough to be immune to the siren song of the Reverend Sun Myung Moon or the Maharaj Ji or Hare Krishna, there are still those other gods of success and prosperity and a growing GNP and the utter secularity of our daily lives. But these demi-gods, however enlightened, cannot deal with the deep questions that face us at the crisis points in life: the reality of sin and suffering, the force of guilt, the mystery of death. He alone is the Word, the Gospel, the fulfillment of the prophets' words.

He Is Heir and Redeemer

One of our bulletin covers several years ago pictured the beauty and joy of the manger scene, but the shadow cast by the barn rafters over the Holy Family formed the shape of a cross. The words from this passage in Hebrews which first suggest the shadow don't sound dark or ominous at all: ". . . a Son, whom he appointed heir of all things. . . ." Those sound like bright words. We can almost hear echoed the Hallelujah Chorus: "King of kings and Lord of lords, and he shall reign forever and ever. . . ."

"Heir of all things." Then all things really belong to him. He is the heir of the wealth of the earth, of its wisdom and learning, of all the achievements of struggling people, of all the glory of the nations of the earth. But heir of all things also means heir to the shame and defeat, to the pain and bitterness, to the abuse and cruelty, to the ignorance and degradation, to the terrors of war and the dread of famine, to the ache of broken lives and the darkness of hate. This is the dark insight of the Gospel: that he who is to reign must bear our sorrows, be wounded for our transgressions, that he must be heir to all the suffering, too.

A new song of Christmas sings of that sadness. It begins by celebrating a stable lamp whose glow wakes the very sky, and stars bend their voices. But by the third verse the song is no longer celebrative. It begins "Yet he shall be forsaken, And yielded up to die."

His suffering is not the kind that so many of us find ourselves experiencing—seemingly meaningless and void of purpose. Hebrews insists that the meaning of his suffering as well as the meaning of his role as Messiah is to make purification for our sins, to be our redeemer; that all this was for us, to free us from the guilt and separation from God that overwhelms us. And that makes the darkness that marks the future of this infant bright with hope.

Through Him—Creation and Glory

Not only is he woven into the tapestry of life as heir, but also, ". . . through him he created the world." At the very beginning something was put into the nature of the world that called for Christ. He was not an after-thought in the mind of God, but was built into the foundation of the structure of all things, and the whole creation groans in agony awaiting his coming. Only in him and through him and for him does the world find its meaning fulfilled.

In the Gospel for today, St. John writes, "In the beginning was the Word, and the Word was with God, and the Word was God." In him God has entered into our world, into the very core of life, and this means that we can affirm life and find it good even in the midst of suffering and sorrow—because he is there.

"He reflects the glory of God and bears the very stamp of his nature." That glory is to be found in the faces of his people redeemed and free, in every patient waiting, in every heroic sacrifice, in every grace-filled home. Because he entered into our world in creation and in the birth of Jesus, "the earth is a theater of the glory," in the vivid words of Joseph Sittler, "It is rich with the ineffable glory because God the Holy One has made it."

Christmas Makes a Difference

Christmas makes a difference, then, far beyond Christmas. It celebrates the birth of him who changes our understanding of all of life, for God speaks his word through him as a Son in the setting of the history of his people, Israel, and also in the setting of all creation, of which he's heir. Heir of all that is good and gracious and beautiful; but also, for us he has taken on himself the hatred and the loneliness, the blasted hopes, and the empty dreams, and he sets us free! So we celebrate as his glory fills the earth and makes it his kingdom glad and good, and we catch glimpses of that glory in the faces of one another on this glad Christmas Day.

In his play, *Our Town*, Thornton Wilder has his central figure,

Emily, realize the joy and fullness and glory of life and of the earth only after she has died. She is given a chance to go back and relive one day of her life but she can't endure it—the joy and glory of life—and so returns to her place in the cemetery. Emily shouts to the stage manager:

> "I can't. I can't go on. It goes so fast. We don't have time to look at one another."
> *She breaks down sobbing—then:*
> "I didn't realize. So all that was going on and we never noticed. Take me back—up the hill—to my grave. But first: wait! One more look. "Good by, Good by world. Good by Grover's Corners. . . Mama and Papa. Good by to clocks ticking . . . and Mama's sunflowers. And food and coffee. And new-ironed dresses and hot baths . . . and sleeping and waking up. Oh, earth, you're too wonderful for anybody to realize you."
> *She looks toward the stage manager and asks abruptly through her tears:*
> "Do any human beings realize life while they live it?—Every, every minute?"
> *The stage manager answers:*
> "No." *Pause.* "The saints and poets, maybe—they do some."

Do *we* realize the glory and the wonder? Do we look at one another and see it? Let this Christmas, filled with the glory and wonder of God's Word in Christ, be the time to realize and to celebrate!

FRED E. RINGHAM, JR.
St. Michael's Lutheran Church
Roseville, Minnesota

GOD'S CHOSEN ONES
First Sunday after Christmas
Colossians 3:12-17

Virtues We Choose

On this Sunday after Christmas, with many college students home for the holidays, it is natural to think with them about their future. What does lie ahead for them, and what will it take for them to find their way as active Christians in an increasingly complex and challenging world. No doubt the common American answers to such a question would go something like this:

> Daring,
>> Imagination,
>>> Drive,
>>>> Determination,
>>>>> Shrewdness,
>>>>>> Ambition

Surely any sales manager, high school principal, or drill sergeant will nod his head in approval of this list. And I nod mine too; they're all good traits. But I want you to recognize that any one of them can be turned into a curse instead of a virtue; all of them lend themselves unusually well to selfishness. In and of themselves, these "manly virtues" are neutral; they need something to guide and fulfill them with a much deeper meaning. The point is worth careful thought if we are going to be in any position to fully appreciate the text for this sermon.

The Virtues God Chooses

The text, you see, has another list of virtues. It's a description of characteristics which are utterly foreign to us by nature; hence quite challenging for us to put great stock in. The list is not a prescription for beating the world. It's intended rather to heal the world. Listen with care:

> Compassion,
>> Kindness,
>>> Lowliness,
>>>> Meekness,
>>>>> Patience,
>>>>>> Forbearing,
>>>>>>> Forgiving

Although these are not virtues that we would choose, they are the ones which God chooses. They describe God's chosen ones, and there lies the theme of this message: God's Chosen Ones.

St. Paul does not congratulate God's chosen ones in Colossae for being selected. That is not my message to you, either. To the chosen ones in this place, as in Colossae of old, goes out this summons to—

> Put on, as God's chosen ones, holy and beloved, compassion, kindness, lowliness, meekness, and patience, forbearing one another, and, if one has a complaint against another, forgiving each other; as the Lord has forgiven you, so you must also forgive.

It is difficult to stop at this point with the text, but the entire epistle through verse 21 of chapter 3 is too rich and meaningful in content to confine within the space of one sermon. So let's digest well the splendid nourishment just two verses provide.

Notable Christians Are Noticeable Christians

First, may we understand that God's plan for life calls for anything but a dull and passive routine. On the surface it might not appear that compassion, kindness, lowliness, meekness, patience, forbearing, and forgiving one another add up to contagious joy of Christian living. But look at these virtues one by one, and see them at work in some notable Christians of the last decade who are very noticeable Christians!

Compassion. A chilling article which appeared in the *Atlantic* magazine entitled "Eichmann and the Private Conscience" mentions among those who testified at Jerusalem the name of Pastor Grueber. This brave old man, a German Christian, helped the Jews openly during the Hitler time and paid for his compassion by imprisonment in Dachau. As great multitudes of his fellow Lutherans did nothing, risked nothing, while trainloads of Jews were led to the camps and to ghastly mass extermination, this man of compassion risked his life by pleading for them to the deaf ears of the embassies of the world and by smuggling out the pitiful few to Sweden and Norway. Is compassion in Pastor Grueber, who returned to shepherd his flock in East Germany, a weak and passive thing? Is it comprised of daring courage and dauntless conviction? It is. Compassion for the human brother, regardless of who he is, is a sign of God's chosen ones at work.

Kindness. There comes to mind a Christian man who has experienced enough hardship in life to dry up the milk of human kindness. He has had to manage his own family without his mate; but instead of clutching to his heart a paralyzing spirit of bitterness, his heart has been opened through adversity to a greater outflow of kindness. He has stretched his resources out across the seas to cover the physical needs of an orphaned child in a distant land. Is such a mark of kindness futile? Is it only the symptom of a soft-hearted individual? I can't help contrasting his kindness for the cause of children with another human being whose answer to a question about supporting a child without parents was a tart "What! Me support somebody else's imbecile?" Is kindness reserved only for those who feel like it or have time for it? Kindness is not so limited; it is a sign of God's chosen ones at work.

Lowliness. It doesn't mean groveling like a worm before God and man. It means marching steadfastly to the lowest corner of human need. The late Kagawa of Japan was a notable example.

A half century ago he took his bride and moved to the most wretched slums of Kobe and Osaka, living in a neat and clean one room house made out of abandoned signboards and newspapers. But he became the rag-picker's brother and all of his enormous, creative genius never turned his head. In the early days of his ministry, whenever the Emperor appeared in a crowd no one was allowed to sit or stand in a place where they might look down on him, the august ruler of the land. But Toyohiko Kagawa, who now sleeps in God, never worried whether there were people higher up than he. His life was an inspiring tale of remarkable sturdiness and drive in serving the lowly. His lowliness was a sign of God's chosen ones at work.

Meekness. Unfortunately, our English word "meekness" calls to mind the Mr. Milquetoast image, a certain spinelessness and failure of nerve. The real biblical meaning of the word, however, has nothing to do with that. It connotes, rather, the absence of arrogance and preening self-will. Do you recognize the name, Albert Luthuli? He made his home in South Africa where he labored tirelessly among the disinherited and disheartened of the Capetown slums. Across the town, in the antiseptically segregated governmental palace lived Prime Minister Verwoerd, the man who stands for the avowed principle that God intended blacks to live the life of servitude. Our Lord himself said that the meek shall inherit the earth. Some years ago the Nobel Peace Prize came not to Verwoerd, but to Albert Luthuli. The determined meekness of Luthuli is a sign of God's chosen ones at work.

Patience. In my rounds among the sick and shut-in I visit a home in which the man of the house has been laid low by a paralytic stroke for several years now. It must require great patience to regain the use of some of the limbs of the body by laborious practice and exercise. But an even greater example of patience is the man's spouse, who has stood by her loved one in time of sickness as well as in health. It requires no small shrewdness and deliberate planning on her part to keep herself spiritually strong and filled with good cheer to help her partner's mind and spirit as well as his body. Patience, in the biblical meaning, signifies more than just bearing with a trying situation. It means actively serving throughout the long stages of waiting until God's hour of fulfillment comes at last. Patience is a sign of God's chosen ones at work.

Forbearing. The word means "putting up with difficult situations or people," and one of the grand examples of forbearance that I know of is a Christian nurse I see when making pastoral calls at a nearby hospital. I know that she is working each day with people who are sick, and therefore who are not at their best emotionally as well as physically. I have no idea of the number of complaints she hears, some tragically legitimate ones and other petty, unnecessary ones. There is no counting the experiences of heartache and woe she witnesses on any day in her work. Yet I can never recall seeing her with a downcast face. Her smile is radiant and her step is light. She possesses the quality of bearing up with people who are having their difficulties, and helping them.

Forgiving. This is the key to all the virtues of God's chosen ones, for it is directly linked with that "love which binds everything together in perfect harmony." One of the great demonstrations of forgiving others as we have been forgiven is a woman in Ecuador. You may recall that some years ago a quintet of young missionaries was ambushed and murdered by hostile Indians of the Auca tribe. This woman's husband was one of those whose heart stopped beating because a poisoned-tipped spear pierced it. Mrs. Nate Saint continued to live and work among those who killed her husband because her life had been grasped by a power that nothing in this world can defeat. In sharp contrast to this daughter of God is another woman who has experienced no sudden loss of her husband at the hands of savage Indians. This woman's child was reprimanded in school by a teacher, perhaps tactlessly and thoughtlessly. The mother's reaction was to arrange a series of anonymous, threatening phone calls designed to undermine the morale of the teacher. This was followed by a long telegram promising a campaign to depose the teacher, and this in turn was followed by sending to the school via a taxi driver an elaborately wrapped coffee can filled with excrement. With which person does the hope of the world lie? It is with people such as Mrs. Saint in Ecuador, for the forgiving spirit is the sign of God's chosen ones at work.

Jesus Christ Is God's Power for New Living

Is it just by natural endowment that some people are the saints of God and others not? What makes it possible for men and women to possess the qualities listed by Paul in these verses? It is Jesus Christ who brings to life that power of God which transforms people. St. Paul speaks of how this is possible in the opening chapter of Colossians. In speaking of God's Son he uses these magnificent phrases:

"He is the image of the invisible God, the first-born of all creation; . . . He is before all things, and in him all things hold together. He is the head of the body, the church; he is the beginning, the first-born from the dead, that in everything he might be pre-eminent.... And you, who once were estranged and hostile in mind, doing evil deeds, he has now reconciled in his body of flesh by his death, in order to present you holy and blameless and irreproachable before him, provided that you continue in the faith, stable and steadfast, not shifting from the hope of the gospel which you heard...." (Colossians 1: 15-23)

God makes it possible to live the life of compassion, kindness, patience, forbearing, and forgiving as we have been forgiven by our Lord through his work for us at the cross.

God Shall Always Have His Chosen Ones

Our times are filled with nervousness, for the center has gone out of the lives of so many. Nevertheless, we may gain an unshakable sturdiness from this truth that God is not nervous or unsure about his purposes in the world. He shall ever have his chosen ones scattered here and there throughout the family of man, people who put first things first and take their lives just a day at a time. As you go about the happy task of applying compassion, kindness, lowliness, meekness, patient forbearing, and forgiving as you have been forgiven by our Lord, remember his words which summarize so beautifully the thoughts of this sermon:

"You did not choose me, but I chose you and appointed you that you should go and bear fruit, and that your fruit should abide" (John 15:16).

F. Dean Lueking
Grace Lutheran Church
River Forest, Illinois

FOR ONE; FOR ALL

The Baptism of Our Lord—First Sunday after the Epiphany
Acts 10:34-38

Peter's words in our Second Lesson for today are nestled in the midst of one of the greatest conversion stories of the early Christian church. Peter is speaking about a man named Cornelius, a man whom we seldom read or hear about today. Who then is this man, Cornelius? What makes his conversion story so unique, so special?

The tenth chapter of Acts provides us with the only account of Cornelius that we have in the New Testament. This is the account that Luke gives.

The Story

In the Roman army regiment at Caesarea there was a captain named Cornelius. He was a religious man and his whole family worshiped God. He also did much to help the poor Jewish people in the area. And he always seemed to be praying to God.

About three o'clock one afternoon he had a vision. An angel of God appeared and said to him, "God is pleased with your prayers and works of charity, and is ready to answer you." The angel went on to tell Cornelius to send some men to Joppa and have them bring back a man named Simon Peter. They would find him visiting at the home of Simon the leatherworker who lives by the sea.

When the angel had gone away, Cornelius sent for three of his men—two house servants and one of his soldiers. This third man was one of his personal attendants and was also a religious man. He told them about his vision and sent them off to Joppa.

Meanwhile, about noon one day, Peter went up to the roof of the house to pray. There he too had a vision. He saw heaven opened up and something that looked like a big sheet being lowered to the earth by its four corners. In this sheet were all kinds of animals, reptiles, and wild birds. A voice said to Peter, "Get up, Peter; kill and eat!" But Peter said, "Certainly not, Lord! I have never eaten anything ritually unclean or defiled." With this remark, the voice again spoke to him. "Do not consider anything unclean that God has declared clean." This happened three times and then the vision left.

While Peter was trying to figure out the meaning of all of this, the three men sent by Cornelius arrived at Simon's gate. They asked if Peter was there. About this time the Spirit told Peter that there were three men looking for him downstairs and he shouldn't hesitate to go with them. So Peter came down, talked to them for awhile, and invited them in to stay the night.

The next morning they got up and departed with some of the Joppa believers going along with them. By the following day, they arrived at the home of Cornelius. Just as Peter was about to go in, Cornelius met him and fell and bowed down before him at his feet. But Peter made him get up for he too was only a man. He went into the house and said to Cornelius and those who were gathered there, "You yourselves know very well that a Jew is not allowed by his religion to visit or associate with Gentiles. But God has shown me that I must not consider any person ritually unclean or defiled."

Peter asked why he had been sent for and Cornelius told him about his vision.

A Unique Conversion

Thus we have the story of Cornelius and Peter—two devout men, one a Gentile and one a Christian Jew. Herein lies the uniqueness and importance of this conversion. For many Jews before this time had been converted to Christianity, but now with Cornelius comes the news of the first Gentile convert to Christianity. If you listened closely to the story you will remember that Cornelius was a religious man for he and his whole family worshiped God. He was not a proselyte though. For he had neither been circumcised nor chosen to obey the strict Jewish laws. But nonetheless, he did much to help the poor and he prayed constantly to God.

And we have Peter, one of the twelve apostles, who had served and followed Jesus and knew him best. After Jesus' death and resurrection he taught, preached, and healed in Jesus' name and even spent time in jail for the sake of the Gospel. It is he who was chosen by God to come to Cornelius with the good news of Jesus Christ. Now Simon Peter had been brought up since childhood under the Jewish law. When Peter saw the vision of all the animals, reptiles, and birds and when he heard the voice saying "Get up, Peter, kill and eat," his only response could be, "Certainly not, Lord! I have never eaten anything ritually unclean or defiled." And when the voice went on to say, "Do not consider anything unclean that God has declared clean," he could not help but be perplexed. What could God mean? This went against everything he had been taught since he was a young boy. But there must be a message for him here for the voice came not once, not twice, but three times.

Now besides the fact that the Jews were not to eat unclean meat, they also believed that they must not have as a guest or ever be the guest of a man who did not strictly observe the law. Here Peter is invited to be the guest of Cornelius a non-law-observing Gentile. Would he only stop outside Cornelius' house and talk to him, or would he go in? The thought must have been on Cornelius' mind as he waited Peter's arrival. But Peter did not hesitate. He went right on in. This had Cornelius a bit perplexed. So Peter said to him, "You yourselves know very well

that a Jew is not allowed by his religion to visit or associate
with Gentiles. But God has shown me that I must not consider
any person ritually unclean or defiled. And so when you sent for
me, I came without any objection."

Peter Speaks the Good News

"I now realize," says Peter, "that it is true that God treats
everyone on the same basis. Whoever fears him and does what
is right is acceptable to him, no matter what race he belongs to."

Only perhaps a few days earlier these words would have been
impossible for Peter to speak. For he had always kept the Jewish
laws and practiced that which he had learned from childhood.
But God had now opened Peter's eyes and his ears. The words
and the deeds that Jesus had spoken and done now came alive for
him. For Peter remembered how Jesus was concerned about and
had compassion for *all* people. It did not matter whether they
were young or old, rich or poor, slave or free, male or female,
good or bad. He cared for them all. He loved them all. He wanted
everyone to follow him, to have faith in him. He showed no partiality. For all people have been created by God.

Peter had now seen the light. It was not adherence to the works
of the law which made one acceptable to God, but faith in the
One who had suffered, died, and risen that all might have forgiveness of sins through the power of his name.

Faith

Faith; this was all that was needed for the conversion of
Cornelius. No works or deeds or any merits of his own, but faith.
The dawning of this for Peter paved the way for Paul's mission-
ary journeys to the Gentiles and for the proclaiming of the Good
News of Jesus Christ for *all* peoples. And so the conversion of
Cornelius to the Christian faith was a great turning point for
the early Christian church.

We too like Cornelius are called to faith. We are to believe and
trust in Christ's promises and we are to share those promises
with others. Jesus told his disciples that they were to go so far
as to the ends of the earth sharing his Word and his love. They
were to love the Lord their God with all their heart, mind, soul,
and strength, and their neighbor as themselves. Christ had shown
no partiality. He treated everyone on the same basis. He even
loved the unlovable. We too are called to love the Lord our God
with all our heart, mind, soul, and strength, and our neighbor
as ourself. We too are to show no partiality. We too are to treat
everyone on the same basis. We too are to love the unlovable. For

genuine faith is action. May we never forget that Christ calls us to reach out to those around us *whoever* they may be. For it always seems easy to love the lovable, but it is not so easy to love those that are hard to love and hard to accept. Is it not true that we by nature tend to shun or forget about that which is different or less than perfect in our society?

What about the sick and dying? What about the old? What about those in prison and institutions? What about the handicapped? What about those whose skin color is different from that of ours? Are we always only loving the lovable and forgetting about or shuning the unlovable? Are we showing partiality or are we treating everyone on the same basis? Jesus was a friend to the sick and dying; to the young as well as the old. He visited the widows and those in prison, and he healed the lame, the deaf, and the blind. It is to this same loving, caring, and sharing that he calls us as his children. For we are to remember that God has created each and every human being and that he wants *all* people to come to the knowledge of Christ Jesus. We are to reach out to *all* those around us. For as Christ has loved us, so let us love one another.

LILETTE E. JOHNSTON
Our Savior's Lutheran Church
Oconomowoc, Wisconsin

A CHRISTIAN VIEW OF THE BODY

Second Sunday after the Epiphany
1 Corinthians 6:12-20

Every person has a body. This much we all have in common. In other things we may be very different. Some are rich, some poor. Some are famous, some unknown. Some are well educated, others poorly. But we are all alike in this one thing. We all have a body. We all have only one body. We can never have another body on earth. We have just one body to nurture, to groom and to use.

Yet there is much confusion today about the body, and society cannot seem to resolve a contradiction. On the one hand, bodies are receiving more loving care than ever before. Billions upon billions of dollars are spent on cosmetics, clothes, medical care, health clubs, and vacations. Sometimes it seems that society almost worships the body. On the other hand, bodies have rarely been regarded so cheaply and callously. Murders, rapes, wife beating, child battering and torture make up so much of the content of our daily papers. On the same day $30,000 is spent to fly a child from Africa to the United States for a series of special treatments on a costly new machine to save its life while two thugs murder a cab driver in cold blood to get $4.17 Urgently needed is a theological understanding of the body.

Back in the first century in ancient Corinth there was the same confusion about the body. The Greeks had a low regard for the body. It was such a distant second in value to the spirit that almost anything a person did with his or her body didn't much matter. Consequently Corinth had a worldwide reputation as a cesspool of sexual promiscuity and perversion. Some of this looseness even invaded the Christian church. So Paul shared with them his understanding of the Christian view of the body.

"I am allowed to do anything," some Christians in Corinth were saying. They based their boast on Paul's evangelical principle that, whereas sin had made us slaves, Christ had set us free by his cross. They had turned liberty into license and even claimed the blessing of Christ on it. To those who crowed, "I am allowed to do anything," Paul responded by insisting, "Yes; but not everything is good for you." Freedom is not the only principle. It must be modified by considerations of what is good for the person and for society. Besides, Paul added, "I am not going to let anything make me its slave." The Corinthians were just trading off one form of slavery for another. In receiving a Freedom Foundation award at Stanford University, Aleksandr Solzhenitsyn coined a new definition of freedom. "Freedoms as conceived by our forefathers," he said, meant "voluntary self-restraint and full consciousness of responsibility."

Others in Corinth were claiming, "Food is for the stomach, and the stomach for food." In other words, God created appetites in the body so what's wrong with satisfying them? Hunger and sex are both physical appetites. Give them free reign. A recent suggestive film was based on the announced principle, "Nothing is wrong if it feels good." On that principle Jesus would have turned stones into bread in his wilderness temptation. He would have called down fire from heaven on the Samaritan village that refused to receive him and his disciples overnight. He would have come down from the cross. Apparently he considered all these things wrong, for he rejected them, even though they would have made him feel good. Paul replied, stomach and food, "Yes; but God will put an end to both." In other words, Christians exalt values which will survive physical death. Then Paul established four fundamental truths underlying a Christian view of the body.

46

Involved in the Resurrection

First, *the Christian's body participates in the resurrection.*
Paul wrote, "God raised the Lord from death, and he will also
raise us by his power." Paul said this in the passage dealing with
the body. To the church in Philippi Paul wrote about God's power
in the resurrection, saying, "He will change our weak mortal
bodies and make them like his own glorious body." Churchmen
used to argue centuries ago about how the particles of matter
that make up our earthly bodies could be brought together again
after a thousand years in the grave to form the resurrection body.
Tertullian, one of the early church fathers, claimed that all believers would be raised with the bodies they had at forty years
of age and that children who died would have the bodies they
would have had if they had lived till forty. But Paul stresses that
the resurrection body will not be a regrouping of the matter in
the earthly body. Instead it will be a changed, transformed, glorified body, and yet it will bear some relationship to the earthly
body. A diamond is a transformed piece of coal. Coal is common,
lowly, brittle. A diamond is dazzling, radiant, strong. God can
change coal into a diamond. If our earthly body is like a piece of
coal, our resurrection body will be like a diamond, but both bear a
relationship to each other.

If a Christian's body participates in the resurrection in that
sense, then it bears a relationship to something that is eternal.
On that score alone it is highly important to keep the body from
immorality and impurity. To pollute it with dope or corrupt it
with sexual promiscuity or damage it with excessive alcoholic
drinking is not in keeping with the body's lofty role. Actually the
human body is one of the most awesome wonders of God's creative powers. It deserves the highest respect and loving care. It
is a holy thing in the sense that God created it. Because, in the
case of a believer, it will participate in the resurrection in a
glorified form, it should be kept pure and inviolate on earth with
the help of the Holy Spirit.

Part of the Body of Christ

Paul's second truth is that *the Christian's body is part of the
body of Christ.* Here is the way he puts it to the Corinthians,
"You know that your bodies are parts of the body of Christ."
Phillips' translation is even more forceful. "Have you realized
the almost incredible fact that your bodies are integral parts of
Christ himself?" Now Paul drives his point home. "Shall I take a
part of Christ's body," he asks, "and make it part of the body of a

prostitute? Impossible!" Some members of the Corinthian congregation were catering to prostitutes. In Corinth there were temple prostitutes for the worship of a pagan divinity. The worshiper would lie with such a prostitute as part of an act of worship in the temple. Christians were being influenced by this practice. Immorality was invading the congregation.

Sexual promiscuity is rampant today. The percentage of illegitimate births among all births in the United States has been increasing since 1952, according to the National Center for Health Statistics. In 1975 a record of 14.2 percent of all births were illegitimate. This increase has occurred among teenagers and adult women of practically all ages, with particularly large increases for women 20 through 29. Illegitimate white births increased the most in 1975. In the same year legal abortions in the United States increased 12 percent over the previous year, one-third of them among teenagers. In Nassau County, Long Island, one out of every three pregnancies was terminated by abortion in that year. A physician has come out with a recommendation for teen paramarriages. He claims that, if teenagers were allowed to live together legally for two years with no long-term commitment, there would be fewer illegitimate children, abortions and less veneral disease. No wonder that Susan Sontag, a writer and film maker, protests despairingly, "This civilization, already so far overtaken by barbarism, is at an end, and nothing we can do will put it back together again."

Paul fought back with a great principle. Life is essentially relational. Sexual intercourse is not an isolated act. It deeply relates two persons. But the Christian is already related to Christ as a part of his body, the church. It is unthinkable for a believer to be a part of Christ's body and at the same time a part of a prostitute's body. It is one or the other. As an integral part of Christ's body, a believer can only participate in such things as would be appropriate for Christ to do. Here is one of the most powerful motivations toward a Christlike life.

Temple of the Holy Spirit

The third truth in Paul's view of the body is that *the Christian's body is the temple of the Holy Spirit*. "Don't you know," he writes to Corinth, "that your body is the temple of the Holy Spirit, who lives in you and who was given to you by God?" The temple of Aphrodite in Corinth, the goddess of love, with prostitutes as priestesses, is sharply contrasted here with the Christian's body as the temple of the Holy Spirit. Not only does the

Spirit making his home in the believer's body elevate immeasurably the worth of the body, but it is also a powerful inner motivation toward a holy life. In addition, the Christian will treat with greatest respect and consideration the bodies of other believers because the Holy Spirit has made his home in them, too.

How strikingly different is the low regard for body and life held by many today! A criminologist told a House of Representatives sub-committee that, according to a recent survey, "about half of the American people will be afraid to walk home alone tonight for fear that they will not make it alive. My parents," he added, "left New York and 22 grandchildren they dearly love to go to live in Florida because they were scared to go out even during the day." New research by the National Institute of Mental Health supports the estimate that seven and a half million couples a year go through a "violent episode" in which one of the pair tries to cause the other physical pain or injury. Wives assaulted their husbands as frequently as husbands their wives, and mothers were more likely than fathers to strike their children. Another statistic: more Americans were murdered during the first four years of this decade than were killed during the entire Vietnam war.

Jesus once referred to his body as a temple. "Tear down this temple," he said to his opponents, "and in three days I will build it again." He was foretelling his death and resurrection. When the body is understood as the temple of the Holy Spirit, it will be treated with supreme reverence and loving care.

Three truths have been presented by Paul in his view of the body. The Christian's body participates in the resurrection. It is part of the body of Christ. It is the temple of the Holy Spirit. But the fourth truth is the most towering of all. *The Christian's body is owned by God.* A Christian doesn't even own his own body. "You do not belong to yourselves but to God," Paul insists; "he bought you with a price." A Christian can't do as he pleases with his body. He doesn't own it. God does. A Christian is using borrowed equipment in using his body for any purpose. God holds title. The price God paid is incalculable. His only Son suffered torture and death on a cross and then came back to life again so that we might henceforth belong to God.

John MacArthur, who is reputed to have been a billionaire, when asked about the size of his personal fortune, gives his usual answer: "Anybody who knows what he's worth isn't worth very much." Certainly a Christian does not know what he is worth, body and soul, because the price God paid runs higher than any calculator could compute. The New Testament letter to the Hebrews declares, "We are all purified from sin by the offering that he made of his own body once and for all." Our worth to God is hinted at in the words of Christ used in the Lord's Supper, "This is my body given for you."

The sixth chapter of 1 Corinthians contains the clearest, most exalted Christian understanding of the human body that can be found in the Bible outside of the teachings of Christ himself. Its conclusion is smashing, but simple. "So use your bodies," Paul wraps it up, "for God's glory." No lesser role will do. Something that is so significant as to participate in the resurrection, something that is part of the body of Christ, something that is the temple of the Holy Spirit and is owned by God—your body—has a holy role on earth and a stake in eternity. Think twice about what you have your body do. God holds title. The cross is his receipt. "So use your bodies for God's glory."

ROBERT W. STACKEL, Director
Love Compels Action/World Hunger Appeal
LCA—New York

WHAT IN THE WORLD DO THOSE WORDS MEAN?

Third Sunday after the Epiphany
1 Corinthians 7:29-31

These weeks after Christmas are the time to be spent with the *epiphanies*. This is the time to be retooled for our tasks—kingdom tasks. Just in case you missed it and even if you didn't, I want to call attention to the Collect for today. We asked for the *anointing of the Spirit* so that we might be about the same work as the Son, *proclaiming the kingdom.* We are God's people—now! We do not need to feel uncertain about the grace of God that enfolds us. All of this doesn't mean that we have overcome the resistance to the common Christian task of "bringing good news to the afflicted, binding up the broken-hearted, and proclaiming liberty to the captive, in the name of Christ." We read about Jonah and easily convince ourselves that we would be neither as foolish nor as disobedient as the prophet. We read the words to the Corinthians and if we aren't careful take them to mean that withdrawing from responsibility in the world is part of the commission to people living in "these last days."

But wait a moment! Interesting games can be played with words, even the words of the Scripture. Interesting games are played with words when it suits what seems to be our best interests. But we are not playing games with God's word. It is for this reason that we ask and ask again: What do those words mean? and what *in the world* do those words mean?

Then the word of the Lord came to Jonah the second time, saying, "Arise, go to Nineveh, that great city, and proclaim to it the message that I tell you." So Jonah arose and went to Nineveh, according to the word of the Lord (Jonah 3:1-3). The word that God spoke the second time was almost exactly the same as that of the first encounter. Did Jonah deliberately plan to disobey God when he ran from that first call? Hardly! He played games with the words from God and he convinced himself that his travel plan should take him in the opposite direction. We, apparently, have no problem understanding what it was that God intended and wanted Jonah to do. God would not have to speak to us a second time. He certainly wouldn't have to go to all the trouble of rearranging a big fish's schedule to turn us in the right direction. We don't know how Jonah would have answered if we could have asked, "What in the world do those words mean?" but let's try it out on ourselves as we're confronted with the kingdom.

We Are Attached to the World

Jonah had his own agenda when he received God's message and we have our own as well. I'm suggesting to you that the agenda with which you approach words, even the words of Scripture, has an effect on the way you receive them. What in the world do those words mean? "From now on, let those who have wives live as though they had none, and those who mourn as though they were not mourning . . . for the form of this world is passing away" (1 Cor. 7:29-31). We find it convenient to detach kingdom values from life in the world. It's not at all unthinkable that the words of this epistle would serve as encouragement to us when we want to shrink our responsibility "out there in the world" toward our marriage, our work, our day by day living. This is the subtle and devastating spiritual and secular division. The point here is that we do have problems because we are so attached to the things of this world. We place such finality in them. Marriage, mourning, rejoicing, buying, general events of life are important considerations. We experience too much irresponsible living in these areas and know what chaos it brings about. So what *in the world* do those words mean? Jesus came into Galilee, preaching the gospel of God and saying, "The time is fulfilled, and the kingdom of God is at hand; repent, and believe in the gospel" (Mark 1:14-15).

The more we look to ourselves, the more we maneuver our lives to find some solid footing, some permanent foundation. "In the world" marriage, mourning, rejoicing, buying and selling, are important matters. They are not permanent. They do not have the eternal value for which we look. The very fact that it could seem harsh for us to speak of marriage in this way, "let those who have wives live as though they had none," indicates the need to hear and to see the reality of the call of the Gospel. There are plenty of examples of people who imagined that they knew when the end time was coming and consequently made light of and even abandoned the responsibilities of the day. Just as challenging is the temptation to attach such value to these everyday responsibilities that the foundation of life is built upon them.

Jonah experienced this attachment to the things of this world. It gave him his understanding of what should happen to the Ninevites. It gave rise to his anger over the dying plant that shaded him. He also learned how futile all of this is over against the gracious direction of God. The permanent things of the world seem less so from the inside of a great fish.

The disciples had their own struggles with what they considered to be permanent. Even though some of the disciples left their families and their nets at the call of the Master there is indication that they struggled with that commitment later on.

What in the world do those words mean? They help us in the necessary action of repentance. St. Paul didn't exhaust the list of things that should be considered "as though they were not." When our Lord prepared the disciples shortly before his death he said, "I have given them thy word; and the world has hated them because they are not of the world, even as I am not of the world. I do not pray that thou shouldst take them out of the world, but that thou shouldst keep them from the evil one" (John 17:14-15).

"In the world, but not of the world." Are certain experiences of my life so rooted that they determine the whole course of my life? It might well be my marriage. As much as the ties of marriage need to be strengthened, and these words do not discourage this, the relationship or the value that we place upon it can get in the way of our understanding of the permanent values of the kingdom. It might be our work. It might be a whole host of things that are so much a part of our living and so vital to our living. What in the world do those words mean? You can feel the tension that develops once you begin to wrestle with them. This kind of tension is an important part of the growing Christian life. "Lord, do I place too much permanence in the things about me; the things that are to my liking or part of my expectation. I just

52

can't tell the difference at times between faithful commitment and false maneuvering. I bring this to you. Give me both forgiveness and guidance."

Unsettled by God

We are most likely to ask, "What in the world do those words mean?" if they unsettle us. And they should unsettle us. Epiphany is an ideal time to remember that when the light of God shines into the darkness of our world, it is unsettling. These words from St. Paul weren't the last that the Corinthian Christians needed. They didn't hear these words with unanimous agreement either. They had an unsettling effect. When God spoke to Jonah he rose to flee. The whole matter wasn't to his liking. The people of Nineveh were about as popular with him as Washington Redskins are with St. Louis Cardinals. In this case it was unsettling and Jonah ran away. This unsettling however, serves its purpose. We can live with it because we can trust the One who unsettles us. To lay bare our reliance on things, our desire to detach life from confession or from our desire to twist the words of God to suit our fancy, must be unsettling.

It is at the same time the beginning of renewal. St. Paul was not suggesting that the Corinthians become some strange group that lived drastically unusual lives in marriage or the other events of life. He was pointing to the centrality of the kingdom, the centrality of Jesus Christ. God is squeezed to the outskirts of life by a whole host of experiences and values. He wants to be back in the center with his grace and his care. Jonah pushed God into the fringes because he didn't want the Ninevites to share the kingdom, and God in his mercy overcame that foolishness. God shows himself to us in the ministry of Jesus Christ, the certain foundation in the middle of everything else. He unsettles us but yet confirms us in the joy of the forgiveness of sins. He knows our fears over the uncertainty of the world; our need to make our marriages, our business transactions and all of the other preoccupations something solid upon which to build our lives. He will not allow it, but he doesn't destroy us in our weakness. In his unsettling, God opens new possibilities for us so that the words do begin to have meaning and to have meaning in the world.

How easy it would be to use the words of the epistle as a rigid directive against one another. How easy it would be to make these words the basis for some kind of cold, moral structure. They are the encouragement of the kingdom and the promise that our God gives us the foundation upon which to stand. There is no need to play games with the words or to fear them or to turn away from them. This is the day of the kingdom of God and we are a part of it. In death and in resurrection God returns to the center of life . . . to the center of our world. We are invited to share in the excitement.

Commissioned by Christ

We have direction from all of the lessons for life "in the world." Jonah was called and ran away. Jonah was disciplined and recalled and he went and accomplished the mission even though reluctantly. The disciples were called by Christ and with startling moves left everything and followed him. "And passing along by the Sea of Galilee, he saw Simon and Andrew the brother of Simon casting a net in the sea; for they were fishermen. And Jesus said to them, "Follow me and I will make you become fishers of men." And immediately they left their nets and followed him" (Mark 1:16-17). And it was the same with James and John.

The call of the Lord comes in different ways to different people. There is something within us that wonders whether the reaction of the disciples was realistic. They left immediately and followed Jesus. Does this mean that I have to interrupt my life, leave my wife or husband, completely change my routine in order to be a part of the kingdom movement? It could be, but it is not necessarily so. This diversity is part of the excitement of the kingdom. Our calling may be that of changing from one way of life to another. Our calling may be, and probably is for most of us, right where we find ourselves. What in the world do those words mean? They can open some exciting possibilities as under the power of Christ we bring good news to the afflicted, bind up the broken-hearted, and proclaim liberty to the captive. It is "in the world" right where we are that these things open up. There are of course people like Simon and Andrew, James and John who make this drastic break with their past and take up their following of Christ in dramatically different ways. Most of us however hear his call where we are as husbands, wives, people who rejoice and mourn, who rise and sleep, who work and rest and who live in a thousand different situations across the face of the earth. What in the world do those words mean? They are the gentle urging of our Lord to see the kingdom and to experience its joy and excitement.

When God stands firmly in the center of our life by the epiphany of our Lord we begin to understand the language that teaches us to beware of making anything in life permanent ex-

54

cept his love. What is equally exciting is that in this very call
to the kingdom those everyday actions of love and work and relationship become filled with greater meaning. "The form of this
world is passing away," but rejoice that God who calls you is un-
movable and his love reaches to the outskirts of Nineveh and to
your very lives.

ALFRED BULS
Bethel Lutheran Church
University City, Missouri

KNOWLEDGE GOVERNED BY LOVE

Fourth Sunday after the Epiphany
1 Corinthians 8:1-13

Our parish is trying out a new idea! We are dividing the entire
membership of our congregation into seven service teams. Each
team will help with various activities of the parish for a month
at a time. In addition to various duties on Sunday mornings, the
service teams take over certain maintenance projects, visit shut-
ins and will assume most of the kitchen work formerly done by
women's circles. In a lengthy session last Sunday evening, we
heard various members of our parish debate the issues—the advantages and disadvantages of this new idea.

Conflict in the Church

With the debate came a number of serious questions: "Will the
leaders of the service teams be sensitive to my situation—I work
every day and can't possibly help to serve lunch after a funeral."
"I'm already helping with the Sunday school; do I need to feel
guilty if I say 'no'?" "Do you really think men will work in the
kitchen?" and "Will the people planning this thing understand
that not everyone enjoys doing certain things?"

In a very real sense, we have the potential for new conflicts in
our own community. Our conflicts are not altogether different
from those experienced by the young church community at Corinth. The Apostle Paul had been with them and at least some
in the community knew and trusted him. We think that he ex-
changed a number of letters with them. In the text before us,
Paul responds concerning the particular problem of food that has
been offered to idols. I hear in his response a strong word of
guidance and counsel for us as well. Paul reminded the community

of Corinth that all new ideas, all knowledge, must be governed and guided by the rule of love.

Meat Sacrificed to Other Gods

"Paul, can members of our community here in Corinth eat meat that has been offered as a sacrifice to other gods?" This question which apparently was sent to Paul might sound at first quite irrelevant. What possible difference does it make, we might ask, whether or not those Christians ate meat that had been sacrificed to idols?

Perhaps a story about Nick, a friendly butcher in Corinth, may help us understand the situation. Like others in his trade, Nick had a special connection—a chute which came through the wall right into the back room of his butcher shop from the temple to Apollo which stood next door. Nick often said: "Everyone knows they have far more meat next door than they can possibly use for their burnt offerings and ritual meals. Sure, we give the priests a kickback. But I still can offer the best bargains on roast beef in all of Corinth. And I've got quality cuts, too—you can count on it! You ought to see the sacrifices these sailors bring in! You'd think they were afraid of the sea or something!"

In fact, the sailors who filled this rough, bawdy seaport city were afraid of the sea. They and the inhabitants of Corinth were convinced that the world was governed by a host of gods, each controlling some sphere of life. To reduce the risk of peril, sickness, or storms, it was best to remember the gods with appropriate sacrifices. No sailor in his right mind would neglect sacrifices for Poseidon, god of the waters and ruler of storms! No one who had experienced illness would neglect Apollo, god of the sun and of medicine as well as god of music and poetry. As for Aphrodite, goddess of love and beauty, honored with a large temple at Corinth, there seems to have been little danger that she would be neglected.

Within the small minority community of Christians at Corinth, the questions were numerous. How much contact may we have with the surrounding world? We can't avoid all contact with fellow workers or neighbors. And really, why shouldn't we take advantage of bargain prices on meat? We don't really believe that this meat has been polluted or defiled, do we?

Paul's First Word

In answer to their central question "May we eat sacrificed meat?", Paul's first word is "yes." Just as there is only one

Jesus Christ for the church, Christian people know that there is only one God who rules over heaven and earth. The powers of pagan gods are not a real threat. Paul writes:

> if there be so-called gods, whether in heaven or on earth, as indeed there are many "gods" and many "lords"—yet for us there is one God, the Father, from whom are all things and for whom we exist. . . ." (8:5-6)

Later in this same letter, Paul is even more specific:

> Eat whatever is sold in the meat market without raising any question on the ground of conscience. For "the earth is the Lord's, and everything in it." (10:25-26)

Now if you were born and raised in Corinth, you might have trouble with these thoughts. For the prevalent stories and beliefs about the various gods were not casual matters. The gods were capricious, unpredictable, and often unreliable—much like people. They held vast powers over the mysteries of life and if they were neglected, they could get back at you in numerous ways. Fertility, birth, illness, suffering, death, storms on the sea and good or ill fortune were all influenced by the gods.

Christian people are called out of this complex and shaky world of polytheism. Paul is not asserting something new with this answer. Abraham, after all, was remembered as the father of a people who made a radical break with polytheism. Abraham dared to go from the household of his father to a new land, believing that Yahweh, the high God and Lord of heaven and earth, went before him to personally guide and protect him. To Abraham and to all of his descendants are given the words of comfort: "Fear not, for I am with you!" Paul is actually affirming the injunction of the first commandment: "Thou shalt have no other gods before me!" This commandment is primarily a word directed against rampant polytheism. It is a word spoken to help people resist chaos and the endless petty or real fears which haunt us in every age.

Paul's Reminder about Love

And yet, the matter doesn't end here. Just when Paul has affirmed Christian freedom regarding sacrificed meat, he tempers the message in a most dramatic way! As a member of the Christian community, he says, you are not free to do anything that you want to do, even when the activity may be all right for you. Rather, you must consider how your actions will be understood by others in your community. This is the rule of love which must govern what a Christian says or does. So Paul suggests that maybe Christians at Corinth should not eat meat that has been sacrificed to pagan gods. In fact, he says, it might be better to abstain totally from all meat rather than risk causing someone else to return to the chaos and slavery of a former way of life. Christian conduct, Paul says, should be tempered by both of these realities—knowledge and the rule of love. Christians are free in Christ yet they are never free from specific situations in the world.

Actions Governed by Love

Now I must confess that I am still troubled by Paul's words in this text. Isn't the rule of love too often used simply to justify or preserve the status quo? Out of respect for the feelings of others, we are hesitant to try anything new, anything that might be controversial. To leave Paul's words at this point certainly misses the full context of his thought and writings.

Our calling is to be the people of God. It is a calling to seek out new ideas and to explore what the phrase "freedom in Christ" really means. In our parish we are now dancing in our parish hall. Champagne has been served at a wedding reception. If we flaunt such activity before people who have serious questions, we must watch out. That is an abuse of Christian freedom. The challenge before us is to allow our knowledge and our actions to be ruled and governed by love. Paul affirmed this challenge with words about human love in this letter which he sent to Corinth:

If I speak in the tongues of men and of angels, but
have not love, I am a noisy gong or a clanging cymbal.
And if I have prophetic powers, and understand all mysteries and have all knowledge, and if I have all faith, so
as to remove mountains, but have not love, I am nothing.
(13:1-2)

It is in this spirit that we are called to think together about our world and our life together as a parish. We are called to use all of the wisdom and the creativity that God has given us. Let's even give the seven service teams a fair chance! The rule of love is not intended to inhibit us. It is intended to enrich and enhance human life for each of us and for those around us.

A. JOSEPH EVERSON
Hope Lutheran Church
St. Paul, Minnesota

58

good - Gospel? ✗

BOUND TO BE FREE/FREE TO BE BOUND

Fifth Sunday after the Epiphany
1 Corinthians 9:16-23

The disturbing alarm rattles off about 6:45 A.M. at our house, disrupting my sleepy escape from pressures and responsibilities. "Just a few minutes more," my sleep-intoxicated mind mutters to itself. "Give me just a few more moments of sleep." But the day bumps ahead, the responsibilities roll on. Soon my feet are on the floor. While I'm adjusting the shower's hot and cold water to just the right temperature, my mind is already cataloging the day's chores. "Chores" they may be at times. Many mornings I'd rather escape them, be free to go and do what I want to do. By the time I have drunk the first half cup of coffee and smeared a little strawberry jam on the toast, I'm ready to hit the deck. The chores of a few sleepy moments ago have now become my purposes and challenges for the day.

What would it be like to have nothing to get up for? I have to have a reason to be. I have to have a reason to live and to die. "This is the true joy in life, the being used for a purpose recognized by yourself as a mighty one, the being thoroughly worn out before you are thrown on the scrap heap. . . ." (George Bernard Shaw, *Man and Superman*).

What is it you are here for? What is your purpose? It seems that many of us fall into the trap of being here for one of two purposes. The first is *sex*. I don't mean sex as just an activity but as "what I am." To be a man. Or, to be a woman. That is why I'm here. The goal of life centers on fulfilling my sexual role. There are a myriad of cosmetic and liquid products sold to us with the promise, "This will make you a real man, a real woman." The second trap is *vocation*. I'm my job. That's right, I become my job. I must confess that is a trap into which I have fallen. Career becomes our sole purpose, our main purpose for living. Each of these roads to finding purpose for living is important. But when either of them is pursued for its own sake, the road suddenly becomes a cul-de-sac. My purpose becomes a prison, my goal becomes a tyrannical god that drives and possesses me. Instead of feeling good about getting up in the morning, I feel bad. "Shut that alarm off! I want out. I don't want to get up. I want to be free!"

Freedom and Purpose

To be free! To have a purpose for living! These two essential ingredients of life are woven together for our meditation by Paul's words to us in the text for this day. "I am free!" he declares. Yet five times in one short paragraph he states his purpose for living as "to win some more for Christ." Paul discovered the secret of freedom and purpose in life.

As I read the Scriptures, examine my own life, study the lives of others, it seems that freedom comes in a variety of packages.

Zephaniah describes for us the legitimate needs to be free from the tyranny of other men. This is a physical freedom. Freedom from terror and physical jeopardy. But I can be free from any threat of physical harm and still be a prisoner of other men. St. Paul says today, "For though I am free from all men...," I experience a tyranny of other men even though there are no physical threats on my life. What you think about me can become so important, so all-consuming that the opinions of others becomes a prison for me. Think of the times, painful situation after situation when you conformed to the desires of someone else even when you wanted to do otherwise, "Yes, I'll go to the stupid party or meeting or what have you."

Mark speaks of another need for freedom in today's Gospel. The need to be free from demons, evil spirits, powers of the universe and the mind which destroy life rather than create and support it. That's old fashioned thinking, you say? I have experienced that kind of need for freedom. My mind gets trapped in sick, negative, destructive thought patterns, the thinking is muddled and I continue to go down the road of self-destruction.

Then there are times when I want to be free just to do my own will, free to do what I want. No other man, no other spirits are going to control me. "Free to be me!" that's my goal. But have you ever noticed that freedom allows you to fall into bad habits but very seldom into good ones? The alcoholic gets what he/she wills. Suddenly the will becomes my god. I'm enslaved to my will. We make very few decisions with the brain, most of them are made with our glands. So, as St. Paul says, our stomach can become our god. The Russian monk in Dostoevski's *The Brothers Karamazov* describes well the slavery of the will. "Interpreting freedom as the multiplication and rapid satisfaction of desires, men distort their own nature ... I once knew a so-called champion of freedom who when deprived of tobacco in prison, was so wretched at the privation that he almost betrayed his cause for the sake of getting tobacco."

The Secret

Paul experienced the secret of freedom and purpose. "For though I am free from all men, I have made myself a slave to all, that I might win the more."

What does he mean? What is the source of his freedom and purpose?

First, Paul experienced that in Christ no man can ever give his heart unconditionally to any other person or cause. Thus he was free of the dominion and opinions of other men. He was free of the dominion of demonic-sick thinking. He was free of the god of his own gut, his own gland-directed will. That is neat . . . to be that free. But, Paul's freedom was not a goal or end in itself. His freedom was a tool God gave him in order that he might achieve God's will. Paul was not free to do as he pleased. "I am entrusted with a commission . . . for though I am free I have made myself a slave to all."

Luther states it this way. "The Christian is the most free of all men." We need not sell ourselves out to any other person or cause. Our salvation, our status with God is secure. But he also says, "The Christian is the most bound of all men," meaning the true Christian is filled with a natural desire to use his freedom not for his own selfish purpose but to serve others for Christ.

Free to be Bound

Five times in one short paragraph Paul states his purpose in life, "to win some more to Christ." Paul was not bound by the traditions and expectations of other men. He did what God would have him do. When he was with the Jews he identified with the Jews in order to win them to Christ. When he was with pagans he identified with pagans to win them to Christ. "I have become all things to all men to win some to Christ." At first that sounds like hypocrisy, Paul switched sides of the street just to win a customer. But that's not his point. His point is that he is not all caught up in protecting his ego, polishing his reputation, preserving his freedom for his own sake. He will do what is God's will to reach another person for Christ.

How different this is from the need to be free from something for my own sake. Paul says that in Christ he becomes so free that he can give up his freedom to help someone else know God's love.

A parable describes Paul's message. A violin string unattached from the violin is free to move in any direction. If I twist one end, it responds. It is free. But it is not free to sing. So I take it and fix it to a violin. I bind it, and when it is bound it is free to sing.

Isn't that strange? When I become bound to Christ I become free enough of my own ego, my fears of what you and others think of me, to give my all to reach someone else with his freeing love. Strange . . . the road to freedom is slavery to Christ.

DENNIS A. ANDERSON
St. Paul Lutheran Church
Grand Island, Nebraska

RUN FOR YOUR LIFE

Sixth Sunday after the Epiphany
1 Corinthians 9:24-27

I can hardly believe my ears. It doesn't seem possible that Paul said or wrote the words of this text. Paul was the man who insisted that we are saved by grace, not by works. He was the man who told the Romans that nothing, not even death itself could separate us from the love of God. And yet the great apostle writes to the people of Corinth that the Christian life is like an athlete running a race or a boxer fighting his opponent. There is no mention of grace here, no surety of salvation. Paul seems to be saying, *Run for your life.* Get busy. There's a prize for the victor. Strain every nerve. Don't miss your goal.

Nor is this passage unique. The same puzzlesome problem appears again and again in the Bible. Sometimes we are encouraged to put our trust completely in God. The other two lessons read this morning emphasize this truth. Yet there are an equal number of passages that counsel us to watch and work, to strive toward an eternal goal. I suppose I add to the confusion by telling you one Sunday to rely on God's grace and then the next week I exhort you to pray and give and help your neighbor. What's it all about? Are you supposed to run for your life? Is Christianity grace or works? Do we strive or do we trust?

Let me put a question to you. This morning, when it was time to get up and get ready for church, did you feel, even for a moment, that it might be nicer to stay in bed? Last week when it was time for choir practice, did you put down with a little reluctance, the interesting book you were reading? Last year when we had our annual meeting at the same time as the Super Bowl, did you come to church with lagging steps or stay home altogether? The fact of the matter is that all of us are tempted from time to time to take the easy way. I must admit that the hardest thing I do all day is get out of bed in the morning, and it isn't any easier on Sunday than during the week.

In other words, all of us are weak, and becoming a Christian doesn't completely change that fact. The old sinful nature still lurks even after we have been saved by God's grace. And it is this which concerns the Apostle Paul, this human weakness which he calls "the flesh" or "the body." The writer of the first epistle of John uses similar terms when he talks about "the lust of the flesh and the lust of the eyes and the pride of life." We are haunted by the force which held us captive until Christ freed us by his grace.

Take that part of human nature that we call the sex instinct. God made it and intended it as a blessing for human beings. And yet how easily it can betray us and lead us away from God. The desires of sex can capture us so completely that our contact with God is lost. Dr. Clarence Macartney, a famous Presbyterian preacher tells how a man came to him seeking help. The man confessed that he had become involved with one of his employees. He said, "It's ruining my business. It's destroying my marriage. My family is beginning to hate me." Then he added: "But Dr. Macartney, I can't give her up. I can't give her up." Can you see why Paul says, Run for your life? Can you see why he talks about keeping your body under control?

And of course it isn't just sex that is covered by the term *flesh* or *body*. Paul is talking about greed and love of idleness and gossip and a hundred other things that can turn our eyes away from God. We all have our weaknesses; They may differ widely—different strokes for different folks—but anything that threatens to drive a wedge between us and God represents a danger to our life.

Paul isn't denying that we are saved by grace. He isn't saying run the Christian race and save yourself. But he is warning us that we can lose the prize that God has given us. We can fritter it away, we can swerve from the true course, we can go to sleep like the hare did and lose the race to the tortoise.

Watch out, Paul says. Keep yourself in fighting trim. Run for your life. That's the only sure way. But what about all those comforting passages of Scripture that promise us salvation? Their comfort isn't lost but you must note that one thing is always omitted—our own actions. Jesus says that no one can pluck us out of the Father's hand. But he doesn't say we can't get out. Paul inscribes a long list of things that we need not fear because these things cannot destroy the love of God for us. But we are not in that list. God doesn't operate a kind of celestial rat trap which captures us and refuses to let us go. He gives us his grace and power. But we must live our own lives under that grace. We must run all the way to the end.

But there is something else in this text that requires our attention. We are to run for our life fully aware of how wonderful the goal is. Paul sets up a striking contrast between the crown of leaves which the victor won in the races of that day and the eternal life which we receive at the end of our race. Athletes strained and trained to be acclaimed the victor in those ancient races and they still do it today. But how trivial is their reward compared to the heavenly crown promised to us. And it is important that we remember the value of our reward.

For let's face it. Sin can be very pleasant for the moment. Lying and cheating can bring a great reward temporarily. Drifting aimlessly through life, being totally unconcerned about your neighbor's needs can help you avoid many troubles. Those who get involved in romantic adulteries, those who take drugs or get drunk may find moments of real pleasure through their actions. We play Satan's game when we picture sin as always ugly and repellent. Listen to the account of the first sin by a human being as recorded in Genesis: "The woman saw how beautiful the tree was and how good its fruit would be to eat, and she thought how wonderful it would be to become wise" (Gen. 3:6). That's sin, alluring, pleasant, easy to take.

But Paul wants us to look ahead, to see what is at the end of the Christian life. He doesn't tell us the race is easy but he promises the reward is great. He doesn't want us to barter away our birthright for a mess of pottage as Esau did. He doesn't want us to sell our salvation for thirty pieces of silver as Judas did. Paul says the goal is worthwhile. Run for your life.

I'm aware that people sometimes sneer when we talk about heaven in the church. Someone once coined the phrase, "Pie in the sky, by and by," and the description has stuck. Omar Khayyam expressed the philosophy of many in this world when he wrote: "Take the cash and let the credit go." But when we are asked to think about the end goal of life, that isn't dreaming or fancy words. The emphasis on eternal life simply puts our existence into proper proportions. It says, is the sin of the moment worth the loss at the end? Was the rich man in hell more fortunate than the beggar Lazarus who found his way to Abraham's bosom? It is only because of the promised goal that Jesus could say, "Blessed are the meek, blessed are the poor in spirit, blessed are you when they say all manner of evil against you falsely for my sake." My Christian friends, we run for our life. We run for eternal life. And Paul tells us wisely that no sacrifice is too great, no earthly loss too much. His advice is to keep in trim. Harden your body against temptation. Keep your flesh under control. For there is a great prize at the end and we do not want to lose that prize.

And now for a moment we must look at the strangest part of this text. Paul says he must keep himself under control or he might become a castaway, he might be disqualified. And that's a disturbing thought. Did he really think he might lose his salvation? Later in life he talked about having run his race and he spoke with great assurance of the crown of life laid up for him. But he doesn't seem so sure here. What about it?

I'm sure Paul was aware that no one should think that, "I've got it made." The Bible warns that the one who thinks he stands should take heed lest he fall. But I believe Paul is more concerned about the spectacle he might present if he preached the gospel to others and then failed to complete the race himself. How embarrassing it is to be in a race and to swerve from your lane or stumble and be disqualified. In other words, Paul says we should run for our lives because of the witness we make to others. And every Christian should be aware that we are under observation at all times. The world looks at us and is either impressed by the strength which we receive from God or is moved to say, "His Christianity didn't do him any good. He's got nothing that the rest of us don't have."

I remember being on a boat one time in the midst of a stormy sea. It was so rough that you couldn't walk around, so my wife and I sat and talked to two women who sat near us. When we finally got into the calm water of the harbor, one of the women said to me: "My sister and I have never been on a boat before. But we knew you had and so we decided we wouldn't get scared until you did."

I wasn't aware I was under observation and yet it happens to all of us all of the time. People watch us. They look at the race we are running. They may even hope that as Christians we'll stub our toe. But the world is impressed by the way we run, not by what we say. We must run, not only for our own life but for the lives of others.

I don't mean that we can expect to be perfect. Every one of us stumbles and falls. We sin daily. Yet we need to keep in mind the influence we have over others. The mean words that we speak may cause someone to say, "If that's the way a Christian acts, I don't want that kind of religion." Or the way we resist temptation may influence someone else to join us in the Christian race. Much depends on us. We dare not become castaways.

Of course no text contains all the truth. Paul's words here seem to leave the impression that it all depends on us, and of course it doesn't. Paul talks about keeping his body under control, hardening himself, etc. But he knows that the Spirit of God is there to help. We run for our life but we do not run under our own power. An anonymous writer has put this thought into a beautiful hymn:

> I sought the Lord, and afterward I knew
> He moved my soul to seek him, seeking me;
> It was not I that found, O Saviour true;
> No, I was found of thee.
>
> I find, I walk, I love, but O the whole
> Of love is but my answer, Lord, to thee;
> For thou wert long beforehand with my soul,
> Always thou lovest me.

You and I are running a race, my friends. It's a race that has been run by human beings in every age. Run for your life. Keep all things under control. There's a crown of life at the end of the course.

W. A. POOVEY
Dubuque, Iowa

GOD'S OVERWHELMING YES

Seventh Sunday after the Epiphany
2 Corinthians 1:18-22

Judged by Jackals, Outdone by Ostriches
(Old Testament Lesson—Isaiah 43:18-25)

It is no compliment to be compared with a jackal. This wild dog hunted in packs, lived mostly off dead carcasses, and sometimes even devoured children. It earned the name "lion's provider" because the lion would hear the yelps of the pack, follow the sound, and share the prey. The jackal is said to have the most unearthly sound of any animal. It would be bad enough to be compared with a jackal, but even worse to be judged by one! Yet Isaiah states that the people of God were judged by the jackal. This creature honored the Lord more than did the people of God.

It's no compliment to be compared to an ostrich either. In the film *OH, GOD*, God admits that the ostrich was one of his mistakes. This bird, six to eight feet high, can't fly, but runs faster

66

than a horse and is described by a Latin name meaning "strutting camel." Momma lays the three pound egg, but Poppa sits on it six times as long as Momma does. Like the jackal, the ostrich has a distinct, disturbing sound. Micah says (1:18), "I will make lamentation like the jackals, and mourning like the ostriches." Yet Isaiah maintains that the ostrich out-did the people of God in honoring the Lord.

When God made streams in the desert, the jackals and ostriches drank of the water. Their howls in the day or night became a praise to God who sustained them. It was their Yes! to God, while his people obstinately replied No! to the offer of spiritual food and drink. God's Yes! has a long history of being given a No! by his disobedient or disinterested people.

Paralytic Legs/Paralytic Hearts
(Gospel: Mark 2:1-12)

You've heard the old exchange:
"I'm tired!"
"Oh hi! I'm Rod!"
"I'd rather be tired—I can get over that!"
The Gospel Lesson could be summed up similarly:
"My legs are paralyzed!"
"My heart is paralyzed!"

I'd rather have paralyzed legs—they are more easily cured!"
The Gospel indicates that the heart problem of the onlookers was a more serious malady than the problem of the paralytic. The scribes' No! was theologically sound—only God can forgive sins. However, sometimes a No! can be theologically correct and yet hinder the good and proper movement of God among people. It was not the first time when propriety has threatened to squelch ministry. But Jesus' Yes! prevailed in both an inner and outer healing. "They were all amazed and glorified God, saying, 'We never saw anything like this!'" Isn't it neat how God's Yes! changes No! into Wow!?

God's Ultimate Yes
(The Epistle—1 Cor. 1:18-22)

There are many ways of saying Yes. An exercise to illustrate this appeared in "In the Worship Workshop with Avery and Marsh" (Vol. V, No. 11, Nov. 1977, p. 3).

yes—as if it means of course
yes—excitedly
yes—"if I have to"
yes—snobbishly
yes—ecstatically
yes—in a hurry
yes—terrified
yes—to a doctor
yes—to the I.R.S. man
yes—encouragingly
yes—with the Good News in mind
yes—to a proposal of marriage
yes—to a baby
yes—to a homosexual

yes—angry
yes—forlornly
yes—with dedication
yes—joyfully
yes—bored
yes—shocked
yes—"if *you* say so"
yes—to a dentist
yes—to your pastor
yes—doubtfully
yes—to a vow for church office
yes—to a bigot
yes—to God

Yes may be spoken in a variety of ways. Though a positive word, it can have negative connotations. We have experienced "yes, yes, yes," as a bore. We associate Yes in a negative way with a "yes" man. We know that the promise of Yes may be given as a shallow response and not seriously kept.

The word "yes" needs life behind it. That is precisely what we have in Jesus. God's Yes became flesh and dwelt among us. All of God's promises found affirmative fulfillment in his Son, our Savior. There was an obedient Yes the world never heard when Jesus agreed to let go of his equality with God and become man. When still a young boy, he was saying Yes under a compulsion to be about his Father's business. There was a Yes to God when faced with tempting alternatives from Satan. His baptism was a Yes in order to fulfill all righteousness. His Yes to the Father held as he determined to go to Jerusalem, as he bowed to the will of God in Gethsemane, and as he "humbled himself and became obedient unto death, even death on a cross" (Phil. 2:8). Whenever you wonder whether God is concerned about you, look at the cross and let it be God's exclamation point— "Yes, I care!". God said his overwhelming Yes to you and me in Jesus. "That is why we utter the Amen through him, to the glory of God," wrote Paul. Our Amen is a kind of liturgical Wow! to God's Yes.

Invitation to Response

God's ultimate Yes in Jesus invites our continual Yes in response. We are not up to that on our own, but we say "Yes, by the help of God." This is what Paul is saying when he writes, "It is God who establishes us with you in Christ, and has commissioned us; he has put his seal upon us and given us his Spirit in our hearts as a guarantee."

The story is told of a wife who yearned to hear her husband express his love for her. Finally she asked him outright, "Honey, do you love me?" A simple "Yes" would have thrilled her. Instead, her husband answered, "Listen, when we got married I said I loved you, and that holds until further notice!" Well, relationships don't do well on only history. They need current events. They need a daily up-dating and renewing and reassurance. God enjoys relationships with his people that are kept current too.

Sure, he said Yes to us in Baptism and has never forgotten this covenant. But he keeps it current through his repeated Word to us and the recurring Sacrament of Holy Communion. Sure, we said a public Yes as our personal response in confirmation, but this was meant to be a rehearsal for daily renewal of our Yes to our Lord. Relationship must also be current event. If you haven't said Yes to your husband or wife, your family, or your friends lately, find some way of doing it. Their hearts will rejoice, and you will make their day.

Also remember to gladden the heart of your heavenly Father with positive responses to him. We have lots of opportunity to exercise a Yes response to the Lord: Worship, prayer, study, fellowship, communion, honest labor, kindnesses to our family, care for the needs of people around us. Let's take these not as heavy obligations but as ways to celebrate God's Yes to us, and as ways to witness the joyful spirit that God's Yes creates in human hearts. He is still in the business of using his Yes to change our dreary No! into a vital, faith-filled Wow!

ROD KVAMME
First Lutheran Church
Havre, Montana

UNVEILING THE TRUTH

The Transfiguration of Our Lord—Last Sunday after the Epiphany
2 Corinthians 3:12—4:2

Religious dissension and controversy are common these days. Such issues as the ordination of women, the inspiration of Scripture and even the doctrine of the virgin birth are being argued and debated. Accusations of heresy are made. Not only congregations but also immediate families are polarized and divided. Amidst all the heated controversies, one is likely to ask—where is the truth? Is the truth being veiled or unveiled, concealed or disclosed?

Adversaries and Arguments

These questions are similar to the ones Paul addresses in today's Second Lesson. He too was involved in a controversy in which the issue of veiling or unveiling the truth was central. His opponents were probably missionaries who held Moses and the Ten Commandments in high esteem. Moreover, they believed that Moses had gained a direct insight into the truth in his encounter with God on Mount Sinai. In order to protect the people from direct exposure to that truth, which would probably have consumed them, he put a veil over his face. But that veil is being lifted now as the missionaries reflect and share and preach the glory of Moses and the Law. They alone possess the truth.

Paul counters by attacking the source of truth for the missionaries, namely Moses and his encounter with God on Mount Sinai. He does not deny that Moses was important nor that there was glory in that religious tradition, but Paul claims it was a deficient, fading glory. That's why Moses put a veil over his face —to conceal the incomplete nature of the truth he had received. Make no mistake about it, Paul says, the truth that came by Moses was accurate and great, but it was only partial. The truth that came in Jesus Christ is full, final and complete. As William Barclay put it, "When the sun has risen the lamps cease to be of use." But Paul also knew a corollary reaction in that the second best is the worst enemy of the best. Moses may indeed be the worst enemy of Jesus. Especially inasmuch as the truth in Jesus Christ is not something people possess; people are possessed by it. It is, in other words, not a possession but a process in which people are freed and transformed into the likeness of Christ. That is the nub of Paul's argument, and it can assist us in exposing the veils that conceal truth and enable us to participate in the process of unveiling the truth.

The Veils that Conceal

The veils that conceal truth are often seductive and alluring. Sometimes they conceal what we don't want to face. Sometimes they make us feel fundamentally in the right even though there is weighty evidence to the contrary. Usually the veils will support us as we are—with our opinions, attitudes, views, prejudices —and will camouflage any need on our part to change.

Notice, for example, one of the veils Paul was contending with —namely, people clinging to what is old even when something far better is offered. There seems to be a long history to that habit. People hanker back to the good old days when life was simple even though the good old days were not always good or simple. People refuse to believe the earth is round because it was understood to be flat in the past. People believe that what was always done must be right and what has never been done must be wrong. And we in the church have often been more at home in looking backwards to what has always been done, than in looking forward to the new things God is doing, to the new glories he has in store for us.

Paul mentions a second veil that affects our understanding of the Bible itself. Almost any viewpoint or issue or attitude can be supported and defended by biblical texts, carelessly lifted out of their contexts. The superiority of certain races of people over other races is defended with biblical texts. Slavery and holy wars are defended with biblical texts. Advances in scientific knowledge are denounced and condemned on the basis of biblical texts. Communism is denounced and the American way of life affirmed on the basis of biblical texts. There is no end to the possibility of biblical texts bolstering and buttressing our own prejudices and viewpoints.

Notice also how selective we can be in reading the Bible. We love to hear of God's love and mercy, but spare us, please, those words on wrath and judgement. We often find in the Bible what we want to find and we disregard what we don't want to hear.

The veils that conceal truth *leave us as we are!* They serve as staunch defenders of our present attitudes, viewpoints and prejudices. They serve, in other words, the status quo.

The Process of Unveiling

And these veils that conceal truth are unveiled in Jesus Christ. He is the truth to which the Bible points, and only when we read it in the light of him do we read it correctly and honestly. That's why Paul says that only through Christ is the veil taken away and the full truth finally disclosed.

What's more, the truth which Christ embodies is not a static doctrine but a life-transforming Spirit. He is the Spirit. It's as though Paul were saying fix your gaze on Jesus, the Christ, and you will end up reflecting him, reflecting his glory, reflecting something kinder and more compassionate, something truer and more honorable, something braver and more joyful than you could ever have known without him.

Some people claim that it's a law of life that we become like the people or things we gaze at. Recall those commercials for dog food in which the master and the dog have very similar appearances. People become like that upon which they fix their gaze and associate with.

Such a transformation occurred in the movie, *One Flew Over the Cuckoo's Nest*. R. P. McMurphy, the central character, has caused so much trouble in jail that he is transferred to the mental institution. There he encounters and confronts the rigid and legalistic approach of the institution, expressed especially in the head nurse, Miss Ratchet. The most beautiful feature of this movie is how the other patients become kinder, braver and truer people through their association with McMurphy. McMurphy, who was blunt, crass and vulgar, a rebel to society, despised and rejected by other people, inspires virtue in the other patients.

It's as we fix our gaze on Jesus, remain in his company and under his influence, that something new comes to birth in us. Yes, but how?

Paul said on another occasion that we were to have this mind among us which was in Christ Jesus, and then later advised, "Whatever is true, whatever is honorable, whatever is just, whatever is pure, whatever is lovely, whatever is gracious, if there is any excellence, if there is anything worthy of praise, think about these things."

And should we be uncertain about what is true, just and lovely, then we can flood our minds and imaginations with the picture of him who both obeyed and confronted the authorities of his day, and demonstrated it by breaking some holy laws for the sake of the brothers and sisters; the picture of him who blasted the proud and self-righteous and sided with the down-and-out; the picture of him who gave himself for a world that rejected him and died as a criminal on a cross. By fixing our gaze on him, staying in his company, we may be changed into his likeness.

And this likeness corresponds to what is deeply and truly human in us. That's why the ancient prayer, "in whose service is perfect freedom," is so appropriate. This combination of service and freedom is not as strange as it sounds. It means, as Frederick Buechner has said, ". . . that to obey Love himself, who above all else wishes us well, leaves us the freedom to be the best and gladdest that we have it in us to become."

That's the process that unveils truth, bestows freedom, and enables us to reflect the glory of Christ Jesus, our Lord. Amen.

MORRIS J. NIEDENTHAL
Lutheran School of Theology
Chicago, Illinois

HIS LOVE DOES IT ALL

First Sunday in Lent
Romans 8:31-39

No doubt about it—HIS LOVE DOES IT ALL. God's love, of course. There it is at bloody bitter Calvary. Paul writes: "He spared not his own Son but gave him up for us all" (v. 32). The words echo those of God to Abraham in today's Old Testament Lesson: "You did not withhold your son, your only son." And so it is the story of that near sacrifice on Mount Moriah all over again, only this time there is no substitute ram waiting in the wings. No angel of the Lord is there to stay God's uplifted hand. The dagger is plunged into the heart of the second Isaac, the nails are driven into his hands and feet, and he dies, that a lost and death-enslaved world might be brought back to God's waiting and welcoming arms. What the Lord commands Abraham to do, he himself does and lays his own bleeding heart on love's altar for us.

And so at Calvary we behold the fierce fervent passionate love of God. And there, if nowhere else in our lives, that love shines bright and clear. Alcohol is destroying your home, a loved one wastes away with cancer, you're out of work, your marriage is on the rocks, suicidal thoughts run through your depressed soul, life is intolerably grim and gloomy, bitter and brutal, and then some pious preacher cheerfully announces to you: "God is love," or "Smile, God loves you." And the temptation to commit murder is almost irresistible. If, as Scripture tells us, the Lord chastens those whom he loves, then you would just as soon that he loved someone else for a change.

And so there's only one place to go—to Calvary. There, if nowhere else in your life, God's love is clear and unmistakable. For this is God himself a broken bleeding body on that torture tree—so deep and fervent is his love for you. Surely a love like that has just got to be at the heart of everything that happens, even the dark cruel mysteries of life. A love like that will never desert, abandon or forsake you, will never lay on your back a burden heavier than you can bear. Surely a love like that will turn tragedy into triumph, crosses into crowns and every sad and dark Good Friday into a bright and beautiful Easter morning.

HIS LOVE DOES IT ALL, there at Calvary and also at that nearby rent and conquered grave. It happened at the crack of that first Easter dawn. He came laughing and leaping and shouting and dancing and singing right out of that gloomy garden grotto and thereby did he become our Coffin-Conquerer and Death-Destroyer. Into the teeth of death God has flung the gloriously stubborn fact of Easter. And now even the final enemy has been vanquished and overcome. Death, the hungry prowling devourer, has been swallowed up in the victory of the resurrection. And that's really good news.

God's love does it all, raises the Christ from his grave and to his own right hand to be King of kings and Lord of lords. In verse 34 the Apostle reminds the Roman Christians of the Jesus who died, was raised from the dead and who is now at the right hand of God. And there he rules. All tears, trials, blows, burdens, sufferings, sorrows, griefs, bereavements, crosses and losses to the contrary, your Savior rules, governs and controls everything in your life, the glad and the sad, for your temporal and eternal good triumph, and blessing. And that's why you can always hang in there with courage and hope.

HIS LOVE DOES IT ALL. Not only does the King govern the universe for your good. He prays for you. As Paul puts it: "He indeed intercedes for us" (v. 34). And so he does what we so seldom do for ourselves and others—he prays, prays that God might make us strong and triumphant in the hour of testing and trial, prays that our weak and wavering faith might be made mighty and mountain-moving, prays that all apathy, indifference and lukewarmness might go and depart and that at last we become his fervent passionate and committed followers.

HIS LOVE DOES IT ALL, enables us to put all our fears and worries to flight. The apostle writes: "If God is for us, who is against us? He who did not spare his own Son, but gave him up for us all, will he not also give us all things with him?" (vv. 31-32). These verses offer two reasons why worry-warts can stop and cease their godless fretting and stewing. First, God is our friend. I challenge you, I dare you to name any sickness or suffering, any tragedy or disaster, any dark demonic force or power in this universe greater or stronger than God. And if God is your friend, you have no foe; if God is your foe, you

74

have no friend. God is on your side and in your corner, and there's no way in the world you can ever be licked, conquered, defeated or overcome! Then how foolish your fears!

We bid our fears a farewell because God is our friend, and second, because the gift of Christ is God's guarantee of everything that we need. When God laid that Baby in the donkey's feed box, when he put that Man on Calvary's cross, he cared enough to give the very best. He literally emptied his treasury with the gift of Christ. He actually gave himself in that crucified and risen Man. And you just can't give, grant or bestow anything greater than God. And so Paul's point is abundantly clear. If God with the gift of Christ tore out his own bleeding heart and gave it to us, then surely he will always provide us with the far less costly gifts of life's necessities. For which is easier to give, an only Son or the gift of health? An only Son or the gift of money or a good job or faith and strength for the daily battles and burdens? God gave us the world in Christ. Will he not then lovingly and lavishly shower upon us every mental, moral, emotional, physical and spiritual gift and blessing that we need? Why then these senseless, silly, godless fears?

HIS LOVE DOES IT ALL, enables us to say farewell to guilt. Oh how the Apostle's words gladden our guilt-burdened souls: "Who shall bring any charge against God's elect? It is God who justifies. Who is to condemn? It is Christ Jesus who died, yes, who was raised from the dead, who is at the right hand of God, who indeed intercedes for us" (vv. 33-34). Good-bye, guilt. Farewell, regret. Jesus, our Savior, has gone into that garden grave and then has gloriously and victoriously emerged again. And now God has amnesia. He can't remember our sins anymore. Well if he can't, why should we?

HIS LOVE DOES IT ALL, enables us to flatten, clobber, demolish and annihilate every foe. Listen to Paul's words: "Who shall separate us from the love of Christ? Shall tribulation or distress, or persecution, or famine, or nakedness, or peril, or sword? ... No, in all these things we are more than conquerors through him who loved us" (vv. 35-37). Are those your enemies, the ones Paul lists here? Maybe "tribulation, peril and distress," but surely not "persecution, famine, nakedness or the sword." Who's making life miserable for you because of your faithful, bold and courageous stand for Christ? When was the last time you fearfully gasped: "I have nothing to eat"? Are you in the habit of running around in tattered rags? Do you live under constant threat of execution because you're a confessing Christian? These were Paul's enemies. Are they yours? Would more of those enemies be there if ever your faint flickering light would really begin to blaze and shine, if ever your salt would get salty and your commitment to the Master become something more than lukewarm and half-hearted? If you were arrested for being a Christian, would there be enough evidence to convict you?

Well, whatever or whoever the foes arrayed against us, they don't stand a chance. They're destined and doomed to defeat. For the love of Christ is stronger than all of them combined. If you'll pardon a grammatical term—oh blessed subjective genitive! The apostle here highlights Christ's love of us and not our love of him. It is Christ's great, deep, strong, everlasting love of us and not our weak and wavering grasp on him that will bring us safely and triumphantly through every danger and distress to the gladness and glory of heaven. Or as the Savior himself assures us: "No one, no person, peril or evil power, no devil, death, casket or grave will ever rob, wrench, pluck or grab you from my arms." And that's why victory is assured.

HIS LOVE DOES IT ALL, won't let anything drive us from his arms. In truly eloquent and inspired words Paul concludes: "For I am sure that nothing in death or in life, no good or bad angel, nothing happening now or in the future, no demon of darkness, no astral deities, no stars or signs of the zodiac, absolutely nothing in this big, broad universe will ever be able to rip, wrench, or steal us from God's great loving arms." The cross proves it. That open, empty grave shouts it. We're simply invincible! *and ever-lasting, all because of God's love for us.*

HERBERT E. HOHENSTEIN
Unity Lutheran Church
Belnor, Missouri

Nothing, absolutely, nothing can seperate the Xian from the love of God that is in Christ Jesus our Lord. Amen

THE CROSS IS THE GIFT GOD GIVES HIS FRIENDS

Second Sunday in Lent
Romans 5:1-11 *To the Good God be all Glory*

We were God's enemies, but he made us his friends through the death of his son.

Say the word enemy and what image comes to mind? Secret agents, robbers, master criminals? Our sins, alas, are not that grand. Most of our exploits seem petty compared to the glorious escapades of the glamorous crooks and criminals whose fame has been highly publicized by the media.

There is not a single Goldfinger among us, nor even a Don

Corleone. None of us has a story like a Charles Colson, a Tex Watson or an Eldridge Cleaver. Even our blaspheming seems mild, our doubts tame.

God's enemies? For most of us, that description seems a bit strong. Yet, who in this wounded time has not felt alienated or alone? Who has not felt damaged, ignored or abandoned?

If that is still too strong, let me try once more. Who has not felt that he has been groping, searching, grasping for something, someone, who will connect him to the rest of the world? Who has not felt at some time that he is a stranger or an alien to God? Paul speaks here of our separation from God.

This separation may not be because we have felt anger or hatred toward God. It may be more a result of our apathy or confusion.

The Cross Is a Gift

Paul's point is that it is precisely at these moments, when we have felt far away, that God acted. God did not wait until we were ready, until we changed, until we made the first move. While the silence of our doubt still rang loud, while our words were nearly erased by our stuttering, while we were reduced to apathy by our confusion, he made things right by the death of Jesus. We were separated, at a distance from God, but he treated us like friends.

We are his friends, and the cross is the gift God gives his friends.

Though we may die for the sake of a saint, Paul says, or even a loved one, seldom does one die for an enemy or a stranger. With God, however, it is different. The cross is the word that there are no enemies, only friends. There are no strangers, just sons and daughters.

Through his suffering, self-giving love, he offers himself to us, and we are changed from aliens, strangers and enemies, to friends. The cross is the gift God gives his friends.

The Cross Is a Way of Life

The Gospel today reminds us that the cross is not only a gift of forgiveness and hope, it is a mark of faithfulness to God. "If anyone wants to follow me, he must forget himself, carry his cross, and follow me." The cross is no mere trinket to be worn around the neck. If it rests only on our altars we have missed its significance. The cross is a way of life.

To bypass the cross, to ignore it, to make it mere decoration, is one of the temptations Satan puts before Christ. "Get away from me Satan," he says to Peter when the disciple wants to shield him from suffering. Images of the first temptations emerge, where Satan wants Jesus to walk around the cross and move directly to privilege and glory.

As a way of life, the cross is an alternative to life as we know it. It is a different story than the one most people tell.

When Clarence Jordan was attempting to organize his inter-racial community in Americus, Georgia, in the early fifties, he was faced with a heap of trouble. Not only was he excommuni-cated from his local church for attending services with black people, his farm was faced with a stiff boycott. He couldn't buy machinery or seeds. No one would deliver gasoline for his trac-tors. The klan rode through his yard burning crosses; bullets pierced his buildings.

In desperation, Clarence turned to his brother Bob, a state senator and, later, Georgia Supreme Court Justice. "Bob, I want you to represent our farm," Clarence began. Bob shook his head, "I can't do it, Clarence. It would ruin both my business and my career."

Clarence's voice rose, "when we went to the altar as boys, the minister asked us if we followed Jesus Christ. I said yes, what did you say?" Bob answered, "I follow Christ, Clarence. I follow him up to a point."

"Could that point be the cross, Bob?"

"Yes, I follow him to the cross, but not on it. I'm not about to be crucified."

"Then I suggest that you go back to that preacher and tell him that you are an admirer of Jesus and not a follower."

No one will accuse Clarence Jordan of only being an admirer of Jesus. Though times were exceedingly tough, though all of the others who began the Koinonia experiment left, Clarence and his family stayed. Risking one's life, Clarence believed, was part of being a disciple. Trying to save our life is folly, for the cross is the gift God gives his friends.

When Dietrich Bonhoeffer was still a young man in Germany, Hitler came to power. Barely thirty, he had already established himself as one of the leading theologians in his country. After he spoke out against the Nazi menace, his friends arranged for him to flee to America where he could live in safety, working on his ethics book.

His time in America, however, was not that peaceful. How could he hope to go home after the war when he failed to share what he believed to be the darkest time in German history?

Finally, it was clear that he must return and work against Hitler's war machine. Bonhoeffer knew that any attempt to save his life, his career, his book was already doomed. He knew that only those who risk their life for the sake of the gospel, will find it. He knew the cross is the gift God gives his friends.

Is there not an easier way to live? Can we not live in comfort without the cross? Of course! But for those who lay claim to the name of Jesus, it must be clear that attempts to bypass the cross are a work of the evil one. It is the ploy of Satan to suggest that we can answer our most difficult questions without suffering. It is his message that we can solve the energy crisis without loss of comfort or convenience. How foolish!

Knowing that the cross lies in our paths does not make this kind of living easy. At times the saints of God scream—enough! Don't be so generous with your gift, God. Share it with someone else.

Like Tevye, the saints declare that though it is no disgrace to be poor, it is no great honor either. With Teresa, they gasp— "no wonder you have so few friends, God, when you treat the ones you have so badly."

The Cross Is an Alternative

The cross can be avoided, but only at the price of losing our lives. Accepting the cross is always accepting an alternative way to the one the world offers. The cross is God's alternative to violence and power-grabbing; it is his alternative to the dominance of the powerful over the weak.

The cross, so easy to accept when it means forgiveness and peace, is so difficult when it is offered to us as a way of life. No wonder it has been a scandal from the beginning.

In a world that preaches the virtue of security and safety, the cross is a word of risk and vulnerability. It is a second voice to the word that rings from our TV screens.

In parenting, the cross is a voluntary surrender of our trump cards. It is a No to strong-armed tactics that reduce children to servants and make them resent us. The alternative, I might add, is not surrender. It is not pure permissiveness that the cross promotes, but a renunciation of power resting only in the hands of adults.

In business the cross is a strong word that ends and means must always be kept straight. Though we need to make a living, our clear and final goal in life must be the human community. Life is more than a balance sheet and vocation more than net profit.

In relationships, the cross is a reminder that it is in giving that we are made strong, in sacrifice that we are free. The cross is a voluntary rejection of anything that is demeaning or that steals dignity from another. It is not the rejection of all power, but the use of a new power, the power of the spirit.

Let us be clear, this new power will not always "work." We are not guaranteed our own way. It is simply the way to be faithful. Nor does the cross make us milquetoast characters. It does not ask us to wither or shrivel when faced with a task. In fact, Luther tells us, it allows us to sin boldly! It encourages us to take an action though that action may prove wrong.

Luther grew impatient with his cool, detached and scholarly friend, Melanchthon, for being so proper. "For heaven's sake," he shouted, "why don't you go out and sin a little? God deserves to have something to forgive you for!"

Instead of retreat, the cross is an invitation to risk. It is an invitation to a robust life where we will err and sin and mess things up. The way of the cross may indeed lead to trouble, but Paul reminds us that troubles produce endurance, endurance produces God's approval and his approval produces hope.

When we fail, and we will, he does not desert us. When we are cowards, and it will happen, he does not abandon us. When we sin, he forgives.

The cross is not *a* word, it is *the* word to us. It is the final word, the last word we will ever hear. That word is simply this: we are not aliens or enemies or strangers; we are his friends, and the cross is the gift God gives his friends.

WILLIAM R. WHITE
Immanuel Lutheran Church
Mt. Pleasant, Michigan

OUR SURPRISING GOD

Third Sunday in Lent
1 Corinthians 1:22-25

Down through the ages men have sought to describe God in varying ways. One of the most definitive and descriptive of all adjectives for God is the simple word *surprising*. The more we learn of our Creator and his ways among us, the more profoundly we realize this truth.

In our text today St. Paul reiterates this theme as he reminds his readers that God can bring wisdom out of foolishness and strength out of weakness. Anyone even mildly acquainted with the many stories of the Scriptures can recall example after example of this truth. Initially the unconditional trust and obedience of Noah to the commands of God looked like sheer idiocy. How ludicrous to build a boat of such size so far from any water! And who would have dreamed that Moses, slow of speech, and fleeing Egypt for the murder of an Egyptian, would one day return to stand in the courts of Pharaoh and emphatically pronounce the judgment of God. Even the patriarch's wife, Sarah, had to learn through her pregnancy in old age that what looks foolish and impossible to men is frequently wise and very possible for God. Perhaps the clearest example in history of God's ability to surprise his creation is found in the foolishness of his becoming one of us and "being born in the likeness of sinful flesh."

Someone has suggested that God has a splendid sense of humor in which he finds delight in surprising those of little faith with how utterly capable and sufficient he really is. Surely there is a quality about our God that can best be described as serendipity. He is in the business of upsetting our selfish, rigid, and arrogant values and replacing them with those of sacrifice, mercy, and humility. God is looking for people and structures in society that can hold the rich and flavorful "new wine" of his boundless love without bursting at the seams.

Paul well knew his audience as he penned these thoughts in today's text. The inhabitants of Corinth, a notorious ancient city, were worldly-wise and thought of themselves as being sophisticated, at least by the standards of their times. For the Greek philosopher, wisdom was one of life's most coveted goals and was diligently pursued. But Paul wished to show how vain and shallow such wisdom could be. He desired to point up how right the psalmist was when he wrote, centuries earlier, that "the fear of the Lord is the beginning of wisdom."

The Apostle meets his audience with language they would be familiar with but noting one important change. He redefines and gives new meaning to such words as wisdom and strength. He attests to the power of God to surprise us with a whole new value system for our lives. In short, Paul is saying that God's foolishness is wiser than our wisdom and God's weakness is stronger than our strength.

The Folly of the Cross

Perhaps nowhere do we see the surprising and table-turning values of God more graphically displayed than at the cross. For

Jew and Greek alike, the cross was a scandalous offense. How could anyone take seriously a God who would send his son not only to die but to die such a demeaning and despicable death? As Paul accurately notes, such talk of the cross is folly to those who seek signs and wisdom. But to those who are being saved it is the power of God unto salvation.

Indeed the entire life and ministry of Jesus ran contrary to Hebrew and Greek thought. Perhaps this is why so little note was taken of Jesus by historians of his day. The Jew sought a Messiah who would restore the throne of David and the glory of Solomon. The Greek, who venerated the spirit and held disdain for the flesh, could not tolerate the notion of a God who became flesh in order that he might dwell among his people. Yet this is precisely what happened. The Christmas narrative reminds us that God has come to pitch his tent alongside ours. He came to be one of us. Even for us today, the magnitude of this event defies full comprehension. The gift God truly seeks to give is himself!

But the surprises did not stop at Bethlehem. God, through his Son, established a kingdom based on mercy, love, and justice. We were taught (of all things!) that it is better to give than to receive, that in losing ourselves for others we will find ourselves, and that in dying to self and sin we find the essence of life in all its abundance. He further taught that by becoming his slave we will find true freedom. He invites us to seek *first* his kingdom and his righteousness and all things shall be ours as well. He even went so far as to take three of life's most common elements and give them a most uncommon and extraordinary sacramental meaning. In fact, he encourages us to treat all of life sacramentally. Perhaps the greatest surprise of all is that God can take the ordinary likes of you and me and use us in a most extraordinary way if we but let him. Who in all the universe possesses more surprises than this One whom we call God and Father?

The Folly of Our Wisdom

God's surprises are most necessary if he is to rescue the human race from its fallen state. The annals of human history are filled with tragic illustrations of the folly of human wisdom. In our arrogance and disbelief we have often created near havoc for ourselves and others. Alexander the Great sought to conquer the world. The Caesars of Rome boasted of their divinity. Napoleon sought to extend French rule over continental Europe. Adolf

Hitler endeavored to establish a thousand-year reign of German supremacy. Richard Nixon became so engrossed in the pursuit of wealth and power that his administration finally toppled when its eroded foundations gave way. The frightening wave of terrorism that is now infecting certain democratic nations of western Europe is but another classic example of the folly of our times. Youthful radicals carry on their death-dealing nihilistic games while the delicate scales of democracy threaten to collapse altogether.

The folly of our wisdom can be seen in other arenas too. A gross national product that become more gross each year while tens of thousands in our world move closer to sickness and death through malnutrition and starvation. A reluctance or unwillingness to initiate effective handgun legislation while statistics prove that easily one-half of all homicides are unpremeditated and were committed as an act of rage or intoxication where assailant and victim were relatives or at least acquaintances. A lack of trust between nations of the world which yearly forces greater and greater amounts of money to be expanded for armaments while a vast array of human needs go unmet. A national ambivalence concerning the proper dispensing of alcoholic beverages despite the fact that HEW now considers this our nation's number one health problem and fully 60 percent of all highway deaths are alcohol-related. In sum, we hardly need go further than our own persons to realize that none are immune to the folly of prideful wisdom. A few moments of honest reflection will reveal the many times in our own lives when our vain wisdom has surely turned to foolishness.

Our predicament, however, is not without hope. For it is in this very situation that God can often act most redemptively. There is comfort to be found in the fact that God can bring good out of any situation, no matter how despairing the situation may look. Corrie ten Boom's *Hiding Place* gives ample testimony to this reality. So also does Eldridge Cleaver, Charles Colson, and Johnny Cash. Each of us can add names to such a list.

The Folly of Our Strength

It is the nature of sinful people to want to "go it alone." First evidences of this truth can be found in the garden of Eden. Jesus himself struggled with this same issue in another garden centuries later. The thought of being totally free of anyone and any responsibility seems to be one of life's illusive dreams. This was the prodigal son's story. It was the story of our first parents in

Eden who wanted freedom from the command of God. They wanted to test their own strength and thereby stand free and clear of God. Moreover, they wanted to be *like* God. Sadly they learned that the true weakness of every man is that he must have a master, and, if it not be God, then someone or something else will emerge. For the prodigal son it was a disastrous enslavement to his own passions. How easily our desire to test our own strength has led us into life's many pigsties.

God's surprising and redeeming answer to this human dilemma is that true freedom comes solely from him. The hymnist stated it so well: "Make me a captive, Lord, and *then* I shall be free." And not unless or until I am his captive will I ever be free! How badly I want to test my own strength, call all my own shots, and prove my ability to control who and what I am. But such a show of "strength" nearly always ends in failure. Thankfully, it is precisely at this point of weakness that God's strength makes its greatest impact on our lives. The old cliche is still true; man's extremity is God's opportunity. When we reach the end of our rope and admit that our strength is nothing, even the weakness of God comes off looking powerful.

No one knows this life-giving truth better than the alcoholic who has been empowered to maintain his sobriety through the spiritual reawakening of Alcoholics Anonymous. By acknowledging the demise of his own strength and his inability to control his life, the alcoholic takes one giant step forward by trusting and experiencing the real strength and power of God. The first three steps of the A.A. program coincide closely with the whole concept of repentance and trust in the life of the believer. "One, we admitted we were powerless over alcohol and that our lives had become unmanageable. Two, we came to believe that a Power greater than ourselves could restore us to sanity. Three, we made a decision to turn our will and our lives over to the care of God." The day we recognize that the "weakness of God is stronger than men" is the day our faith increases a hundredfold.

In the first book of Kings the writer tells of an especially intriguing incident in the life of Elijah. The prophet had gone into the wilderness to escape the hot anger of Ahab and Jezebel. He is beaten and tired. He despairs so greatly for his ministry that he hopes God will take away his life. His own strength and wisdom have dried up like parched earth.

In time the word of the Lord came to Elijah and invited him to a mountain where he witnessed earthquake, wind, and fire. But the Lord was in none of them. Not until the still small and persistent voice of God was heard did the message reach Elijah's ears. God's surprising activity was seen again. Not only was Elijah given hope but he was shown that this amazing God frequently imparts his wisdom and strength—not through events of sound and fury which may signify nothing—but through unspectacular means which sustain, direct, enlighten, and strengthen his faithful people. By faith we appreciate the surprises of the past and look with anticipation to those of the future.

Come, O Lord, and surprise us once more.

PAUL L. HARRINGTON
Sylvan Lake Lutheran Church
West Bloomfield, Michigan

THE PAST AND GOD'S PRESENCE IN YOUR FUTURE
Fourth Sunday in Lent
Ephesians 2:4-10

Time flies. It also is a-wastin'. It gives us a sense of past, present, and future—moving slowly at some times and quickly at others—but always carrying moments and days into history, never to be relived. Like an ever-rolling stream it bears all its sons away, giving us a sobering sign of our seemingly finite life. But time may be a category of our experience that confuses our faith. It is possible that only by an all-things-made-new understanding of time will we begin to perceive the biblical proclamation about the infinite.

Listen carefully to one of the most important texts for Lent, a portion of the Second Chapter of Ephesians. Listen for the tenses of the verbs, in particular, and what these tenses do for your experience of time within faith.

> But God . . . made us alive together with Christ,
> . . . and raised us up with him . . . that in the
> coming ages he might show the immeasurable
> riches of his grace toward us in Christ Jesus.
> For by grace you have been saved through faith.

What we have here is one of the clearest examples of the way in which the original authors of our faith merged the tenses of things. The timelessness of things and events in Scripture are so puzzling because there is nothing timeless about our experience. Each of us has a beginning and seems to have an ending—

and that face-to-face confrontation with finite facts obliterates our true appreciation of infinite things. Time is full of what has happened, what is happening, and what will happen. But faith is not to be so confined.

Chronos and Kairos

The language of Scripture uses two words to describe what we mean by the single word, "time." *Chronos* is time that is measurable. It is regarding chronos that we speak of days, months, years, and about which we divide it into even smaller sections called hours, minutes, and seconds.

Kairos, on the other hand, is the "accepted" or "acceptable" time, according to Scripture. The Bible speaks of time being "fulfilled," or the "crucial moment," as we might put it. For example, a couple may date for a long time, in terms of chronos. The time for their engagement and marriage is called kairos. Athletes speak of the need to "peak" in their preparation for a particular event. They are looking for kairos, that exact time when their preparations climax.

Add the biblical word for "eternal" and you have another puzzling but potentially powerful insight. It means that the divine has no ending or beginning. It means that God's timeline has no start or stop. Hard to fathom? Yes, but a crucial point if eternity is to be appreciated and if the everlasting is to be grasped.

Science and Seasons

R. Buckminster Fuller speaks of time in scientific and philosophical terms that approach the theological ("Time Present," 1975). "Time is not the fourth dimension," he says, "It is only a relative observation. . . ." He suggests that intellect is top-speed, faster than the speed of light, and exceeded only by the speed of human intuition. The implications for those who contemplate the mind and methods of God are most helpful. Listen to his application of these suggestions. "Life is the eternal/present in the temporal. With death the individual probably loses nothing but gains the insight of all others."

As we move through Lent, in particular, there is no end to the possibilities that a new understanding of time may present. Think of what Scripture is getting at if time has no relevance for God. If the Creator-God is outside our understanding of time, then consider the results for our time-oriented framework for faith.

"For a thousand ages in thy sight are like yesterday when it is past." "Do not ignore this one fact, beloved, that with the Lord one day is a thousand years, and a thousand years as one day." "From everlasting to everlasting, thou art God." It was this mystery that prompted St. Augustine to ponder what God did before he created heaven and earth. Most of us have asked the same question of ourselves or a besieged confirmation pastor. St. Augustine's response was that God did nothing before he made heaven and earth, for time was created along with heaven and earth.

Our faith is plainly and simply full of the timelessness of God. We at once affirm that the kingdom of God is at hand and that it is not yet here. In Christ the kingdom has come, and yet he taught us to pray for it because in the reality of this world it is yet at a distance.

The ancient Creed, "Christ has died; Christ is risen; Christ will come again," puts the Christ-event in timely terms, but terms that transcend watches and calendars.

The Church Year is full of past, present, and future applications of the God of "all-times" and of no-time. Advent is the arrival of something new. For the most part we think of that as Christmas, the approach of the Baby-in-Bethlehem celebration. It is much more than that if our sights can once be expanded to see God's arrival today. Even more exciting can be the anticipation of his arrival again in glory—on the horizon—perhaps today.

Lent, moreover, is meant to focus on the salvation-event, culminating in God on the cross. It happened once-and-for-all, but it is not over-and-done. You and I participate in its reaffirmation daily. To say that Christ is risen is to say something very different from saying that he rose. It is to say he lives, and that you have a chance to live with him.

Time has to be transcended or the prophets who looked forward to the imminent intervention of God to put an end to history —were wrong. They spoke with a kind of urgency that looks slightly mistaken several thousand years later. Unless their excitement was timeless. In Revelation we are urged to get ready, for the "time is near." Two thousand years later it is still "near" but only if we move out of chronological concepts into the kairos of God's creativity.

"Remember ..."

This is why Jesus chose such a special word when he instituted communion. "Do this to remember me," means to do a unique kind of remembering. The Greek word puts you in the upper room with him and the apostles. To remember him in this special way brings the event forward into the present and brings Christ along with it. It is a word for "remembering" that even moves you off into the future and puts you at the Lord's Table at the messianic banquet that will celebrate the beginning of the world to come. It is a timeless remembering that suggests something like a combination of magic and science—fiction with a spiritual application. The word is "sacrament."

The Cross and Glory "Today"

In the final experience of our Lord's ministry of salvation—the experience of the cross—the experience toward which Lent seeks to focus our attention, we have the most explicit and direct scriptural example of the eternality of God invading the present. Jesus said to the thief who repented, "Truly, I say to you, today you will be with me in paradise" (Luke 23:43).

Hear once again the words you have heard for years. Reflect on what you may often have neglected. The word was "today." He did not say, "In three days, you will be with me in paradise;" or "In 40 days, after the Ascension;" he did not say "someday." That would have corresponded to the chronology of the event and theologically would have made it all much less fantastic and more dull.

One cannot look at that statement and penetrate its purpose without realizing that Jesus was speaking within a frame of reference that is totally unlike our concept of chronological time. To put it quite bluntly, Jesus did not experience paradise that day himself. On the other hand, he spent three days in the tomb, or elsewhere, depending upon your understanding of the very complex issues. After that there were many days with the disciples.

One is faced with three very precise alternatives. The first is that Jesus was mistaken on this matter. For whatever reason, he didn't understand the order of things and said "today" clearly indicating he didn't know what the next few would be like. The second is that Jesus was using the term "today" in the most poetic of ways. His use of the term "today" makes the approach of resurrection poetically present, if not historically precise.

There is another interpretation which may even be more exciting. It is quite possible that our Lord chose the term, "today" very deliberately. It is even likely that he knew as clearly as can be known that humanity must not project its concepts of time upon God, and thereby limit God to ours. A far more faithful interpretation of Jesus' experience on the cross and with the penitent thief might be to know, if even for the first time, that Jesus' experience of crucifixion included the experience of his resurrection and even ascension. With God all the events of ultimate meaning have a way of occurring with a kind of immediacy that is not possible with chronos but which is possible in the kairos—or time of faith.

To look at the experiences of humanity with the eye of God, as it were, and to experience salvation as he planned it and provided it *that* day, is to know that Jesus rose from the dead and ascended to the Father all on the same divine day. The moment of death is the moment of resurrection.

Think about the implications. The moment of your Baptism *is* the moment of your salvation. You *were* baptized. You *are* saved. You *have been given* new assurance of God's love on your behalf—you *will* rise in glory. You *have seen* the Christ and have committed yourself to him, you *have stepped* from your grave. You *know* the Lord as Christ—you *have been* raised from the dead.

You are now, today, experiencing the resurrection unto eternal life. You do pass from death to life, and do so again and again. God made you alive together with Christ. He raised you up with him. By grace you have been saved. You have died. You are risen. You can stay that way. The kingdom is now.

GLENN SCHOONOVER
Messiah Lutheran Church
Fargo, North Dakota

POWER TO ENDURE

Fifth Sunday in Lent
Hebrews 5:7-9

There are many slogans around which talk about achieving smashing victories in life; but in day to day living most people are not looking for any big victories. They will gladly settle for the strength to hang on. Nor is this goal necessarily aiming too low. Some instinct tells us that most victories do not come through a sudden burst of power or a brilliant flash of inspiration. They come as one finds the strength somehow to endure. This was part of the appeal of the Academy Award winner, *Rocky,* a story of a second-rate fighter discovering something important about himself as he drove himself to the point where he was able to go fifteen rounds with the champ. Scores of young people and old also flocked to theaters to see the movie, *One on One*, the story of a young basketball player who took an enormous amount of pain, ridicule and abuse, but refused to quit the team until he had vindicated himself.

The Cause of Our Lack of Staying Power

There are countless people every day who are looking for the same power to endure within their place of work or within the four walls of their home. Pressures, faithlessness, illness, or ill-will have been knocking them around to the point where they have had it. They may get a momentary charge out of a story which shows someone holding on to be a winner, but then they are back to reality where faith itself seems to be nothing more than a word. It's nice to talk about enduring, but where do you get the power?

The writer of the Letter to the Hebrews knew that his readers were going to need power to endure, and he also knew that they were drifting away from the source of that power. He reminds them of the power they once knew as he writes:

> Remember how it was with you in the past. In those days, after God's light had shone on you, you suffered many things, yet were not defeated by the struggle. You were at times publicly insulted and mistreated, and at other times you were ready to join those who were being treated this way. You shared the sufferings of prisoners, and when all your belongings were seized, *you endured* your loss gladly, because you knew that you still had for yourselves something much better which would last forever (10:32-34 TEV).

But something had gone wrong, and the writer can see it plainly. They were forgetting what had sustained them. He can see that their grasp on the confession of faith which they once made is slipping (4:14). Now that earlier tests had passed, the practice of their faith was receding instead of deepening. With great sorrow he says, "For though by this time you ought to be teachers, you need someone again to teach you the first principles of God's word" (5:12). They have stayed at the point of needing what he calls "the milk of the word," meaning the A-B-C's of the faith such as children require, when they should be going on to Christian maturity (5:13 and 6:1).

This case of arrested development can happen to us as it happened to them. The pattern is all too familiar. You come to faith in Jesus. You are tested and your faith carries you through. You know what it means to find the help and strength of God. But then the crises diminish, the practice of the Christian way becomes routine, and the sense of importance about what you have found grows dim. You become preoccupied with satisfactions which have little to do with the quality of life and much to do with the luxuries of life. The appeal of pastors and teachers to go beyond the A-B-C's of the faith fall on deaf ears. You are no longer ready for the tests ahead.

Growth Through Testing

Above all, the danger of drifting away from the source of our power comes when, no matter how much you hear God's word and no matter how many courses you take, you avoid that learning which comes only through doing and testing. For there is a certain point at which further learning can take place only through doing. You may read an auto repair manual or a cook book and think you've learned something, but the real learning takes place only when you put your information to the test. But it is at this point that the need for endurance comes in. It is at this point that a man may throw down his tools in disgust or a young bride burst into tears over a mess on the stove and say, "I will never learn!"

Whether we like it or not, however, a faith which is to be more than dry and arid intellectualism which is of no value at all *must and will be tested.* This testing is an essential part of our growth in fellowship with the Savior himself. There is a line from a poem which reads, "Ne'er morning did pass to evening but some heart did break," although we never want to think that this will be our lot. Our greatest illusion is that we can rise to places of spiritual leadership without being tested, or become mature Christians without experiencing suffering, or speak with authority to others about the importance of faith without having our own faith put to the test.

So there we are, in the same condition as those to whom the writer to the Hebrews addressed himself. We are easily led astray toward lesser goals than we once envisioned by the grace of God. We become content with a superficial and untested knowledge. We are duped into thinking that the way to eternal life, since it is the gift of God, will also be easy.

Jesus Is the Source of Our Power

As we exist with such weaknesses, the writer does more than reprove us. He offers us the way back to that source of power which we need if we are to endure. He offers us Jesus. The appeal which he repeatedly makes in this letter in order to strengthen fainting hearts could be summed up in the phrase, "Think of Jesus." In the twelfth chapter we hear him saying: "Let us keep our eyes fixed on Jesus, on whom our faith depends from beginning to end. He did not give up because of the cross! . . . Think of what he went through . . . (and) so do not let yourselves become discouraged and give up" (12:2-3 TEV).

It is in the context of such a call to renewal that our text is cast as the writer calls people to think about Jesus in the "days of his flesh." It is a picture we concentrate upon in the Lenten season and should think about in every season. How often Jesus in weariness and sorrow offered up prayers and supplications for himself and others! How often those prayers were mixed with loud cries and tears! He wept over the blindness of the people as he stood before the grave of Lazarus (though people thought he only wept over dead Lazarus). He wept as he looked down on the Jerusalem which was to reject him. He wept in the garden of Gethsemane as he thought of the cup given him to drink. He cried out on the cross as every consolation was taken away from him.

What does such anguish mean? The writer says that the meaning was this: although Jesus was higher than the angels (1:4), although he was appointed an eternal High Priest after the order of Melchizedek, and yes, even though he was the begotten Son of the Father in heaven, it was necessary for him to learn obedience in the only way it is ever learned: through testing and through suffering (5:6). And because he was willing to be put to the test and—in the face of all evidence to the contrary—trust in the Father alone as the one who could save him from death, Jesus was heard, and he did become the resurrected Lord who could be the source of eternal salvation to all those who call upon him.

Now we come to the big question for those of you who have been called upon to endure and wonder if you will be able to make it. Since you are promised salvation through Jesus, does this mean you will also be exempt from testing? The answer is, "No!" Jesus is the source of your salvation or rescue, but not in the sense that his cross has gained for you an exemption from being called to endure what he once endured. Your sins are fully paid for, but salvation has not made unnecessary for you the kind of prayers, supplications, cries and tears which Jesus once uttered.

He is the source of your salvation also in the sense that as he once endured, so he will give you the same power to endure. He is the source of our salvation in the sense of being the starting point for being able to endure whatever God calls upon us to endure.

If ever there was a writer who calls on people to expect hard going, it is the writer to the Hebrews. If ever there is a writer who promises that God will give us the necessary staying power, it is the same writer. This is his offer:

> a Lord who knows in every respect what you are going through;
>
> a Lord who is a high priest who has made a perfect sacrifice for sin, once and for all;
>
> a Lord who shows you that you have the same loving Father as he had;
>
> a Lord who shows us by his own resurrection victory that the Father will give us the same victory and a city eternal, the foundations of which shall never be shaken.

Hang On!

For some, I know, the testing seems so hard. As a pastor I have often confessed to people that I can't understand why they seem to have to bear so much more than others. I only know that Jesus, looking ahead to the suffering in store for his disciples once said, "The servant is not above the Master." But even as I confess my own bewilderment and insufficiency to give the answer I would like to give, I hear them say to me, thus ministering to me, "Pastor, we know that Jesus had suffered the ultimate for us. That's what keeps us going."

The word to one and all is, "Hang on!" "Endure!" The story is told of a boy who, during a severe winter when the drifts and cold had made the delivery of his morning papers a chore almost beyond his strength, announced that he was going to quit for sure. One morning he found a note in his bundle, written by his father. "You may quit your route in the summer, when the sun is shining, but not in the winter, when there is snow." If by this word a father would help a boy grow into a man, how much more is your Father in heaven calling upon you not to give up, but to find in Jesus the power to endure.

VERNON R. SCHREIBER
Lutheran Church of the Resurrection
Yardley, Pennsylvania

DO WE WEEP OR DO WE REJOICE?

Sunday of the Passion—Palm Sunday
Philippians 2:5-11

Once again it is Palm Sunday. In many ways it is a day of contradictions and opposite moods. Good Friday casts its deep shadow over this day. But just beyond the shadow is the dawn of Easter morning. Do we weep or do we rejoice on this Palm Sunday?

Palm Sunday Glory

Lo, your king comes to you;
    triumphant and victorious is he,
humble and riding on an ass
    on a colt the foal of an ass.

Zechariah 9:9

There was glory on that day. Jesus the king arrived in Jerusalem riding on his donkey. He was welcomed like a hero. The crowd waved their palm branches and spread their garments on the road. "Hosanna to the Son of David! Blessed be he who comes in the name of the Lord! Hosanna in the highest!" We are invited to rejoice and shout with gladness, but the story has another side.

Palm Sunday Humility

Tell the daughter of Zion,
Behold, your king is coming to you,
humble, and mounted on an ass,
and on a colt, the foal of an ass.

Matthew 21:5

There was humility, too, and in and around the day, a sense of sadness, sorrow, betrayal, death. King Jesus rides into a death trap. The enemy waits to ambush him. The cruel events of Holy Week are before him when the Palm Sunday crowd would be crying, "Crucify him, crucify him."

It is in this context today that we are confronted with Paul's words to his Philippian friends. This is probably the most moving passage that Paul ever wrote about Jesus. He presents the paradox of the servant king whom we proclaim as Jesus Christ our Lord.

He Humbled Himself

Servanthood was the central theme of Jesus' life here on earth. At the heart of his work was the humble, selfless desire to serve. He "emptied himself, taking the form of a servant." The Palm Sunday king didn't want to dominate, he wanted to serve. Always he considered the needs of others before himself. Remember the many places during the years of his public ministry where these words are found, "He who humbles himself will be exalted." The life of the servant king was a powerful witness to these words.

Remember the foot-washing incident that is told about in John's Gospel? Jesus and his disciples were in the Upper Room preparing for the Last Supper when he "poured water into a basin and began to wash the disciples' feet, and to wipe them with the towel with which he was girded." They protested. He insisted. "If I then, your Lord and Teacher, have washed your feet, you also ought to wash one another's feet. For I have given you an example, that you also should do as I have done to you" (John 13:5, 14, 15).

He humbled himself. We have his example. Our days are full of humble tasks. This daily work ought to take on new meaning as we think about our Lord's example of servanthood and remember again and again that "He who humbles himself will be exalted."

There are so many humble tasks involved in parenting: diapers, dirty noses, bloody knees, late hours on the living room couch as you wait for the son or daughter to come home. The housewife is constantly aware of the humbling monotony of her daily routine. The farmer goes about the same chores day after day, really a servant of his farm animals. All of us long for the glamour job that is always exciting, always creative. And yet for most of us, a good part of the work day and a good part of our daily living involves the sameness of routine. Oftentimes our role is that of the foot-washer. But Jesus was a foot-washer.

All of us have known some poignant examples of his kind of servanthood. I think of Lois. Her brother Ed had Parkinson's disease. Their mother was in her eighties and very feeble. There were other brothers and sisters, but Ed and his mother preferred to live with Lois. For years she patiently cared for them. And always she did it as though it were a real privilege. I remember her tears at Ed's funeral and her words, "He was such a beautiful guy and he gave so much meaning to my life. I'll miss him so." As I observed her over the years, I thought of our Lord's words on the Sermon on the Mount, "Blessed are the merciful."

Lois was so full of mercy and compassion. She had faithfully followed Christ's admonition to "wash one another's feet."

God Highly Exalted Him

Being a servant is not easy. The Loises of this world know this to be true. But in their serving they find meaning. Our Lord Jesus is the perfect example of this. "He humbled himself and became obedient unto death, even death on a cross." He teaches that the way to life and glory for all of us is the way of cross-bearing.

The hosannas of Palm Sunday help us to see the cross in all of its ugliness and also in all of its glory. We look at the cross and see the ugliness of sin. Our sin. How false our hosannas can be. How our pride and lust for power destroy. They took the finest life in all the world and smashed it on the cross. Jesus Christ died as a despised reject. And we hang our heads, overwhelmed with guilt and sorrow.

But even more, the cross shows us the depth of Christ's love. The cost of his servanthood was the agony of the cross. But the scandal of that cross became his glory and our glory. "God highly exalted him and bestowed on him the name which is above every name, that at the name of Jesus every knee should bow, in heaven and on earth and under the earth, and every tongue confess that Jesus Christ is Lord, to the glory of God the Father." As we lift our heads to see his glory, we are overwhelmed by his love.

Palm Sunday worshipers: Weep over your sins. Rejoice over your Savior.

O Saviour, precious Saviour, Whom yet unseen we love;
O Name of might and favor, All other names above;
We worship thee, we bless thee, To thee alone we sing;
We praise thee and confess thee, Our holy Lord and King.

SBH 419

THEODORE J. VINGER
First Lutheran Church
Kenyon, Minnesota

E PLURIBUS UNUM

Maundy Thursday
1 Corinthians 10:16-17 (18-21)

We have come together tonight by the invitation of our Lord. We have come to a meal where Jesus is our host and where the menu is deceptively simple—bread and wine. We come remembering—memories of a downtrodden people who through divine intervention as the angel of death passed over their homes, were liberated to begin life anew in a new land; memories of a Galilean who in a borrowed room entertained his closest friends and followers; memories of the deceptive nature in each of us as we hear the words "one of you will betray me."

But we also hear the assurance that Christ is here, present among us to take and bless and break and share. With the grim cross brooding on tomorrow's horizon, we know that his words about body and blood are not hyperbole but bitter and brutal reality. The new covenant is sealed tonight—it is a covenant not of death but of life and salvation for with this meal comes the promise of the forgiveness of sins.

The Temptation of Pluralism

In our Epistle for Maundy Thursday, Paul refers to this holy meal, not in the context of its institution but as it relates to the temptations and turmoil of everyday life. One of the major problems in Corinth was the variety of religious options. As a commercial crossroads and melting pot, religious claims and calls of every kind could be heard in that city. Paul therefore, speaks of the Lord's Supper and its consequences in the midst of the religious pluralism of that day. Our old Adam or the natural man likes to shop around for the most convenient religion and for the best bargain. We would like to be polytheists, and have a whole range of choices without committing ourselves totally to any of them. (This despite the fact that we know full well that there is only room for one god at the center of our lives.) Thus, just before speaking of the loaf and the cup of the sacrament, Paul offers the injunction, "my beloved brethren, shun the worship of idols."

Of course, we sophisticated Americans of the last quarter of the twentieth century need not be reminded of that, or do we? We may not be aware of graven images or statues or shrines to strange and unknown gods, but I would suggest to you that they are with us. For example, every age builds cathedrals to house its deities. The best and most lavish construction is employed to show that only the finest should be offered. That was the significance and meaning of the magnificent churches that dot our landscape or are even more evident in Europe. It was common that when approaching a city or town that the most prominent building on the horizon was usually marked with a steeple and a cross. That is becoming increasingly less so.

It has been my observation—and please test this against your own experience—that our newest and most elaborate structures are either banks or insurance buildings. If that is an accurate observation, it would indicate that two of the chief deities in our culture are money and security. This is not to imply that those who own and operate or work in banking or insurance institutions are any more in the service of idols than the rest of us. These cathedrals have been built with the money of all of us and reflect our desires and value systems as well. It is because of this example that the title of this sermon has a deliberate ambiguity. Pull a coin out of your pocket—any coin—and you will find printed on it somewhere, *E Pluribus Unum*—out of the many, one. The reference there is of course to the union of the Thirteen Colonies and the federation of states that we call the United States of America.

One God

Tonight, while still using the same phrase, "out of the many, one," I should like to change the perspective considerably. Out of the many deities and claims for our loyalty, there is only one who is worthy and demands our all. "I am the Lord your God, you shall have no other gods before me" has been the clarion call ever since the children of Israel were liberated from their Egyptian bondage. It is not accidental that Paul reinforces his advice to shun the worship of idols with his reference to the Lord's Supper. Even as the Passover meal immediately preceded the Exodus and marked the beginning of Israel's covenant relationship, so the Lord's Supper as the Lamb of God slain for the sins of the world precedes the resurrection and the triumphant assurance of new life for those who are bound to him in the new covenant. Paul maintains that when we participate in the sacrament we are *bound* to our Lord. Paul here takes up an idea as old as religion itself, namely, that when we take part in a cultic meal, we become a companion of and are united with, the God whose guest we are.

This has much to say about how circumspect we must be with our loyalties and commitments. Strange deities take on subtle forms but whatever it is that concerns you ultimately has become your god. It may be your work, or your profession, or your hobby, or your club, or your lodge, or your country, or your habits, or your prestige, or your power, or your bank account, or your prejudices —the list of possibilities is endless. In the last analysis, however, it usually boils down to a two-fold option—either some extension of my ego as reflected in my narcissistic drives and desires (and this is greatly enforced by the navelgazing tendencies of our age) or, the living God as revealed in Jesus Christ. Out of the many options, one god—either the old Adam or the new Christ. No man can serve two masters. To partake of Holy Communion therefore, is to make a choice, to be united with, to share in, and to be faithful to, the crucified and risen Lord.

One Body

But Paul does not stop there. The implications and ramifications of being united with our Lord in table fellowship has profound sociological consequences. We are united with one another. And not just with those we like, or those who fall in our line of vision but with all people in all times and in all places, who are, or have been, or will be, guests at the Lord's Table. Our unity is not in our commonality or homogeneity. We are not alike—we are of different backgrounds and experiences, of varied languages and races, of disparate cultures and nationalities, of varying ages and inclinations—yet like spokes of a wheel we are joined at the center, in Christ. "All of us, though many, are one body, because we share the same loaf."

That loaf symbolizes the unity of the Body of Christ as well as the source of its life. Let's pursue the analogy of the loaf a bit further. The loaf of bread that Christ shared then and shares with us tonight is the product of some farmer's labor. The grain had been sown and tended. When ripe it was harvested and ground for flour. The thousands of individual kernels had been milled and mixed and kneaded together to form a single loaf. That loaf was taken, blessed, broken and shared.

In a real sense, that same process applies to the church. As separate individuals, each of us distinct and unique, we are taken and formed into a unity. Yes, there may well have been some grinding and milling that we experienced. But in the hands of the Master we are shaped and molded. He has taken us and blessed us. He forgives us and grants us new life as he claims us in Baptism and sets us apart for his use. He feeds and nourishes that life in the Lord's Supper. He unifies us in order again to separate us and distribute us to become pieces of new life in the world he loves.

One Mission

The action of the Eucharist is not only a historical portrayal of Christ and his life, it is also a model for all those who name his name and have been joined with him through his supper.

To put it another way, we see in the Sacrament of Holy Communion both the centripetal and centrifugal forces of God's strategy and intention. That force which draws us to the center of life, to Christ, where we are reborn and renewed is primary. Jesus spoke of the magnetic power of the cross when he said, "And I, when I am lifted up from the earth, will draw all men to myself" (John 12:32). Thus the invitation to come to the table of the Lord is that centripetal force that reminds us that being precedes doing. Here he takes us and blesses us.

There is also a centrifugal force which sends us or impels us outward from the center. We do not spend our lives at the table. We are nourished and strengthened in order that we might be sent and distributed as witnesses and bearers of what we have tasted, seen and heard. "For as often as you eat this bread and drink the cup, you proclaim the Lord's death until he comes" (1 Cor. 11:26). On this night, the words at the empty tomb ring proleptically in our ears—"come and see, go and tell."

In this sacrament a new covenant is established, a new people called into being, and new freedom and life is given. He who is the Bread of Life has incorporated us into his body and through us would share that bread with a hungry world. He who is the True Vine has made us branches that are to bear the fruit of love in a hostile world. Out of the many gods, there is only one God and we know him through Jesus Christ. Out of the many people, he has made one body which he in turn disperses into his world as obedient members who are to serve, witness, and transmit his love.

But now, come, this meal is ready.

LaVern K. Grosc
Christ Lutheran Church
York, Pennsylvania

OUR GREAT HIGH PRIEST

Good Friday
Hebrews 4:14-16; 5:7-9

When Jesus was hanging on the cross on Good Friday, just before his death, he said " 'It is finished'; and he bowed his head and gave up his spirit" (John 19:30). His time on earth was past. He had finished the work which his Father had given him to do. He had lived a perfect life, he had offered the one final sacrifice for sin.

Today's Old Testament Lesson, written centuries before his coming, tells us that the Lord's Suffering Servant "was wounded for our transgressions, he was bruised for our iniquities." This was all planned beforehand by the Father, for "it was the will of the Lord to bruise him; he has put him to grief; when he makes himself an offering for sin . . . because he poured out his soul to death, and was numbered with the transgressors; yet he bore the sin of many . . ." (Isaiah 53:5, 10, 12).

Modern people find it difficult to accept the teaching that Christ sacrificed himself for us. A priest, a sacrifice, always presumes the reality of objective evil and the seriousness of sin. It is hard, even impossible, for some to confess that they have sinned "by thought, word, and deed."

Who needs a priest now? The concept of priesthood is unpopular, out of favor. The idea is downgraded even in parts of the Roman Catholic Church. "Priestcraft" fosters an old fashioned, outdated type of religiosity. There are overtones of medievalism and superstition associated with it.

Yet, it is good that the theologians and liturgical scholars who arranged the new three year lectionary chose this passage from Hebrews as the Epistle for Good Friday. Our text deals with *Christ's* priesthood and sacrifice in a fresh, lively, winning, and deeply personal manner. It points to Jesus Christ, calls him and shows what he means to us in faith and in all the perplexities and trials of life.

Our Great High Priest

"For every high priest chosen from among men is appointed to act on behalf of men in relation to God, to offer gifts and sacrifices for sins." The reference is, of course, to the Jewish high priest. God himself established the office with all its magnificent and moving rituals and ceremonial. The Lord did this in order to satisfy the deepest need of men and women and to point forward to the Coming One.

A true priest in ancient Israel enabled the people to recognize and cope with the reality of sin and evil in life. The priest brought people into contact with almighty God. He was appealing and open in his relationship to ordinary Jews. He understood the problems of the sinner, he had deep sympathy and understanding. "He can deal gently with the ignorant and wayward, since he himself is beset with weakness. Because of this he is bound to offer sacrifice for his own sins as well as for those of the people."

God himself provided his people with a priesthood and with a high priest. Aaron was the first in a line which extended down to the time of Jesus Christ. "And one does not take the honor upon himself, but he is called by God, just as Aaron was."

People Need a Priest

Who needs a priest now? We all do, everyone does! The signs of this need are all around us.

People in large numbers have cast off the moral restraints of the Ten Commandments. They proclaim their freedom, liberation, and independence. The idea is to affirm one's life, to reach the human potential, to express the individual will.

Yet, people have difficulty with themselves and with each other. And they can't believe in God or relate to him. There is much mental and emotional stress. Millions depend on tranquilizers or drugs just to be able to cope with the problems of daily life. It's nice when people say, "Have a good day!" It seems to be harder and harder to have one. People are all mixed up. Have you ever heard so much complaint about the hassle connected with almost everything?

Psychologists and psychiatrists are kept busy because there are many with deep seated feelings of inadequacy, emptiness, even guilt. Many seek out a professional healer or helper, they desperately need someone to listen to them. People seek in others that which they will find only in the Priest which God has provided for them.

The solution to our need is not a return to Judaism! The Jews themselves no longer have a priesthood or a high priest. There is no Hebrew temple, no tabernacle, in Israel or anywhere in the world today. Sacrifices are not offered in a synagogue, A rabbi is not a priest. The pastor in a Christian church is not a priest in the Old Testament sense of the word.

A Priest for Ever

God has provided his promised One to be our great high priest. "So also Christ did not exalt himself to be made a high priest, but was appointed by him who said to him,

'Thou art my Son,
today I have begotten thee';
as he says also in another place,
'Thou art a priest for ever,
after the order of Melchizedek' "

It was Jesus Christ who was "designated by God a high priest after the order of Melchizedek."

Melchizedek, that mysterious sacerdotal figure mentioned in Genesis, king of righteousness and peace, was a type and forerunner of the Redeemer. Christ took up that which was valid and essential in him and in the Old Testament concept. He brought the old priesthood to a glorious end through his fulfillment of all of God's promises. He offered himself as the sacrifice for the sins of the world upon the altar of the cross.

> Offered was he for greatest and for least,
> Himself the Victim and Himself the Priest.
>
> (*SBH* 273)

Christ calls all to come to him for cleansing, forgiveness, peace of heart. He is the One through whom we have a blessed relationship to God.

The Pain and the Paradox

Sacred prophesy tells us of Christ's agony. "He was despised and rejected by men; a man of sorrows and acquainted with grief; and as one from whom men hide their faces, he was despised, and we esteemed him not" (Isa. 53:3). The gospels tell us how he prayed: "Father, if thou art willing, remove this cup from me; nevertheless not my will, but thine be done. . . . And being in an agony he prayed more earnestly; and his sweat became like great drops of blood falling down upon the ground" (Luke 22:42, 44). Our text gives us a further description of the Lord's anguish. "In days of his flesh, Jesus offered up prayers and supplications, with loud cries and tears, to him who was able to save him from death, and he was heard for his godly fear."

We can't fathom all that took place within the body and spirit of Jesus Christ as he bore the pain and load of our sins. "Although he was a Son, he learned obedience through what he suffered." How could he, in whom was hid "all the treasures of wisdom and knowledge" (Col. 2:3) learn obedience in what he suffered for us? How could the perfect One be made more perfect? This is simply stated, in all its mystery, earlier in our Epistle. "For it was fitting that he, for whom and by whom all things exist, in bringing many sons to glory, should make the pioneer of their salvation perfect through suffering" (Heb. 2:10). The mystery and the miracle that is Jesus Christ is our only hope. For "being made perfect he became the source of eternal salvation to all who obey him."

We Live by Faith

This part of the Bible was written over 1900 years ago. Even then, Jesus had already "passed through the heavens." Contact with this great priest is only by faith.

Cling to Jesus Christ as you have come to know him and to believe by the power of his word and Spirit. You can hold to him as you cannot grasp anyone else on earth—loved ones may die, friends may move away or turn away, ministers and pastors are all too imperfect, they may be hard to reach and face. Recall the gracious words of Christ, repeat the Apostles' Creed on occasion, not only in church, but also when you are all alone. Let us hold fast our confession.

Jesus makes it possible for you to come to God in spite of all your frailties and sins. Our text emphasizes aspects of Christ's priesthood which are deeply comforting and encouraging to sinners. "For we have not a high priest who is unable to sympathize with our weaknesses, but one who in every respect has been tempted as we are, yet without sinning."

Just think of what this means to every one of us. Guilt and shame may be deeply inbedded within heart and soul. You may wish that you could obliterate the memory of certain things you have done. There may be people whom you dread to meet because of what they know about you. You may hope and pray that certain letters may not be written, or revealed. You may be guilty of sins which you have never been able to confess to any pastor even though you know that they could never be told to anyone else because of the seal of the confessional.

Christ is your priest. Confess everything to him! He was, in every way, tempted as we are. That which has been a part of your life also came to Jesus. The only difference is that he coped with everything and overcame it "without sinning."

The revelation concerning Christ's temptations can move us to do that which is impossible without him. "Let us then with confidence draw near to the throne of grace, that we may receive mercy and find grace to help in time of need." Tell everything to Jesus Christ. Learn what it means to commune with him in spirit and in truth under the inspiration of his word. You'll find the forgiveness, the understanding, and the acceptance which you desire and need.

He is *Our Great High Priest*. The One we need, a priest forever, human and divine, tempted during his time on earth as we are now. He proves himself if we simply trust and follow him.

There is power, grace, and a peace that is larger than life. There is a steadfast love which is "better than life" (Ps. 63:3), which "surpasses knowledge" (Eph. 3:19). There is a place in God's eternal temple for every penitent and believing sinner because of the work of the great high priest. "For by a single offering he has perfected for all time those who are sanctified" (Heb. 10:14).

We Are Priests

It is significant that the New Testament never uses the term priest in naming and identifying Christian ministers. They are simply called pastors, preachers, shepherds, servants, stewards, elders, overseers. It is the Christian people, all who confess and believe, who are designated as priests in New Testament times: "You are a chosen race, a royal priesthood, a holy nation, God's own people, that you may declare the wonderful deeds of him who called you out of darkness into his marvelous light" (1 Peter 2:9).

It's humbling, isn't it, even a little bit embarrassing, to know that *you* are a priest of God? We're all so frail, so fickle, so imperfect! There is so much that we would prefer to forget. People have often said, "I could never be a minister! It's not for me!"

How can we think of ourselves as priests? How can we do the good works, and speak the good words, which are expected of them? "You shall be to me a kingdom of priests and a holy nation" (Exod. 19:6). That which God spoke to his people in the time of Moses is fulfilled in a more glorious manner in his church, the new "Israel of God" (Gal. 6:16).

There is One who is the hope and the assurance for all. Jesus Christ alone is our great high priest. Stay close to him, hear and use his word daily, rejoice in his promises, pray to God in his holy name. He understands you perfectly, far better than you understand yourself. He knows how it is to live in this world, in times like these. His great sacrifice was offered also for you, it is sufficient to atone for the sins of the world.

JAMES G. MANZ
First St. Paul's Ev. Lutheran Church
Chicago, Illinois

ON A CLEAR DAY YOU CAN SEE FOREVER

The Resurrection of Our Lord—Easter Day
1 Corinthians 15:19-28

I love the mountains. It isn't hard for me to know why I love the mountains. I can trace it back to the time when I was a smokejumper and fire fighter for the United States Forest Service in the Montana Rockies. Something deep within that wilderness country stirs my spirit. As a result of that I take every opportunity I can to go back to the mountains. One of the ways that I maintain my romance with the Rocky Mountains is by going skiing or camping as often as possible in that gorgeous country.

Last winter I was standing with a friend on the top of a ridge in the Colorado Rockies. The azure sky stood out against the snowy brilliance of the sun-washed mountains we were skiing. As we stood on that ridge, we looked back down the valley and saw the road switchbacking its way up the valley like a gigantic serpent. We looked out across the vast expanse of those beautiful peaks. It was as if we were on top of the world. We reminisced about our experience the night before when we were able to gaze billions of miles into space at all of the stars that you can never see when you live in the city. My friend turned to me and said, "You know, out here on a clear day or night, you can see forever."

Easter and our text for today reminds me of that great truth. On a clear day you can see forever. You can see forever because that's the message of Easter. The message of Easter is being able to *see*. It is a message about forever and ever more.

Standing on that ridge and looking across space a person can be speechless and breathless. The sense in which one comes to Easter is that same way. Easter is being able to glance into the forever and to stand speechless and breathless at the wonder, the awe and the presence of knowing that you can live forever.

There's a kind of parable, too, in the experience that I had with my friend because we were looking back at the road, we were celebrating where we were and we were looking beyond that which we could comprehend.

What I'm going to talk about today is that Easter is God's day. It is a day filled with wonder and awe as we look back, as we celebrate the present and as we look beyond today into the future.

Easter Enables Us to Look Back

Our text for today tells us about that. One can't properly understand the text unless one looks back. The words of the text say, "For as by a man came death, by a man has come also the resurrection of the dead. For as in Adam all die, so also in Christ shall all be made alive."

My friend and I had to look back far beyond the miles that we had traveled to get to that majestic ridge. The journey of man goes farther back than the time when those majestic mountains were formed and became the towering spires of granite that they are.

It goes back to the old story in the book of Genesis. It was Adam's sin that brought death into the world. Paul reminds us that it was a direct consequence and penalty of that sin, and that all men literally sinned in Adam. We see that his sin and a tendency to sin came to us as his descendants.

We don't need to go very far to be reminded of that. The conclusion to the Ten Commandments in our catechism reminds us that the sins of one generation are passed on to another and that there is no way that any of us can escape the consequences of sin. All have sinned in Adam—the whole world of humanity has.

That may seem like a strange idea to us, and even unfair, but that was the Jewish belief and it is our belief. All had sinned in Adam, therefore all were under the penalty of death. With the coming of Christ the chain was broken. Christ was sinless and conquered death. Just as all men sinned in Adam, so all men escaped from sin in Christ, and just as all men died in Adam, so all men conquered death in Christ. Our unity with Christ is just as real as our unity with Adam. This destroys the evil effect of the old, and we get two contrasting sets of facts. First, there is Adam and then sin and death.

Second there is Christ and goodness and life. Just as we were all involved in the sin of him who was first created, so we are all involved in the victory of him who recreated mankind. However we may estimate that way of thinking today, it was convincing to those who heard it for the first time, and whatever else is doubtful, it remains true that with Jesus Christ a new power came into the world to liberate all mankind (and you and me) from sin and death. When one reads this text one has to remember that—the "looking back" process.

But Paul just doesn't leave it there either. He talks about something that may seem strange to us in another way, but it was also a looking back. Paul looks back to the feast of the Passover, just like we celebrated it again a few days ago. Only we celebrated it as the Sacrament of Holy Communion. The Passover was a reminder of the deliverance from death, from slavery and from bondage. The new meaning that Christ gave it in that night in which he was betrayed, we celebrate and continue to celebrate.

When Paul speaks of Christ as the "first fruits of them that sleep," Paul was thinking in terms of the picture that every Jew would recognize, but that we really don't. The Feast of the Passover had more than one significance. We remember the one I just spoke about as a deliverance of the children of Israel from Egypt, but it also had a great harvest festival connected with it. It fell just at the time when the barley harvest was due to be gathered. The law laid down the rule, "You shall bring the sheaf of the first fruits of your harvest to the priest and he shall lay the sheaf before the Lord, that you may find acceptance; on the morrow after the Sabbath the priest shall wave it" (Lev. 23:10-11). Some sheaves of the barley must be reaped from a common field. They must not be taken from a garden or an orchard or from specially prepared soil. They must come from a typical field. When the barley was cut, it was brought to the temple. There it was thrashed with soft canes so as not to bruise it. Later it was parched over a fire in a perforated pan so that every grain was touched by the fire. Exposure to the winds blew the chaff away. The grain was then ground in a barley mill and its flour was offered to God. That was the first fruits.

It is significant to note that not until after that was done could the new barley be bought and sold in the shops and bread be made from the new flour. The first fruits were a sign of the harvest to come and the resurrection of Jesus was a sign of the resurrection of all believers which was to come. Just as the new barley could not be used until the first fruits had been duly offered, so the new harvest, the new life, the new eon of life could not come until Jesus had been raised from the dead.

When Paul speaks about this he is saying that you can see forever but you have to first of all look back.

Easter Enables Us to Celebrate Where We Are

Our text says, "If for this life only we have hoped in Christ, we are of all men most to be pitied. But in fact Christ has been raised from the dead. . . ." We'd better remember that sense of pity. If Christ hadn't been raised from the dead, what a pity our lives would be.

"But in fact Christ has been raised from the dead!" That's the proclamation and the celebration of Easter and that's what we celebrate now.

We celebrate it because Christ comes to us in the situations of life.

The meaning of Easter may take on its greatest meaning where we are. If I were to rephrase my friend's statement I might say, "On a *dark* day, you can see forever."

Yes, life reaffirms itself between persons in that invisible geography of crisis in which we sense the presence and person of Jesus Christ. When I am the lowest, he propels himself into my life. When I feel most like I am lost, sick, tired, miserable and dying, He propels himself into my life. The power of Jesus Christ is in all of those situations, that he is in the midst of life. The resurrection reminds me that he is not bound by space or time. He is not bound by a tomb with a rock in front of it, but he is present in my life here and now.

The open tomb always says, "Open your eyes."

In Tennessee Williams' play, *Camino Real,* a man and a woman talk about life. They talk about their past—their future. They speak of tenderness. Her name is Marguarite and his name is Jacques.

Marguarite says sadly, "We're lonely, we're frightened . . . so now then, although we have wounded each other time and again, we stretch out hands to each other in the dark we can't escape from."

"We held together for some dim communal comfort. What is this feeling between us?"

"What is it we feel in whatever is left of our hearts?"

"Something, yes, something delicate, unreal, bloodless! The sort of violets that could grow on the moon or in the crevices of those far-away mountains. . . ."

And then she says, "But tenderness, the violets in the mountains, cannot break the rocks!"

And Jacques replies, "The violets in the mountains can break the rocks if you believe in them and allow them to grow!"

We know that it's true, not only poetically but almost literally, that divine life and the power of God in Jesus Christ in the universe makes violets split rocks with the same divine force that makes delicate daffodils and tender tulips, as well as crabgrass and toadstools push through the frozen ground in the early spring. You've seen it. It may be that you look at the daffodils or the tulips in the garden and you think to yourself, "Surely this is a miracle!" You can look at the crabgrass in the driveway and think, "I have to get some weed killer because this stuff is destroying the entire driveway." I remind you that both were pushed through the earth and the pavement by the same life force of the universe. That life force is called God.

It's the same life force that's hidden and yet revealed, like Christ always is.

In a world of human life and a world of personal relationships that life force, that moving thing, that aliveness of Christ will go through concrete, anger, and hostility.

It is something called love.

Kindness may go by other names. You may call it grace. You

may call it mercy. You may call it peace. You may call it love. When we act it out among ourselves in the crisis and the aloneness of all that is in life, we discover its tenderness and love. We discover the person and power of Christ who is risen and set free. He shows himself in and through other people.

I know it and you know it. I know it in the human kindness in all of its shapes. I know it in human mercy. I know it in human tenderness. In human compassion. In human sympathy. All of this is the life force in Christ that breaks through and reaffirms itself and brings back life between people.

The quality of tenderness, mercy and sympathy is the affirmation of human life and the life of a risen, powerful, dynamic, all alive Christ.

He is risen! And that makes a difference.

That difference enables us to celebrate where we are.

Easter Enables Us to Know What the Future Holds

The resurrection proves that life is stronger than death. If Jesus had died and never rose again, it would prove that death could take the loveliest and best life that ever lived and shatter it.

William Barclay tells about an experience during the Second World War. In a certain city church in London the parish was all set for a harvest festival. In the center of those gifts was a sheaf of corn. But the service was never held for on the Saturday night before the service a savage air raid laid the church in ruins. The months passed and spring came and someone noticed that on the bomb site where the church had stood there were shoots of green. The summer came and the shoots flourished and in the autumn there was a flourishing patch of corn growing amidst the rubbish. Not even the bombs and the destruction could kill the life of the corn and its seeds.

We know that Jesus will reign. He has put all enemies under his feet; the last enemy to be destroyed is death. We can know that the future that all of us will be involved in, is in his hands.

What the future holds is a chance to laugh at death.

The great American playwright Eugene O'Neill, has written a play about that event. Its title is *Lazarus Laughed*.

The play begins with the dramatic event of Jesus raising Lazarus from the dead. The family is there. Guests are there. Guests have come for what they felt was going to be a funeral. Now their funeral grieving has changed to gladness and it's mingled with curiosity.

They ask Lazarus, "What happened?"

110

What had he seen during four days of being dead? What was life beyond like? People gathered around him, followed him into the house and amidst all of the animation, the conversation, the father of Lazarus poses a toast. He says,

"A toast! To my son Lazarus, whom a blessed miracle has brought back from death!"

Lazarus speaking in a voice like a loving whisper of hope and confidence says, "No! There is no death!"

The people, holding their goblets motionless in mid-air, all ask him, "There's no death?"

And Lazarus laughed.

He says in exaltation, "There is only life. I heard the heart of Jesus laughing in His heart. It said, there is eternal life in 'no', and there is the same eternal life in 'yes'. Death is the fear between. And my heart reborn to love of life, cried, 'Yes!' and I laughed in the laughter of God!"

And Lazarus laughs. He laughs, and laughs and laughs. Not only does he laugh because he knows the joy of life, the joy of love, and the joy of Christ, but he also laughs at the many things that those around him think are so important in this life.

Gradually, the guests pick up his infectious laughter.

Eventually, everyone laughs and Lazarus says,

"Laugh! Laugh with me! Death is dead! Fear is no more! There is only life! There is only laughter!"

And he is right, and this is the good news of the Easter message.

Life affirms itself.

Life is mystery and it swims against the flow of time; it's born again and again.

Life affirms itself when our spirits rise above our nature and we swim against the natural tide of meanness, badness and selfishness. And we bring into their places:

Kindness—love—gentleness—faith—hope—and trust.

The good news is that he is here in our lives and we discover that the beauty of life, and the joy of living is present because Christ is present.

Yes, on a clear day, or on a dark day, we can see forever because Easter enables us to look back.

The Presence of Christ enables us to celebrate where we are.

And the Resurrection enables us to know what the future holds.

REUBEN D. GROEHLER
Westwood Lutheran Church
St. Louis Park, Minnesota

THE DEBT THAT'S NEVER PAID

Second Sunday of Easter
1 John 5:1-6

How much in debt are you?

As you reflect on that question, you may think of the balance on the family mortgage. Or, maybe it's the remaining payments on the family car. If you're in college, you may be mentally tabulating the size of your student loan. Even the younger set may recall a loan from a friend or the advance on the weekly allowance. There are very few of us who can honestly say that they have no debts. Even these would have to admit to their share of the national debt, so essentially no one is debt free. There's always someone who has a claim on our resources.

Another Kind of Debt

For Christians, there's another kind of indebtedness. A debt greater than financial. A debt of love. As Christians, we are under obligation to all mankind. Wherever a need exists, and we are capable of meeting that need, there is a rightful claim upon our love. In that sense, all of us are debtors to one another. St. Paul put it this way in his letter to the Romans, "Owe no man anything but to love one another." He knew that this kind of debt could never be repaid. The reason for this is spelled out in the formula that we read as a part of our text for today. It is very simple and uncomplicated. "Everyone who believes that Jesus is the Christ is a child of God, and everyone who loves the parent loves the child." In other words, the claim that people are able to make upon our love grows out of a particular relationship that we sense with God. Because he is our Father, all of mankind are our brothers and our sisters.

This is a startling truth! We ordinary mortals dare call God our Father and ourselves his children. We do it because we believe in Jesus Christ, God's anointed, as our Savior and Lord. We stand in the long tradition that goes back to Peter the apostle, those who have confessed, "You are the Christ, the Son of the Living God." We say this with no boasting, as if we had done something to earn that status. We believe in Jesus Christ only because the Holy Spirit has called us to that faith and enabled us to believe. The interesting truth is, that the moment faith unites us to God it automatically unites us with all of God's children. We have both a Father *and* brothers and sisters.

The very idea that a believer in Jesus Christ would attempt to dwell in isolation and not feel drawn into a fellowship is unthinkable. It was distressing for me, therefore, to read the results of a survey of some evangelistic campaigns of Billy Graham that showed that only 15% of the new converts actually united with a Christian congregation after a year's time. The results of the "Here's Life, America" campaign were even more disturbing. Among those in Indianapolis who claimed, "I Found It," only 3% joined churches. This is a serious distortion of the Christian faith. It's not enough to be satisfied with our own salvation, as if somehow we could be related to God and ignore everyone who lives around us. When the Holy Spirit calls us to faith in Jesus Christ and God becomes our Father, we automatically have others as our brothers and sisters. All these have a claim on our love. That's what John is talking about in today's Epistle.

Example of Early Church

Now the early Christians understood this well. They did not dwell in isolation, ignoring others around them. They sensed this community into which they were brought. It says, for example, in the book of Acts: "Now the company of those who believed were of one heart and soul, and no one said that any of the things which he possessed was his own, but they had everything in common. . . . There was not a needy person among them, for as many as were possessors of lands or houses sold them, and brought the proceeds of what was sold and laid it at the apostles' feet; and distribution was made to each as any had need" (Acts 4:32, 34, 35). It's very obvious that they sensed the claim which other people had on their love. They knew that wherever need existed, it was their responsibility and opportunity as Christians to deal with that need. The Christian cannot call God his Father unless he is ready to call others his brothers and sisters.

The needs among our brothers and sisters are so vast that the claims they make on our love can never be fully settled. You can never burn the mortgage of the indebtedness we owe others. It's a debt that is never fully discharged. Origen, a great Christian scholar of the third century, put it this way: "The debt of love remains with us permanently and never leaves us. This is a debt which we both discharge every day and forever owe." It is a debt which is manifested first in the household of faith by those who are brothers and sisters in Christ, and is seen throughout the entire world wherever needs exist in the human family.

Taught by Example

Personally, I feel very fortunate that I grew up in a home where this was not only taught but also practiced. Some of my earliest memories reach back to the small home we lived in before I started grade school. It was located just a few blocks from the main line of the Northern Pacific Railroad. These were the days of the depression and many people were out of work. It was common then for unemployed men to hop a freight and ride the rails from city to city. When they got off in our community and started their walk toward town, they invariably walked through our neighborhood. Supposedly they had ways of identifying receptive families, and a steady stream found their way to our home. They usually asked for work to earn a meal. Sometimes there was a little wood to chop or some other chore to perform, but no matter what the circumstance my mother never refused a single person who asked for food. I can still see those men sitting on the porch munching sandwiches or joining us at the kitchen table for the evening meal. Why did mother do it? Was it customary? Not necessarily, for there were many homes in the neighborhood which absolutely refused them. Was it because we had so much? Frankly, no. We operated on a very limited budget. There was only one reason. Here were people in need and my mother felt obligated to help. Why? Well, about two blocks from our house was our church. In fact, from our yard you could see the steeple. Every Sunday morning our family was there worshiping. I came to learn how my mother felt. She could not go into that little church, worship God, confess the Creed, profess love for God, and then return to our home and reject any of God's children who were in need.

John writes in this letter that anyone who does not love his brother whom he can see, cannot possibly love God whom he has not seen. And when he speaks of love, he is not referring to sentimental or emotional feeling. Frankly, some of these transients were difficult to love in that sense—some were coarse or unfriendly and carried offensive odors. Some were even surly and didn't seem to appreciate what was done for them. But Christian love is more than an emotion. It is the giving of self for the sake of another. "If anyone has the world's goods and sees his brother in need, yet closes his heart against him, how does God's love abide in him? Little children, let us not love in word or speech but in deed and in truth" (1 John 3:17-18). Christian love is meeting the needs of those who put their claim on us.

114

Claims on Our Love

These childhood memories made an indelible impression on me. They serve to reinforce in my mind and heart the importance of the claim others have on my love. This is needful, because in our busy rush through life we are often tempted to pass by on the other side and ignore our needy brothers and sisters. I thought of that recently as I was returning to Bloomington from a meeting. It was late and I was hurrying to keep an appointment. Suddenly I came upon a dangerous scene. There in the main line of traffic on the interstate, a car was stalled. As I pulled off to the shoulder of the busy highway and looked across, I saw the driver, a young lady. She was frantically trying to lift up the hood. I must admit I really did not want to stop and help. In addition to the appointment to which I was hurrying, it was raining. Fortunately the sense of obligation, implanted in early childhood, overcame the desire not to get involved.

This woman had a claim upon me, upon my love, because God is my Father and she was my sister. She proved to be an African student enrolled at our local university. After determining that the car could not be started, we pushed it off the highway. By now we both were drenched. In attempting to open a can of motor oil with an improvised tool, I accidentally spilled the contents all over my new suit. After further attempts to start the car failed, we transferred her goods to my car and rode on together. The net result was that she got home safely, but I was late, drenched, and coated with oil. No wonder we are tempted to pass by on the other side. Thank God, our selfishness is curbed by the still, small voice that reminds us, ". . . everyone who loves the parent loves the child." Love means practical help in time of need, and everyone in need has a rightful claim upon the love of a Christian. We are debtors to all of God's children. And that debt cannot be discharged apart from some sacrifice and cost on our part.

Transforming a Burden

But, couldn't this become a burden? It is not meant to, for our text tells us, "This is the love of God, that we keep his commandments, and his commandments are not burdensome." If this is true, what removes the burden? The key is found in realizing that the God whom we love is served in the needs of our neighbor. It is easy to sacrifice for the one we truly love.

A woman discovered this who had recently re-married after being a widow for some time. Her first husband had been a demanding tyrant. She remained with him out of sheer loyalty, but resented every moment. One day he did her the biggest favor of his life. He died. Finally she felt free. After being a widow for several years, she met a very fine man, they were married, and it was like the fairy tale—"they lived happily ever after." The whole relationship was a beautiful one. He was sympathetic, understanding, tender, warm, sensitive—all the qualities which the first husband lacked. One day she was cleaning out some desk drawers and came across an old, yellowed piece of paper. When she unfolded it and saw what it was, she reacted with the same sick feeling that she experienced when she read it for the very first time years before. For this was a sheet of instructions her first husband had given her on the second day of their marriage. At the top of the paper it read, "Duties for a Diligent Wife." Then it spelled out in clear detail all the tasks she was to perform. Superimposed upon her by a man for whom she had no real love, they were seen only as a burden. Each time she performed that round of duties on the list she resented them more and more. Out of curiosity she now re-read the list, and was surprised to discover that every requirement on that list she was now doing, but none was seen as a burden. The difference? She was doing them now for a man whom she loved. She wanted to serve him. She was responding to his love for her, and it transformed the whole situation.

Now, something of that is what this lesson is trying to get across to us. For after all, when somebody lays a claim on our love, and we respond, that response is really to God himself. It is an act of devotion and sacrifice to the One who has loved and given us his all. Our neighbor provides us a way to love God, for there is no way to serve God except through our neighbor. When Jesus said "What you have done to the least of these, my brethren, you have done it unto me," he meant that any act of service done for the benefit of another person, is essentially a service to God. That is, I may see the face of Christ in the face of every person who lays a claim on me. What a difference that makes! "We love because he first loved us." This transforms an obligatory task into a willing act of devotion. Our service is to the God we love. All sense of sacrifice, inconvenience, or cost fades when it is measured against the love we want to share with the One who is our Father. What kept the feeding of transients from becoming a burden was my mother's realization that she was serving Christ. What delivered me from resentment over lost time and a soiled suit was the certainty that it was Jesus Christ who stood by that stalled car on a rainswept highway.

That's what transforms the oppressiveness of drudgery and

116

duty into a delightful experience of joy and celebration. In our neighbor God gives us fresh opportunities to return a small portion of the love he has first given us. No one of us would refuse a chance to serve Christ, no matter what the cost. Think of it, every time a neighbor puts his claim on us, it is Christ giving us an opportunity to serve him. There will be many of those opportunities for all of us in the years ahead. Let us rejoice that because God is our Father in Christ, we can serve him through his children who are our brothers and sisters. They have a rightful claim on our love. It is a debt that we'll never discharge, but each day is a fresh opportunity to make a payment.

If we are faithful, it will be said of us, as it was said of the early Christians, "Behold, how these Christians love one another."

HAROLD C. SKILLRUD
St. John's Lutheran Church
Bloomington, Illinois

THE RESURRECTION OF CHRIST MAKES OUR FELLOWSHIP POSSIBLE

Third Sunday of Easter
1 John 1:1—2:2

John tries to make clear that eternal life has appeared in the concreteness of life in this world. He doesn't want to have us think that it is some abstract, vague thing or idea. He talks about hearing it, about seeing it with his own eyes, about touching it with his own hands.

The resurrection of Christ makes our fellowship possible

He says eternal life appeared among us as a Person. That Person is Jesus Christ. John writes about his own concrete experiences with Jesus.

Why does he want to talk to us about Christ? John does so because he sees this as the way we, too, can experience what he experienced. John is convinced that, as we accept Jesus' words about eternal life, we will share in that life.

On the first two Sundays of Easter, we were busy celebrating the event of the resurrection of our Lord. We are, of course, still doing that, but today there is a new perspective. Today we are reminded that the resurrection goes with us into our life in this world. The resurrection of Jesus is the source of eternal life now, and that life calls us to live in the light of the truth in this world. Thus, the resurrection of Christ from the dead takes root in our lives and we live in it. We share in it. The resurrection does not remain merely an event in the past to be celebrated; the eternal life established by the resurrection of our Lord takes root in our lives here and now.

This gift comes to us through words about Christ and his resurrection

The first thing we observe is that it is for us a life created by words. We don't have the opportunity that John did of saying, "That which was from the beginning, which we have heard, which we have seen with our hands, concerning the word of life —that life was made manifest, and we saw it. . . ." Only John, and those like him, can make that statement.

But for us, the gift of eternal life, the gift of the resurrection of Jesus, comes through words. Some of those words are words joined to actions, as in Holy Baptism and the Holy Eucharist, but nevertheless, words.

Eternal life consists of closeness to Christ and to one another

They are remarkable words, though, because they do for us the same thing that John's seeing, hearing, and touching did for him: they bring us into fellowship with John, with one another, with Christ, and with the Father.

This eternal life, which is the gift of God through the resurrection, pushes us close to other people. And as we get close to other people, and to God, we find ourselves closer to the light. John says, "God is light and in him is no darkness at all." To live with the word of the resurrection in your heart is to live in the light.

It is good to be close to one another and to God. This is the purpose for which we were created. To live with the new life of the resurrection in us is to be most fully human. John says, after talking about this fellowship of people in the resurrection, ". . . we are writing this that our joy may be complete." We are glad that we have been given this gift of life, and that we can share it with one another. We are glad that John experienced it. We are glad that Christians through the centuries have received the powerful words bringing new life. We rejoice that it has come down even to our own day. And we are determined to pass it on to the generations that follow us. All of this is what makes the joy of John complete. And it is what makes our joy complete.

The words we share about Christ and his resurrection, bring

about the fellowship of people with Christ and the Father, and with one another. Barriers are broken down. People today often find that words divide them from one another. Individuals and nations are pitted against one another by words. But here, in the words about Christ, walls come tumbling down. Relationships are restored and built up. Life is created by these words, just as God created life in the beginning. And so the Christian congregation, the community where the words about Christ are spoken, becomes an instrument for creating eternal life.

Closeness to God and one another reveals our shortcomings

The words of the Gospel bring the light of God into the midst of the congregation. We know light has a way of revealing things that would otherwise remain hidden. This is true also of the light of God.

The light of the Gospel reveals that our fellowship is not perfect. It reveals that we are sinners. This fellowship we have been talking about is, after all, a fellowship among us, a fellowship involving you and me. You know yourself and I know myself. Sometimes the words about the resurrection and eternal life seem to fall on deaf ears. We do not hear. And we don't live in that new life. We have seen the enemy and he is us! In the light of Easter, our sins stand revealed.

In today's First Lesson, we have an example of how Peter used words about the resurrection of our Lord to call people to make a change in their lives. "Repent therefore," he says, "and turn again, that your sins may be blotted out. . . ."

And in today's Gospel, our Lord says to his disciples, "Thus it is written, that the Christ should suffer and on the third day rise from the dead, and that repentance and forgiveness of sins should be preached in his name to all nations, beginning from Jerusalem." The resurrection of Christ makes it possible to speak realistically about the forgiveness of sins. Without the resurrection, forgiveness of sins is either not seen as necessary, or it is trivialized and sentimentalized.

In the light of Easter, we can see our sins and know the need for forgiveness. The light of Easter reminds us that if we deny our sins we are kidding ourselves. Easter gives us the courage to be honest with God, with ourselves and with one another.

In Christ, we dare to confess our sins

Let's confess our sins. People with the eternal life of the resurrection in them can afford to do that. Playing games with God, with ourselves and with one another is definitely not part of the new life that came with Easter. The truth of Easter makes it possible for us to confess. John writes, ". . . if any one does sin, we have an advocate with the Father, Jesus Christ the righteous; and he is the expiation for our sins, and not for ours only but also for the sins of the whole world." Sinlessness is not one of the characteristics of life in the church. Confession of sin is. Confidence in forgiveness is. The power for this confession and this confidence in forgiveness comes from our risen Lord, Jesus Christ. Christ suffered and died for your sins and mine. He made the great sacrifice for us. That's how much he cared for us. He is not about to lose us to our sins now. He represents us before the Father. He speaks for us. Knowing this should free our consciences to recognize our sins, our hearts to turn from them, and our tongues to confess them.

And, with such a Lord, we are freed up to live in fellowship with one another. If all of us know that all of us are and continue to be forgiven sinners, then we don't need to hide from one another. We can accept one another in the fellowship of eternal life. We dare to get close to one another. Not only do we dare to do so, we want to do so. Easter is the key to our living together in home, community, and church. It is the key because Easter spells the end of phony innocence. We can be honest with ourselves about ourselves. We can see ourselves as sinners, but as forgiven and beloved sinners through Christ. We can look at the sins of our spouse, child, parent, friend, enemy, and remember that Christ sacrificed himself for them, too.

The power of our Lord's resurrection is among us today, calling us to new and eternal life in him

And so, Easter comes alive in our congregation. It isn't just an event that took place years ago in a distant place. Easter is here and now among us as we turn from the darkness of this world to the light of the Gospel of the resurrection of Christ. But we need to be aware that this is a continuing turning, a daily turning. It's real; it's a daily turning from our sin to the new life in Christ. The water of our Baptism, the bread and wine of the Eucharist, and the words conveying the Good News, all make this turning happen. The existence of sin among us is part of the reality in which we live. But an even greater part of the reality of our lives is the forgiveness of sin brought into our midst through the suffering, death, and resurrection of Christ. That forgiveness is the glue that holds us to God and to one another. Let's help one another to know the meaning and joy of this life which is the gift of God through Jesus, our Lord.

ARNE KRISTO
Executive Director for Social Ministry
Lutheran Council of Tidewater
(Virginia)

WHO AM I?

Fourth Sunday of Easter
1 John 3:1-2

Self-identification is one of man's basic problems. "Who am I?" That's the question that plagues people as they try to find their places in a complex society.

A lady says, "I am 48 years old. I have been married for 23 years. My husband credits me with being a good homemaker and a faithful wife. My three children have left home. Now I have a lot of free time but have no occupational skills. Who am I, anyway?"

Such a person is frustrated and unhappy. She entertains thoughts of being a failure. Such an attitude has worn many labels—inferiority complex, low self-image, or personal identity problem.

In Search of an Answer

This question, "Who am I?" has moved people to search for answers. Seminars dealing with "Know Yourself" are well attended. Book publishers have read the signs and are enjoying excellent profits on books that deal with the subject of self-identification. An example of such a book is Jess Lair's *"I Ain't Much Baby—But I'm All I've Got."* Samples of chapters in this book are "Accepting Yourself—Five Minutes at a Time," or "When We Go in Search of Ourselves."

The Youth Research Center in Minneapolis has been studying the needs of youth for the past five years and concludes that low self-image is the underlying problem of youth.

But it is not only youth's problem. The 48-year-old woman mentioned above is bothered with self-identification. Even people in their prime who can write a great success story, find life unfulfilling and are asking, "What's my place in this world?" A visit to any home for the aged will enable you to hear people asking such questions as "Who am I? Where am I going? What does life have in store for me now?"

An Answer from God's Word

For all those who are asking questions about self-identification, God has a word. Listen! "See what love the Father has given us, that we should be called *children of God; and so we are* (1 John 3:1).

It is natural for people to enjoy being identified with prestigious groups. A student at one of our midwestern professional schools tells how one of his classmates never lets the others forget that he is a Harvard man. A friend of mine continually makes reference to the days when she was a student at a prestigious school for women in New England.

If it does something to our ego to have some relationship with prominent families or institutions, what must it do to us if we feel the real impact of these words, "We are the *children of God*"? Perhaps an honest reaction to this statement is, "It should thrill us, it should give us self-worth, but really what does it mean to be God's child?"

Popular opinion says that we are all God's children. God created us. In that sense, we are his children. Thus we talk about the fatherhood of God and the brotherhood of man. It is a beautiful picture, filled with sentiment; but biblically speaking, it is not true.

When John writes, "We are God's children," he is referring to a comparatively small group of people, those who confess Christ as Savior.

It is true that we are God's creation but God saw his intended sons and daughters turn their backs on him and walk out of a personal relationship with him. God wants to move beyond the impersonal relationship of Creator. He wants to be our Father.

In spite of God's disappointment with us, he did not give us up. Rather he sent his Son Jesus Christ to die for us. His death was a payment for our sins and his glorious resurrection wins for us victory over sin, death and the devil. Having completed his work of redemption, Christ assures us that "whoever believes in him will not perish but have everlasting life. For God sent not his Son into the world to condemn the world, but that the world might be saved through him."

The Bible continually emphasizes that by grace, through faith in Christ Jesus, we become the adopted children of God. This explains the difference in our understanding as to who are the "children of God." The popular voices say, "All people are God's children." The Bible declares, "In Christ we are God's children." This teaching is very offensive to the non-Christian and is sometimes confusing to the Christian.

I believe that Professor William Poovey has said it well, "Christianity is an intolerant religion. It is not for us to sit in judgment on other groups. God will judge them, but we are to maintain the truth. On the Gospel we are not tolerant."

Our Mission

It is this teaching that only in Christ are we God's children that is the primary motive for our mission and evangelism programs. For nearly two thousand years our missionaries have gone to distant lands, often at great sacrifices, to share the Gospel with those outside of Christ that they too might become the children of God. Any congregation that takes seriously its mission is involved in teaching the members how to share the faith that the people in our own community might be introduced to Jesus Christ. It is only in Christ that they too can know God as their Father.

A Potential Child

God's Word makes it clear that every person is a *potential* child of God. "God so loved the *world* that he gave his only Son. . . ." Paul writing to Timothy says, "This is good and it pleases God our Savior, who wants *everyone* to be saved and to come to know the truth."

No one needs to be excluded from God's family. If you are outside of this family listen to this invitation, "Repent, and be baptized everyone of you in the name of Jesus Christ for the forgiveness of your sins; and you shall receive the gift of the Holy Spirit. For the promise is to you and to your children and to all that are far off, every one whom the Lord our God calls to him" (Acts 2:38-39). It is this glorious Gospel that the Christian carries to his friends and relatives who are outside of Christ.

The Departed Child

There are also those people who can be called, "the *departed children of God.*" According to the Scriptures, God makes us his children in Holy Baptism. It was through this initiating act we were brought into the family of God. How good it is that many, by God's grace, walk in this covenant with God throughout their entire life.

However, we know that our Father has also given us the right to walk away from the family of God. In such case we are God's sons and daughters who are away from the Father.

Our Lutheran Church has always reckoned with this possibility. Thus our confessions teach us,

> Our churches teach that Baptism is necessary for salvation, that the grace of God is offered through Baptism, and that the children should be baptized, for being offered to God through Baptism, they are received into his grace. (*Augsburg Confession*, Article IX)

But the confessions also say

> Our churches teach that those who have fallen after Baptism can receive the forgiveness of sins whenever they are converted, and that the church ought to impart absolution to those who return to repentance. (*Augsburg Confession*, Article XII)

During these past years some of our young people have rebelled and left home. A few years ago I visited an area in San Francisco where some of these young people were living. One young lady said, "I will never return to my family." Her spirit was filled with bitterness. A young man said, "I would like to go home but pride will not permit me to return to the family."

Last summer I visited with a mother who told me that seven years ago her daughter had left home. They have tried every means to find her, but she is still missing. This mother's heart was desperate. "Where do you suppose my daughter is?" was her question as her eyes filled with tears.

One thing was evident. The rebellious child who had left home was not hurting as badly as the parent who stood waiting for her son or daughter to return. In wonder if that is not the way it is with God. We rebels live as though we can get along famously without God, but our Heavenly Father waits for us to come home.

Are you one of those departed children? You might be a member of a church but you have rejected any personal relationship with the Father. Listen to the Gospel, "You can come home. Your Father is waiting for you."

A Child of the King

There is also that person who lives with the Heavenly Father in a personal relationship. He is not bothered by the question,

124

"Who am I?" He knows he is a child of God who can rely on the promises of God, "I am with you, . . . As your day is so shall be your strength . . . I forgive you." These are the very foundation of his or her life. The good counsel, "Love those who hate you, . . . Forgive as you have been forgiven, Seek first the kingdom of God" are his guide through life.

And the child of God never forgets that his or her relationship with the Father is eternal. "Beloved, we are God's children now; it does not yet appear what we shall be, but we know that when he appears we shall be like him, for we shall see him as he is."

Here we have the note of mystery but how exciting to know that our relationship with the Father knows no end. That is enough. We leave the details until that day when he comes to receive us.

Who am I? Whatever else you might say in answer to this question just remember, you are a child of the King.

HOMER LARSEN
Nazareth Lutheran Church
Cedar Falls, Iowa

ONE TRUTH IN A SUPERMARKET OF IDEAS!

Fifth Sunday of Easter
1 John 3:18-24

"For the message about Christ's death on the cross is nonsense to those who are being lost; but for us who are being saved, it is God's power" (1 Cor. 1:18 TEV).

"This then, is how we will know that we belong to the truth. This is how our hearts will be confident in God's presence" (1 John 3:19 TEV).

My mind went tip-toeing across the lawns of our area and in my imagination, found the house of Mr. and Mrs. John Q. Jones, 1234 Iowa Avenue. John Q. works in the Collins Division of Rockwell International in the management end of engineering. Let's imagine a typical day for J. Q. Jones.

John Q. eats Post Toasties, likes his eggs and bacon and likes it done in a matter of seconds in the radar range. He eats quickly, reads the morning paper and never stops for prayer because John Q. Jones really doesn't think God is involved in his Post Toasties or his eggs and bacon. *The message about Christ's cross is foolishness to those who are being lost. . . . How will we know we belong to the truth?*

At work, John is familiar with all the problems and joys of engineering. He thinks well and the basic natural laws of life are very clear to him. Computers are tremendously exciting to John Q. Very seldom, however, does any God-consciousness get into his mental processes while he is at Collins. And Collins really doesn't consciously need God on a day-to-day basis to meet their competitors. Skill, knowledge of the market, and a good product will take care of that. *The message about Christ's cross is foolishness to those who are being lost. . . . How will we know we belong to the truth?*

One of John Q.'s children is in eighth grade and is studying science and the evolution of man. But no one is really taking time with John Q.'s son to try to put together his belief in God and the whole evolutionary process. So the son struggles to try to make sense out of creation and the Book of Genesis. You see, *the preaching of the cross is foolishness to those who are being lost. . . . How will we know we belong to the truth?*

John's wife, Betty, is having a morning coffee party for the neighborhood wives who are not employed. Religion gets into the chatter. Betty is surprised to learn that one of her neighbors is now going to the Baha'i temple in town . . . another is visiting the Islamic mosque . . . another is studying spiritualism . . . another is going to the Roman Catholic church and another is studying Judaism. The other two in the group . . . well, they just prefer to stay home on Sunday and when spring finally comes, they like to be on the golf course on Sunday morning. *The message about Christ's cross is foolishness to those who are being lost. . . . How will we know we belong to the truth?*

John Q.'s oldest daughter is home on semester break. As a junior, she is plunged into the philosophy of Plato, Socrates, and Aristotle. It is tremendously exciting to her and as she has moved into the philosophical realm of ideas both ancient and modern, her mind is stimulated. Her own feelings about the Christian faith are being challenged. The Bible is something else. *The message about Christ's cross is foolishness to those who are being lost. . . . How will we know we belong to the truth?*

This past week, tragedy hit one of John Q.'s friends. His son was killed in a car accident when a drunken driver moved over on the wrong side of the highway. The veil of depression and sorrow has hit the family and John is having a terrible time trying to put all this together. How can a loving God conceivably permit this kind of tragedy? *The message of Christ's cross is foolishness to those who are being lost. . . . How will we know we belong to the truth?*

126

At the end of John Q.'s day, he sits down to watch the 10 o'clock news. He sees the latest on a kidnapping story . . . the hot news of the Mideast crisis isn't so hot at the moment . . . the President's decision on the latest national strike is splashed before him on the screen. Hoping for some kind of joy, he finally turns to Johhny Carson and watches the humorous cynicism and satire until he is ready to go to bed. For John Q. Jones, *the message of the cross is foolishness to those who are being lost. . . . How will we know we belong to the truth?*

Where does the Gospel of Jesus Christ fit into the kind of life lived by John Q. Jones? If you are open to the age in which we find ourselves, you must admit as I do, that to many a sophisticated person, the cross is nonsense.

At no time in history have we seen so many different faiths and beliefs. We have been plunged into such a world of ideas and philosophies because of the media and also because of accelerated knowledge. And so, life offers a supermarket of ideas on any given subject:

A supermarket of ideas about God.

A supermarket of ideas about religion.

A supermarket of ideas about how to become saved from sin and death.

A supermarket of ideas of how we can find forgiveness and freedom from guilt-laden consciences.

We live in an age of pluralism. Dr. George Forell of the University of Iowa has hit it straight in the head of his book, *The Proclamation of the Gospel in a Pluralistic World.* Let me quote this word from Dr. Forell:

> Pluralism, the existence of various and contradictory approaches to life simultaneously, which can neither be uprooted nor overcome, absorbed or ignored, is the ideologically most threatening aspect of the modern world. It is so threatening because it undermines the notion of "one truth" and thus jeopardizes equally the claims of atheists and theists, nationalists and internationalists, totalitarians and democrats. As Peter Berger has said, "The man in the street is confronted with a wide variety of religious and other reality-defining agencies that compete for his allegiance."

The thrust of my word today is simply—this is the way it is—it is not going to change—it is going to become more tense. The supermarket of ideas and religions will be more abundant the older we become. *Yet God calls you and me to be faithful to the cross, though it is nonsense to those who do not believe. We can know we belong to the truth.* The insights of St. Paul and St. John are valid!

I am reminded of St. Paul's word in 1 Corinthians 2:

> When I came to you, my brothers, to preach God's secret truth to you, I did not use long words and great learning. For I made up my mind to forget everything while I was with you except Jesus Christ, and especially his death on the cross. . . . Your faith, then, does not rest on man's wisdom, but on God's power. Yet I do speak wisdom to those who are spiritually mature. But it is not the wisdom that belongs to this world, or to the powers that rule this world—powers that are losing their power. The wisdom I speak is God's secret wisdom, hidden from men, which God had already chosen for our glory even before the world was made. None of the rulers of this world knew this wisdom. If they had known it, they would not have nailed the Lord of glory to the cross.

That is the way it is. We who believe in Jesus Christ are now thrust into a pluralistic world, into a supermarket of ideas in which we exist. Somehow we must maintain our allegiance to the cross.

I believe there is one truth that exists in the supermarket of ideas which must be marketed . . . moved . . . presented amidst all other religious ideas on the shelves of modern humanity's religious supermarket. It is that God fully revealed himself in Jesus of Nazareth. You can walk up and down the rows of the supermarket. You can inspect all the price tags and values. You can look at the commodities as they are presented in all kinds of packages. Yet, there still is this one truth in Jesus Christ that we Christians believe and must sound with clarion call:

On a hill far away, stood an old rugged cross, the emblem of suffering and shame. . . .

When I survey the wondrous cross, on which the Prince of Glory died. . . .

Beneath the cross of Jesus, I fain would take my stand. . . .

You see, *the preaching of the cross is nonsense to those who are being lost but for those of us who are being saved, it is the power of God. Knowing this truth in our hearts we can become confident in the presence of God.*

Back to John Q. Jones and his family. Though living in a supermarket of ideas, he and his can experience more than the nonsense of the cross. *The power of the cross can be theirs as well! They can know they belong to the truth . . . and be confident in God's presence!*

May this be your experience as well!

GEORGE W. CARLSON
First Lutheran Church
Cedar Rapids, Iowa

FROM BEWARE TO EMBRACE
Sixth Sunday of Easter   *O.K.*
1 John 4:1-11

This Word of God seems to place us on a teeter-totter. Part one sounds an alarm, "Beware! Don't be gullible!" Part two emphasizes a tenderness, "Love one another. He who loves is born of God." The initial call to be judgmental is followed by an appeal to rise up and show affection. We move from criticism to a loving embrace. Two different moods, yet they are to fit together. They are two sides of a single coin. The spirit of truth with which we detect the evil is to live in the same apartment with the spirit of love through which we lift our brothers and sisters and give them support.

Our Problem

We have a problem with this text. It isn't only that we may be sluggish in our role as doctrinal detectives, or shy in developing an extrovert expression of encouragement of others. Our problem includes our inclination to reverse the responses we ought to be giving. We are critical and suspicious at the wrong places. We zig when we should zag. We can be highly critical of Christians of other denominations while at the same time adopting distorted bits of philosophy in our personal life. We are guided by some superstitions or we consult astrology or biorhythms for directions. Meanwhile we shut ourselves off from the guidance which Christian kinfolk could give us. We strain at gnats in judging other believers in Christ while we swallow camels in permitting materialistic whisperings of the tempter to shape our daily decisions.

"Beloved, believe not every spirit!" That warning leaves us uneasy. "How can I know what's right?" is the anxious question we raise.

The problem is comparable to one faced by a missionary family upon their return from a ministry in the New Guinea highlands. Entering an American supermarket after an absence of several years proved to be a cultural shock. Such changes that had occurred! So many choices—so much computing needed to determine the best buys—so many items on the shelves that no one really needs. What a contrast to the simple pattern of buying basic foods at a rural market.

Although skills need to be developed in shopping for groceries, making choices at the spiritual marketplaces is even more difficult. We are to evaluate prices and the quality of goods received —the warning is out that there are dangerous products interspersed on the religious shelves. Neither are there any warning labels attached. Cigarette manufacturers must state that their product has been judged to be injurious to health, but no similar designations are posted by religious merchandisers. Everything is available. Let the buyer beware!

What then shall we do? Those whom St. John addresses as "little children" may well imagine that wise theologians are needed to refute successfully the invasion of false spirits. Obviously such men of God can be a great asset. But if we don't have an expert living in our neighborhood we can run the likelihood of facing the attack of the spirit of evil when there is no one else around to help.

Our Helper

St. John's solution is far better. It's a bit of a surprise to listen to his words. When diabolical foes seek to discredit the Lord Jesus, the holy writer does not rouse the troops to valiantly "Stand up! Stand up for Jesus." He rather pictures the reverse. The Lord begins to protect us. When the false spirits move in on our life, the God of history does not watch us critically from some vantage-point in the heavens, but he is again in action in the wondrous role of our Redeemer. "He who is in you is greater than he who is in the world," is the Apostle's assurance. Our great defense against evil voices is not dependent on our ability to give a brilliant refutation of untruth, but our help is in the name of the Lord, who not only made heaven and earth, but who also knows his people and dwells with them.

There's a second little surprise in the words of St. John. "Every spirit which confesses that Jesus Christ has come in the flesh is of God, and every spirit which does not confess Jesus is not of God." That sounds naively simple. Does it imply that everyone who sings a Christmas carol concerning his birth in a manger is to be identified with the solid truth of God?

Not quite. The writer also states that whoever knows God listens to his messengers. God has communicated through chosen spokesmen who through the inspiration of the Holy Spirit have revealed God's good and gracious will through the sacred word. People then and now who belong to God listen to that eternal voice coming through apostles and prophets. As believers share God's Word with each other, there is a wave of strength and light that continues to bless the people of faith.

But all of the revealed Word finds its fullness in the coming of Jesus Christ. St. John uses this incarnation of our Lord as the dividing line between truth and error. It is the all-important event. It is the moment of warfare but also of peace. Mighty forces resented his appearance. The evil of the world is serious because it is anti-Christ. Demonic powers want no one to interfere with their materialism. God would be acceptable if he would remain in the abstract, but the coming of the Son of God into the flesh is intolerable. They see this Immanuel who is God-with-people as invading their terrain. They marshal the forces against the implications of the incarnation.

But why would God come where he wasn't wanted? Didn't he know what would happen?

In St. John's earlier chapters we can feel the heartbeat of the Almighty Father and we catch some of the tremendous urgency behind this action. The Creater sees the human family in a most pathetic plight. The darkness is so thick that people don't even know themselves. We commonly designate humans as being part of the animal world, only to hear God speak through this tiny concept of life in urgent tones. "You are more than animals. I formed you in my image. You are my beloved! You are to be children of God!"

Our Father

The Father sees and loves. His children are confused and wrong and lost in their shallow life. They are in the power of an unholy trinity—the lust of the flesh, the lust of the eyes and the pride of life. They don't know what they are doing and they don't know what they are missing. The little enjoyment they possess does not last. "The world passes away and the lusts thereof." Dismay and panic set in as life slips out of control. There are cracks in the foundation of life. Man is afraid and he begins to hate. He turns on his God in resentment and on his brothers and sisters whom he views as competitors. When the day inevitably comes that he too passes from the scene, materialism has left only nothingness. Even more tragic is that the creature whom the Maker designed for achievement, fulfillment, and joy, has lost his great birthright.

Into this sad setting, God sends his Son. He comes without shouts or threats. He comes as a child. He enters in love. He appears in our world to share our humanity and to knock at the door of our lives. The Apostle earlier describes the Savior's mission as one that was to destroy the works of the devil. He became the Son of Man in order that he might meet the forces of evil in their own backyard. He faced entrenched iniquity and conquered it! At the same time he reached out to all who were victimized by sin. He searched out the bruised and the broken. He absorbed the pain and sorrow they suffered. He climaxed his ministry in walking into death itself, entering it via the shame of the cross. But he came a-conquering! There was victory beyond death. And he came a-loving! He shared his triumph with all the children of men.

No wonder that Christ makes a difference to us. When he is downgraded, maligned or dismissed, God's people react. To minimize Christ is to tear the heart out of our faith and hope. He is all-important. False prophet, be gone! Christ is supreme in our life!

Our Task

With reliance on the resurrected and abiding Lord for our victory over the evil spirits, a peace comes upon us. However, it is not a stagnant or inactive mood. Our Lord has called a new spirit into action. In releasing us from facing spiritual powers beyond our capabilities, he commissions us for a new task. He excuses us from the need of destroying evil on the basis of our wits, so that he could use our energy in a new beautiful way. He has a mission for us that is exciting and fulfilling.

The new assignment is to love. Christ's mission of ministry to a broken humanity must go on through us. The need is great. People are hurting and bleeding. Those who do not have the beauty of God's grace shining in their hearts are running into brick walls and destroying themselves. Those whose lives are empty because of loneliness or worry need the touch of loving agents of the merciful Savior.

"Beloved, if God so loved us, we ought to love one another." Practice this spirit of love on people you know. Share it in the family circle. Extend it to other Christians who have a goodness to return to you. But then reach out to those who do not yet know how to love. They may hate for they live in fear and in desperation. But the Christ who unlocked eternal beauty and love for us has enough grace for them too. Live the love of God in the outreach to other people. Show them that you care because God cares for both you and them.

The circle is now complete. The false spirit is gone. The new spirit has been formed. The evil is conquered so that we might live the good. Thanks be to God!

VICTOR L. BRANDT
Lutheran Church of the Good Shepherd
Palos Heights, Illinois

ABSENCE MAKES THE FAITH GROW STRONGER
The Ascension of Our Lord
Ephesians 1:16-23

Forty days after Easter Sunday the church celebrates the Ascension of Our Lord. Because it falls on a weekday, Thursday, just ten days before Pentecost, most local churches tend to forget about it. Some make a valiant effort at a special worship service, but most give it simply a passing honorable mention on the following Sunday. Here in our congregation we have for several years now held a special liturgy on the eve before the Day of the Ascension, hoping that the crowd will be somewhat more respectable in size.

Ascension: What Is That?

The church should never quit celebrating the festivals of the work of Jesus Christ through worship services, no matter how minor a certain festival, no matter how few people might come to worship. Besides, it isn't just the small attendance that has caused the demise of Ascension Day. I believe that the church in many places is somewhat embarrassed because it does not quite know what to make of the ascension story to begin with. What really happened back there in A.D. 33 or thereabouts? What does it really mean?

One of our Lutheran congregations recently held what they called The Big Balloon Ascension on the Sunday after Ascension Day. They tried to make something meaningful for the children out of this almost forgotten day. Here is how, in part, they described it: "Sunday schools often fall into a rut—never doing anything above and beyond the call of duty to jolt youngsters out of the routine Sunday lethargy. It is a fact that Sunday schools can become so cluttered with trivia that we fail to give enough or any stress to special days on our church calendar. Ascension Sunday is one of these days when we should aim to bring the glory of Christ's ascension in such a way that children will remember it for years to come. Our Sunday school tried a tactic which we hoped would stress the importance of the ascension as well as provide an opportunity for the youngsters to do some tract ministry." For weeks in advance this Sunday school had rallied resources throughout the congregation in order to finally pull off The Big Balloon Ascension.

Then the occasion arrived. "We held our Ascension Day opening devotion for Sunday school on the lawn behind the church. Each teacher was given enough inflated balloons for every child in his or her class to have one to release on a given signal. Up, up, they floated in a riot of colors, and off they sailed on an obliging breeze. As the youngsters watched the balloons disappear on their tract mission, we hoped the children were also seeing the symbolism of Christ's ascension into heaven."

First Century Imagery

That was a notable effort, but it still lacks basic insight into the essential meaning of the ascension. As twentieth century Christians we continuously want to escape into first century imagination. Consequently we are bothered by the idea of someone making his way up into the clouds, to heaven, to some God sitting there with his Son next to him. Given the first century understanding of the universe, what else should we expect but their witness to the faith be shrouded in the kind of imagery that Luke of today's First Lesson and the Gospel is so familiar with. Now in matters of our witness to the same faith, we must be true to our age. We must struggle to discern the truth of the ascending and ascended Christ and then tell it using our twentieth century imagery.

I thank God for many of you who have helped me in shaping my witness to the faith in imagery that is appropriate in your lives. And there are saints in other times and places who through their writings help me understand our risen and ascended Lord Jesus Christ, "the riches of his glorious inheritance in the saints, and . . . the immeasurable greatness of his power in us who believe."

In his monumental book *On Being a Christian*, Hans Küng

speaks in very helpful ways to us about the Ascension of our Lord.

> The heaven of faith is not the heaven of the astronauts, even though the astronauts themselves expressed it that way when they recited in outer space the biblical account of creation. The heaven of faith is the hidden invisible-incomprehensible sphere of God which no journey into space ever reaches. It is not a place, but a mode of being; not one beyond earth's confines, but bringing all to perfection in God and giving a share in the reign of God. . . . The Ascension is not to be understood and celebrated as a second "salvation fact" after Easter, but as a specially emphasized aspect of the one Easter Event.

Referring to the Gospel reading for today, Küng adds: "Luke wants to say that only those have understood Easter who do not look up to heaven in amazement but bear witness to Jesus in the world" (pp. 352, 354).

First Century Witness

That is exactly what Paul was doing in the Epistle today and, it appears, what Christians in Ephesus were doing: giving witness to Jesus in the world. They refused to stand around belaboring or bemoaning the departure of Jesus. They did not get disabled by the sudden absence of Jesus. They simply got to work, the work of prayerful and active thanksgiving for all that this Jesus Christ had done for them while he had been on earth, and for all that he now was for them and, through them, for all people and things everywhere. They now were the body of that truth in action, pervaded by the fullness of Christ's love through and through.

I am quite sure that already then members in that congregation had different perceptions of the details of the Ascension of our Lord. Amazingly even Luke in the First Lesson and Gospel for today presents two slightly different descriptions of the same event. Of the disciples who "watched it happen," I am sure, no two would have been able to agree on the same detail a short time later. What they all agreed on, however, was that the absence of their Lord now did in no way weaken their witness. In fact, being freed from the obsession to run to Jesus with every little question and disagreement—"Master, where will I sit in the kingdom of heaven?" and the like—they now learned how to walk by themselves in faith. The muscles of their minds and the

tuggings of their hearts were being shaped by this new freedom
into a stronger faith, freed from the necessity to have everything
by sight, right here and now, in easily manageable terms. Thank
God for Christ's absence, they prayed. Thank God for his wisdom
and revelation so that now "having the eyes of our hearts enlightened" we can see more clearly who Christ truly is. It is in
his absence that he is closer to us, more totally available, and in
command of all!

Our Congregation's Witness

What is the meaning of the ascension for us? It is the same,
though our imagery might have changed over the centuries. Or
has it changed all that much? We continue to witness to Christ
through our creeds, hymns and prayers as the first Christians at
Ephesus did through theirs. In fact, scholars are pretty much
agreed that the very phrases in the Epistle selection for today
(as is much of the remainder of the Ephesian letter) are creedal
and liturgical sentences out of their growing worship life. It is
good for us to look at *our* worship life and see with what words
we celebrate the truth that Christ's absence makes the Christian's
faith grow stronger.

The *Service Book and Hymnal* includes two of the three ecumenical creeds. We use them as part of our liturgical worship.
The Apostles' and Nicene Creeds, as well as the Athanasian, in-
clude that little statement about Jesus Christ: "he ascended into
heaven." There are some clues to the meaning of that phrase in
those other witness statements that go right with it: he arose, he
sitteth at the right hand of God, he will come to judge. That is the
church's way, that is our way of joyfully affirming that we are
all in God's hands, under his rule, his loving care. Nothing, not
even death, not even the world's greatest powers of nations and
technocracies hold supreme rule over us. God in Christ does!
And so do we, faintly just now; but when all is said and done,
when he returns, in all clarity.

The same book lists seven hymns as special Ascension day
hymns. These hymns contain some of the insights of the ages
for our faith-growing today. Walk with me through the pages
covering hymns 110 through 116 and consider the insight of
these Christians of past centuries.

> By a new way none ever trod
> Christ mounteth to the throne of God,

May our affections thither tend,
And thither constantly ascend,
Where, seated on the Father's throne,
Thee, reigning in the heavens, we own!

The Venerable Bede of the eighth century witnessed to the ascension in these words. Ten centuries later John Wesley sang out the same truth, very much affirming the basic theme of the ascension event:

See, he lifts his hands above, Allelulia!
See, he shows his prints of love; Alleluia!
Hark! His gracious lips bestow, Alleluia!
Blessings on his church below. Allelulia!
Lord beyond our mortal sight, Allelulia!
Raise our hearts to reach thy height, Alleluia!
There thy face unclouded see, Allelulia!
Find our heaven of heavens in thee. Allelulia!

And the hymn writers of the nineteenth century add still more perspective. Let two selections suffice, by Christopher Wordsworth and Johan Wallin:

Thou hast raised our human nature On the clouds of God's right hand;
There we sit in heavenly places, There with thee in glory stand;
Jesus reigns, adored by angels; Man with God is on the throne;
Mighty Lord, in thine Ascension We by faith behold our own.

How blessed shall those servants be,
O Lord, at thy returning,
Whose hearts are waiting still for thee,
Whose lamps are trimmed and burning.

Christ's Absence, Our Growth

We often wish that Jesus would not have gone away, up, up and away. We would like so very much to cling to him, to run to him with all our questions, frustrations and hurts and let him handle it. But Jesus has said no to that. He will not permit himself to be the one who stands in the way of our freedom, freedom to struggle and to grow. He loves us enough to let us go, freeing us from our dependence on sight. He steps out of our lives so that we can truly step into fullness of living. In all this he relates to us as he did to those first disciples. It was good for them that he should go away. It is good for us!

Crucified, dead, buried, risen, ascended, at the right hand of God—at one with the Father, "Through him, with him, in him, in the unity of the Holy Spirit, all honor and glory is yours, almighty Father, now and forever." His Father and our Father in heaven "has put all things under his feet and has made him the head over all things for the church, which is his body, the fullness of him who fills all in all." In a way, Jesus is for us less in order to be more, for us and for all things and people. He is absent in order for us to experience more profoundly his presence. He challenges us thereby to be more, to be greater, to be more totally present in love to all and in all things, to be more than we would otherwise be, if he were bodily and specifically present.

So with Paul I give thanks for Christ's absence, for his being everywhere in glory, for all of you who enflesh this church, Christ's body, the heart and hands and voices of his fullness. I give thanks because as Christ's body you help me understand what it means to live joyfully during Christ's absence, what it means to grow fonder of his grace and love. I give thanks for Christ's presence in and among you. I join you and all the saints of yesterday, today and for ever "rejoicing to receive all that he accomplished for us . . . and awaiting his coming again to share with us the heavenly feast." Pray with me the prayer of the Great Eucharist: "Join our prayers with those of your servants of every time and place, and unite them in the ceaseless petitions of our great High Priest until he comes in power and great glory as victorious Lord of all." Amen.

GUSTAV KOPKA, JR.
University Lutheran Church
East Lansing, Michigan

LIVE IN LOVE AND GOD LIVES IN YOU
Seventh Sunday of Easter
1 John 4:13-21

Love! Such a simple word and yet so complex. It is said so easily. We love ice cream and movies. We love certain brands of processed food. We sing about it. We talk about it. It sounds so beautiful. It rhymes so easily—"All the world needs now is love sweet love." No one really seems to be against love and we no doubt nodded our heads in agreement as the Second Lesson was read. How beautifully it reads. We live in God, God lives in us for he has given us his Spirit. We know and believe the love God has for us. We agree that whoever lives in love lives in God and God lives in him. We do not fear punishment or judgment for God's love is unconditional. He has first loved us and we reflect his love in love and service to each other.

Then why do we react so differently? Why do we argue and fight and hate and kill in anger? Why do we live so selfishly? Why do we not really let ourselves go on this love trip?

While these questions remain unanswered, it might prove wise for us to consider what it actually means to give ourselves in love, to God and to one another. For it is in the giving that we finally receive the answers.

Love and Believe in Yourself

The point of beginning in love must have its origin in God but it finally works itself out in you and in me. How important it is to properly love ourselves. You are a most important person. God created you so very special. There has never been and there never will be another you. You are that rare combination that is especially you. It is important that you get in touch with *you*. That you learn to love yourself. The best beginning is to realize that God loves you; that God cares enough about you to send you his very best; that he himself comes into your life through his Holy Spirit to bring you to faith; to assure you that the "Word became flesh and dwelt among us." In Christ, God himself comes into the world to show his love and concern for you and for me. He gives up his life because the world will not accept and yet in this giving up he conquers the world. He prays for us as he prays for his disciples. "Holy Father! Keep them safe by the power of your name. Keep them safe from the evil one. May they be truly dedicated to you."

Love yourself! Love God. When Jesus quotes from the Scriptures what some have called the eleventh commandment, he emphasizes "Love the Lord your God with all your heart, with all your soul and with all your strength, and with all your mind and love your neighbor as you love yourself." This self-love is almost an assumption. We need, however, to realize as Erich Fromm points out in *Escape from Freedom:* "Selfishness is not identical with self-love but it is the very opposite. Selfishness is a kind of greediness—the selfish person is always concerned with himself;

he is never satisfied, is always restless—selfishness is rooted in this very lack of fondness for oneself." The selfish person neither loves himself or others.

The self-love that Jesus emphasizes is best described as self-worth, a sort of being able to say—It's good to be me—I am very happy to be me." Rabbi Joshua Liebman advocates a rewording of the biblical commandment to love so that it will read "Love and believe in yourself properly and you will love and believe in your neighbor." Transactional Analysis is a movement which has as its central goal, a learning to feel okay by adopting a kindly, positive and accepting attitude toward yourself.

Jesus implies that we cannot really love others unless we love ourselves. In other words, it's a package deal. You have two people you must love: yourself and your neighbor.

To Love Requires Decision—Commitment

We often think of love as primarily a feeling or an emotion. We talk about "falling in love" or "falling out of love." But feelings are fickle things. They are yo-yos, up and down. To love demands decision. God's love for us was surely his decision to express this love through the incarnation, through the Word becoming flesh, through Christ coming and giving finally his life. John puts it so aptly. "For God loved the world so much that he gave his only Son, so that everyone who believes in him may have eternal life." Paul in his first letter to the Corinthians describes love as being patient, kind, not jealous, conceited or proud. It never gives up, he states. It is eternal. Effective, unconditional love is forever. Love really isn't love until it gives itself away.

Answering the Call of Love

To really give ourselves in love we have to take chances. It demands self-exposure. And self-exposure always involves risks. The risk of being rebuffed; of being refused; of having our feelings seriously hurt. In our Adopt-A-Grandparent Program, Donna gave herself to a lonely elderly resident in one of our nearby convalescent homes. Everything seemed to be going great. She visited her ninety-year-old adopted grandparent on a regular weekly basis. She brought little gifts and spent much time. The relationship was very rewarding for both. But then a stroke came and disabled the senior citizen. Paralysis resulted and then followed refusal. She would have nothing to do with Donna. She refused her visits. Giving yourself in love is risky and if we love as Christ loved us we must take the risks.

Love Expressed

How important it is to communicate our love for each other. John Powell in his book *The Secret of Staying in Love* tells of the day his father died. His father died in his arms in a small hospital room. "It's all over Mom. Dad is dead."

And his mother said to him, "Oh, he was so proud of you. He loved you so much." He said these words were like a sudden shaft of light on a thought he had never before fully absorbed. Later, as the doctor was verifying death, he was leaning against a wall crying softly. A nurse put a comforting arm around him. "I couldn't talk through my tears but I wanted to tell her, I'm not crying because my father is dead. I'm crying because my father never told me that he was proud of me. He never told me that he loved me. I was expected to know the great part I played in his life and the great part I occupied of his heart, but he never told me."

Love needs to be expressed and communicated; needs to be verbalized and activated. Love is expressed is so many ways. A small child without a mother to care for her remembers a woman across the street who always took the time to pin up a snow jacket with a broken zipper; another woman who always baked one extra small pie for her especially; her sisters who let her sleep between them, in the middle of the bed to keep her warm in a bedroom made so cold by the wind of winter blowing across the Kansas plains, that frost formed on the outside of the covers.

Live then in love and God lives in you. Realize first that you are a very special person; that God loves you so much that he brought you to Christ; that God gave of himself for you. Learn to properly love yourself, knowing that God loves you and then give yourself away in love; give yourself away unconditionally. "He who loses his life for my sake will find it."

The love we know, we know in Jesus the Christ. Jesus, the Master, the teacher who symbolically washes the disciples' feet, becomes the servant of all. We, his followers, who bear his name need to follow his example, expressing our selves in loving service to one another. "He who serves the least, serves me" are his words. "God is love and whoever lives in love lives in God and God lives in him." Amen

HOWARD A. LENHARDT
Lutheran Church of the Good Shepherd
Buena Park, California

(with assistance from the Sermon Seminar Group:
Pat Akers, Pat Eggert, Dorothy Jensen and Nancy Peralta)

PENTECOST TODAY

The Day of Pentecost

Acts 2:1-21

It must have been an exciting moment—that 9 o'clock Sunday morning several thousand years ago—when the Holy Spirit descended on the congregation that had gathered together. The strange noise, the flames of fire, the speaking in tongues, the inspired preaching, it all added up to an impressive birthday for the Christian church. But there is no reason why the experience of this first Pentecost should be entirely a one time event. The same Holy Spirit is still alive and active in his church today. As I thought about this this week—the events of the first Pentecost and the church as we see it today—I could not help but think how much the church in our generation needs a Pentecost experience. It would revolutionize the church in our day and inject into it a new life. There are several thoughts that struck me as I began to draw some parallels.

The Zeal of the Apostles

The first was the zeal of the apostles. They were filled to overflowing with the Holy Spirit as they spoke to the international congregation gathered before them. You can be sure that their preaching was something more than quietly reading a carefully prepared speech, or reciting some selected Scripture passages on evangelism that they had memorized for the occasion. They were on fire with enthusiasm—so much so in fact that some of the listeners thought that they might have had a little too much to drink. They had a cause that they felt compelled to proclaim. They were zealous about moving out into their community, and subsequently to the world, with courage and conviction. People might misunderstand them, hate them, persecute them, make martyrs of them, but they certainly would never be able to accuse them of being complacent or apathetic about their faith.

Compare that to the church of our generation. In the intervening generations we have grown rich and fat and in many ways lazy. We have lost some of the apostles' fire of being alive in the Lord. At 9 o'clock on Sunday morning, or 11 o'clock, or whatever the time might be, we join together with other respectable, well-dressed people to sit for an hour in a comfortable church, sing a few hymns, listen to a sermon and then often without too much further thought go back to our lives unchanged, unmoved, untouched.

At a luncheon I recently attended a group of Christians around me were discussing whether one had to believe in the deity of Christ to be a Christian or whether or not his resurrection was important to the Christian faith. The early Christians wouldn't have asked those questions. The words of Peter to the surprised gathering that morning were based on the unequivocable conviction that the Christ whom these people had crucified was now alive. "This Jesus God has raised up, whereof we are witnesses," Peter thundered. Then he went on to say, "therefore . . . know assuredly that God has made this same Jesus, whom you have crucified, both Lord and Christ." Here was the foundation for their zeal: He who had been crucified was alive.

If we don't have the conviction—more than a catechism truth, you understand, more than a spoken confession in a creed—if we don't have the conviction that Jesus Christ is a living Lord vitally involved in our lives today, then we aren't going to be very zealous Christians and we aren't going to have very much influence in our world either—no matter how large a church we might have or how many activities we might have on our church calendar. What the church needs today is a stronger conviction of and commitment to what it believes and is. It needs to recapture the spirit of the first Pentecost.

Whenever people work together, also in the church, there has to be organization and structure. That is necessary to accomplish anything. The church today though often spends more time talking about its budgets and its programs than it does about its Christ. When concerns about the organization become more important than our commitment, then they hinder rather than promote the mission of the church. To be effective at all as the church, in our generation or in any other, we have to arouse ourselves from organizationitis and activity for activity's sake and recover the Pentecost zeal for the risen and living Christ. He is its only reason for existence. Without him there is no church. Active congregations, beautiful church buildings, new missions, beautiful liturgies, complicated programs, oversubscribed budgets, you name it—it is all a waste of energy unless throbbing at the center of it all is an excited commitment to a living Lord.

A Scattered Three Thousand

Another thing that struck me about the Pentecost story is the list of countries that furnished the listening audience. People of 16 different nationalities are listed as being present. It was perhaps one of the most international congregations ever to gather.

I know of only one congregation in the world where we have something similar today. Our Lutheran church in the international city of Geneva lists on its membership roster people from 19 different countries and from every continent of the world who have come to Geneva because of their work in one of the more than 200 international organizations located in the city. Well, here in Jerusalem devout Jews from 16 countries had come to celebrate the Passover and they became the first Christian converts—3000 of them, the account tells us. But these 3000 didn't stay in Jerusalem. They returned to their home countries spreading the word of the living Christ. Here, ten short days after the ascension when Christ had challenged his disciples to go and make disciples of all nations, a dramatic beginning was being made. The Christian church was not to be a group of Christ-followers isolated from the world, set apart in a given place, holding to a truth they had come to know and to cherish. It was to be more than an organization. It was to be an organism of committed people infiltrating society, a community of people who had the vision of a worldwide conquest of people's lives to the God of love.

It is easy for us who are Americans living in a country where being a Christian demands no special sacrifices, where in fact it may even at times be popular to be a Christian—there are some advantages to it—it is easy for us living under those circumstances to become somewhat lackadaisical and sluggish and to convince ourselves that we are being good Christians simply because we go to church regularly, give to church generously, become involved in our local church's program and exercise some religious practices in our homes. Somehow we've got to take seriously the Savior's injunction to get out of our myopia and to move into "the uttermost parts of the earth." Ours is nothing if it is not a global mission.

The Church's Challenge Today

"The uttermost parts of the earth" challenge the Christian church today more than ever before. As church members, too, we are living in a global village and we simply cannot retreat to the point where our vision is limited to our own little sphere of existence. Our Baptism has made us members of a worldwide church, not just a local congregation. We were baptized, not into a Lutheran church or even *the* Lutheran church. We were baptized into Christ, into the body of Christ that is spread throughout the world. We are a part of that body. And we are also part of the world into which as members of the body of Christ we are to live, a world that is tottering, much of it, on the brink of starvation, of revolution, of war, of death, of struggle for social and economic justice and equality. As Christians we are part of a worldwide Pentecost movement that began several thousand years ago and was meant to be not a static event but to continue as a dynamic force. We are not only identified with it; we are extensions of it. We have been additions to that original 3000 as responsible for people's struggles and the church's advance in Africa and India and South America and the whole United States as much as we are right here in our own community.

A few years ago a paraphrase of the New Testament called the Cotton Patch Version appeared on the market. I very much like the way the author consistently translated one word. Whenever the phrase "kingdom of God" appeared in the Gospels he always translated it "the God movement." Let me repeat two familiar little illustrations where Jesus told what the kingdom of God was like and see what a difference it makes to your understanding. "What is the God movement (the kingdom of God) like, and with what shall I compare it? It's like a mustard seed which a man plants in his garden, and it keeps growing until it becomes a big bush, and the birds in the sky make its branches their home." And again he said "With what shall I compare the God movement? It's like yeast which a housewife mixes in three cups of flour until it rises." We are not just members of a church, we are part of the God movement, the great Pentecostal movement of the Spirit, that was let loose to be at work on our planet earth.

The Wonderful Works of God

This is very important for us to understand. The Pentecost story tells us that that group in Jerusalem heard the apostles speak to them of "the wonderful works of God." Do you remember the incident when John was languishing in prison, having his doubts about the Christ whose ways he had prepared, sent his disciples to Jesus to inquire whether he really was the Christ and Jesus sent them back with the words, "Go and tell John what you hear and see: the blind receive their sight and the lame walk, the lepers are cleansed and the deaf hear, and the dead are raised up, and the poor have good news preached to them." That was the evidence that he was the Christ, the things that he did, that he made happen to people. When we in our lives, both as individual Christians and as the church, emulate what Christ did in his ministry, when we are agents in "making the wonderful works of

God" happen, that is evidence of the fact that we are a part of
Christ's spirit let loose in the world, part of the God movement
unleashed on the first Pentecost through the first disciples and
continuing on in the world through us today.

W. J. FIELDS
Evangelical Lutheran Church of Geneva, Switzerland

A LIVING TRUST IN THE TRIUNE GOD
The Holy Trinity—First Sunday after Pentecost
2 Corinthians 13:11-14

NOTE: *As this volume was going to press, the ILCW announced
that the Epistle texts for The Holy Trinity in Series B and A
would be transposed. Therefore this sermon should be used in
connection with Series A, and the present Series A volume of*
AUGSBURG SERMONS *contains the sermon for today.*

Do modern Americans want heroes any more? Or are we too
cynical, too much bombarded with the bad news about everybody
and everything, to reach out and up to one who stands high above
the crowd?

Many have been telling us that this is an age strangely lacking
in heroes, a time, actually, of the antihero. Maybe, I say with
sadness and nostalgia, that is true. The fanatical sports addict
realizes that the athlete-hero is not nearly enough. The most
ardent militarist knows that generals and admirals have their
day in the sun only briefly. The most productive scientists,
churchmen and statesmen may be chosen for the cover of *Time*,
and yet their fame is just as fleeting as the paper it's printed on.
At the same time, cultic figures, often ugly and raucous, draw
people like moths to a flame.

Heroes of Trinitarian Faith

Our hero's name is Athanasius. A little fellow physically, barely
topping five feet, he was unassuming and modest, yet often in
trouble with the political and ecclesiastical powers of his time.
Five times he was exiled, and five times permitted to return to
his work, as the winds blew now against him, now for him.

And what was his work? It may not seem important to our
generation which features religious emotion rather than Scriptural revelation, but his God-given task was to affirm, and keep
on affirming, the historic and classic doctrine that Jesus Christ

is God, not merely divine, and that we are the people of the Holy Trinity. Jesus seen as a creature of God, however he may be loved and exalted, cannot save my soul. Only Jesus the Christ, one with the Father and the Spirit from eternity and to eternity, can be Savior.

It is quite true, as many sects and cults quickly remind us, that the word "trinity" is not in the Bible; but the doctrine of the Holy Trinity, and the confession which the great majority of the historic Christian church confesses, comes from the heart of the Scripture.

Thus when St. Paul ends his highly personal and dynamic second letter to the church in Corinth, he closes with a benediction which is more than a ritual or a tired formula. It is a classic confession of trinitarian faith. It is deliberately worded in such a way as to convey to the leaders of all generations the unshakeable belief that Father, Son, and Holy Spirit are One. The church's three powerful early creeds, called ecumenical because they bespoke the faith of the universal church, were formulated to help us know, believe, and confess that God is One, and that he makes himself known to us in the three persons of the godhead. *Credo:* this is what I believe; and on this belief I stake my whole body of belief, my values, and my life.

Some of those who hear these three verses from the Epistle for this Sunday might have had their attention focused not so much on the Triune God as on Paul's farewell to the congregation he founded. Others may have caught the emphasis Paul gave to Christian living, to peace and love within the family of God. Or you may have wondered at Paul's suggestion that Christians might greet one another with a "holy kiss," and may have wondered what a holy kiss is, and how and when it should be practiced. (Phillips' paraphrase, "A handshake all around, please," is not quite what St. Paul had in mind.)

But the church's reason for selecting this passage for Trinity Sunday is that Paul's closing benediction is the glad confession of trust that God is Three in One.

Does it matter? Are Unitarians, universalists, and others who deny or disregard the Holy Trinity correct when they consider Jesus to have been a noble figure indeed, but not God in the flesh? This is not an academic question, of interest only to a handful of theologians, although a great many of today's church members who belong to denominations which officially subscribe to the trinitarian doctrine pay little or no attention to it. Many have noted that today's emphasis is on instant and one-time conversion experiences. Millions of Americans have appropriated the phrase "born again" as all they need to know or say about the Christian faith. Ignoring the God of creation, and invoking the Holy Spirit as a kind of personal presence, they tend to destroy or distort the balanced revelation of Holy Scripture. In their emphasis upon immediate religious experience of Jesus, usually mystical or emotional, their faith is inwardly directed. But we are redeemed from sin, death and the evil one not by our much believing, or by any ecstatic experience, but by him who said, "I and the Father are one."

Also numerous are Christians whose thinking about God is unbalanced in another way: God is the Holy Spirit who gives gifts of himself, usually tongues, "prophecy" or healing, to or through certain individuals; but the crucified and risen Christ, as well as God the Creator, all too often takes second place to "my experience," or to the most dramatic—and most easy to claim—of the charismatic gifts.

Bedrock of Our Faith

Athanasius, and many others of the earlier heroes of Christian faith, were captured by the whole of God's self-revealing in Scripture. They knew intellectually and saw with the eye of simple faith, as their opponents did not, that no mere demigod Jesus, however different from us creatures, could save us by his example, by his teaching, or by his own relationship to God. They believed and proclaimed, in the words of the Nicene Creed, that Jesus Christ is the

> only-begotten Son of God, begotten of his Father, before all worlds, God of God, Light of Light, Very God of Very God, Begotten, not made, being of one Substance with the Father: By Whom all things were made, Who for us men, and for our salvation came down from heaven, and was incarnate by the Holy Ghost of the Virgin Mary, and was made man, and was crucified also for us under Pontius Pilate. He suffered and was buried, and the third day he rose again according to the Scriptures, and ascended into heaven, and sitteth on the right hand of the Father. And he shall come again with glory to judge both the quick and the dead: whose kingdom shall have no end.

An "outworn creed" which belongs to a dim and ancient age, no longer comprehensible or important to the late twentieth century? Hardly! It is still the bedrock of our holy faith, not a kind of intellectual frosting.

The third great early creed which we affirm in our congregations' constitutions, as well as in the ordination promise of the pastors, bears Athanasius' name. Athanasius, however, did not live to see this creed approved by the entire Christian church of the fifth century. But apart from his strenuous struggle for truth it might have very well happened that the church would have been captured by such men as Arius and later unitarians. No wonder a favorite catchword in the history of the church is "Athanasius against the world."

A Faith to Live By

Do creeds matter anymore? Some say no, "we have no creed but Christ;" but when you ask, "What Christ?" their answer becomes a creed, and usually a faltering reduction of the Son of God on the cross. Does doctrine matter any more? Is "dogma" to be regarded as an oppressive and repressive word? The late Dorothy Sayers answered with a ringing denial, that unless we believe *rightly*, there is not the faintest reason why we should believe at all. She insisted that "the dogma is the drama" of our faith, and that we have seen so much debasement of doctrine that the average churchgoer has fallen far below Scriptural truth to chattering about "Christian principles" or, worse, the "Christian life-style." No, declared Miss Sayers, we cannot remain little children; let us move from the pablum of babes to strong meat. Christ is the friend of little children, but he is also the food of the full-grown.

Yet it will come as no news to anyone that what we are talking about is not mere repetition of a creedal statement, but thinking it through—and allowing the Spirit of God to help us live out our confession.

The divine mystery of the Trinity calls for the best use of our minds and our keenest apprehension of God's self-disclosure. No parking of our brains as we enter the church! We are called "to set our minds on things above where Christ dwells with the Father." He, the Father, he, the Son, and he, the Spirit, commands mind, will, and spirit. No part of life is untouched by the godhead. How filled with pathos and loss, then, is the life of anyone who reduces the high and holy treasures of our faith to moralism, to a vain striving for human goodness and worth! Or to meaninglessness or despair.

What we are given, praise God, is a living trust in the Triune

God and nothing less. From it flows a living of the life of grace, with attitudes and behavior and moral values which do not contradict grace.

Another "yet." With all the proper emphasis on doctrine in general, and the doctrine of the Holy Trinity in particular, yet, face to face with God in personal crisis, I am not brought savingly into his eternal presence by knowing so much, or understanding so well. To be a living witness, I cannot be content with knowing and understanding the minimum that I do, or with formulations which touch only the cortex of my brain.

When everything is at stake in my life, including its ending in this body, I simply rest my case with him who has never broken any promise he has made to me. For this I thank and love him, and seek to serve and obey him.

A good friend, a Lutheran theologian and pastor, died last year. A few weeks before his death, which he knew was soon to come, he told me, "When you're dying, you can't believe how simple your theology becomes."

Simple, indeed. Not ignorant, not stupid, not foolish, not impudent. Rather, so deep, so personal, so all-in-all is the simplicity of glad trust in Father, Son, and Holy Spirit. You and I wish to live out our days in the holy love of the Holy Trinity, and see the way to eternity open.

GERHARD L. BELGUM
Director, Center for Theological Study
Thousand Oaks, California

GOD'S PENTECOST PEOPLE

O.K.

Second Sunday after Pentecost
2 Corinthians 4:5-12

Jesus' resurrection and the gift of the Holy Spirit created a new people. We could call them Easter people. We could call them Pentecost people. They were the first Christians. Jesus' living presence and the Holy Spirit within changed them and changed their living—every day. They were different and their lives were different. Today's lesson from Paul's second letter to the Christians at Corinth pictures this great difference that our Lord's resurrection and the indwelling of the Holy Spirit made in Paul and other early Christians. This picture stirs us. It quickens in us a sense of possibilities. We glimpse what the Lord is ready to be and do in us here and now. The Lord still lives. The Holy

150

Spirit still calls through the Gospel. Given in Baptism, the Spirit still creates among the people of the world a new people, Christ's people, Pentecost people.

Let's see what Paul's word picture, painted for the Christian congregation at Corinth, shows us has happened in every year and century since that first Easter. Let's see what can happen and still happens in people like you and me. God's Pentecost people receive a priceless treasure; they see themselves as servants; and they live by a power not their own. In them the life of the risen Christ is openly shown!

Receive the Priceless Treasure

But what is the treasure that we receive when we are open to the Gospel and welcome it? In the second verse of the lesson for today, Paul writes: "It is the God who first said, 'Let there be light' who has shown in our hearts to bring us the knowledge of his glory, shining in the face of Jesus Christ." That's part of the treasure: to have our hearts and minds illuminated by God so that we can see who Jesus really is. Martin Luther said that God the Holy Spirit calls through the Gospel and brings light through his gifts. The treasure includes recognizing the glory of God in Jesus Christ. The treasure is in seeing that Jesus is Lord, Jesus is the Lamb of God that takes away the sin of the world. The treasure is knowing these things within our hearts and minds so that we become filled with trust in Christ and give ourselves to him. The treasure is the mercy of God; it is love and forgiveness; it is life and salvation. It is the privilege of being chosen by God, of belonging to him and being led and protected by him. It is the risen Christ living in us.

The treasure also is the miracle and responsibility of being partners with God. His Pentecost people receive the treasure of faith and salvation. They also receive the treasure of work to do for God. It is the privilege of following his lead and example. It is the gift of sharing his love with others. This priceless treasure, received through the work of the Holy Spirit, is also a gift of power. In Pentecost people Christ lives. In them the Holy Spirit bears his fruit. In them the Spirit's strength works to show Jesus Christ to others. The priceless treasure is to be openly shown in them.

See Themselves as Servants

So God's Pentecost people see themselves as servants. As Paul put it, "What we preach is not ourselves, but Jesus Christ as

Lord, with ourselves as your servants (slaves!) for Jesus' sake." The Christian's goal is to help others for Jesus' sake. God's people aim to show Jesus Christ as Lord. They strive to do for others anything that Jesus would. Where help is needed, there they want to give help as though they were helping their Lord. God wants others to enjoy the priceless treasure of his love in Christ. He gave his Son that whosoever believes in him may not perish but have everlasting life. Thus persons who received the treasure, see themselves as servants, helping others to know the glory of God shining in Jesus Christ.

God's Pentecost people—Christians—don't come to lord it over people as though they were better than others. It isn't their place to condemn others, or to put them down, or to lay a guilt trip on them. It isn't their place to stun other people with their arguments or to snow them with Bible quotations. Christians present themselves as servants. "If we can be of any help to you, that's the way we want it." We want it that way because that's the way Jesus did it (Mark 10:45) and that's the way he commanded it (Matt. 25:40).

The Lord gives his people what Dr. H. C. Moule called "a new grammar" in which the personal pronouns are reversed. God the Christ, he, is the first person. Others, you, are the second. Self, I, am third. Therefore Christians point to Christ both by loving words and helpful deeds.

See Themselves as Clay Pots

But these Pentecost people who have received the priceless treasure also see themselves as clay pots. Paul writes, "We have this treasure in earthen vessels." The containers that hold the treasure are like common earthenware. Every pot has its flaws; every pot is fragile and breakable. These containers don't look like much, especially in comparison with the beauty and value of Christ and the gifts of the Holy Spirit.

Normally earthenware vessels can't do much except hold or display something. They can hold water or wine as a pitcher does, or they can display colorful fragrant flowers or beautiful plants as a vase does. Christians, too, have limited powers although persons can do much more than cups and saucers, vases and pitchers.

Isn't it amazing that God gives his treasure to limited, sinful, breakable persons? Isn't it even more amazing and somewhat scary that he makes us partners in showing and sharing this gift of heaven? Just the other day we read in our local newspapers that for the first time ever in the United States Jean-Francois

Millet's masterpiece painting "The Gleaners" is to be shown at the Minneapolis Institute of Arts. That means extra security precautions, special guards and equipment. Although there is a chance that the painting may be damaged or stolen, it will be shown, no matter how valuable it is. It must be shown! Something so special, so skillfully done, so able to speak to the heart, just can't be kept hidden, no matter what the risk. It's meant to be seen and appreciated. It's meant to have opportunity to touch us and even to change us. Good reasons prompt the Institute of Arts to make this exhibition, even if it costs to do so. In the same way, God has strong reasons for giving his treasure to people like us and counting on us to exhibit it before our fellow men, even if we don't feel up to it or right for it. Once a man said to me about trying to share his faith, "I feel as though I were holding in my hands a rare, costly vase and am afraid I might drop it."

God doesn't expect us to be perfect. He asks only that we turn ourselves, our minds and emotions, our imagination and skills, over to him for his use. He asks that we consecrate our energy and effort to him even if we are uneasy or afraid. All that is asked of us is to be willing. The treasure is ours if we are willing to receive it and willing to share it. God has a real purpose in mind. Paul wrote: "We have this treasure in earthen vessels, to show that the transcendent power belongs to God and not to us." Through people like us it can be perfectly clear that the Gospel's power to attract, change and bless others belongs to him, not to us. God's Pentecost people live by a power not their own.

Live by a Power Not Their Own

Paul knew from experience that God's strength is "made perfect in weakness" (2 Cor. 12:9) and that his grace is adequate for every need. God's power is strongest when we are weak. His weakness is far superior to our might (1 Cor. 1:25). Not our skill but the splendid power of God's grace changes ordinary people into Christ-persons, cross-persons.

God's Pentecost people live by a power not their own, superior to all difficulties and danger. God's ways, God's thought and God's power are not our ways, our thoughts or our power. They are higher than ours as the heavens are higher than the sea.

Thus we don't need to be alarmed about our weakness, or the loose ends we leave lying around, or the errors we make. We don't need to hold back because of the pressures and problems or the knock-down-drag-out that we may experience as bearers of the treasure.

By the power that belongs to God, Paul and early Christians could declare: "We are often troubled, but not crushed. We are pressed by difficulties on every side, but we are never concerned. We are frustrated but not to the point of despair."

Although these Christians became perplexed and couldn't see why things happened as they did and sometimes even were in doubt, they never felt hopeless. They never lost heart even though they couldn't see an answer to their problems.

God's power in his Pentecost people meant that they never had to stand things alone. Ridiculed, shut out and faced with many enemies, they were never without a friend, "All the way my Savior leads me, Cheers each winding path I tread, Gives me grace for every trial, Feeds me with the living bread."

The power of God sees to it that although Christians may be badly hurt at times and even knocked down, they are not destroyed. The world can never count out either Christians or their churches. "For us fights the Valiant one whom God himself elected." Lincoln Steffens once wrote of an interview that he had with Mark Fagan, then mayor of Jersey City. He asked how Fagan had been able to take the smear tactics, to withstand the temptation to take bribes and to face up to the graft. His one answer was, "I have a way!" Asked, "What is it?", Fagan pointed to a picture of Christ on the wall of his office, illustrating the words of John 14:6: "I am the Way."

Life Openly Shown

One more thing is to be said here about the people created by Jesus' resurrection and the gift of the Holy Spirit. In them the life of the risen Christ is openly shown. It's a matter of his life in ours.

Paul wrote: "At all times we carry in our mortal bodies the death of Jesus, so that his life also may be seen in our bodies." The promise of God is that by Baptism and faith we become partners in Christ's death and resurrection. "You were buried with him in baptism, in which you were also raised with him through faith in the working of God, who raised him from the dead" (Col. 2:12). United with Christ, we know both the suffering and the triumph of our Lord. God's purpose is to show openly in our mortal bodies the victorious life of Jesus Christ.

When we're up against it is exactly the time that Christ's life can best be seen in ours. Paul wrote: "Throughout our lives we are always in danger of death for Jesus' sake, in order that his life may be seen in these mortal lives of ours." It's in the high risk situations that Christ's life can be seen most clearly in ours, if we want it to be, if we count on him for it, if patiently we welcome the grace that he grants us. "Let the beauty of Jesus be seen in me, all his wondrous compassion and purity."

God's purpose is, as Paul states in verse 12 of our text, that others may know more and more of life in Christ. It's a life where God works through suffering and death to bring new life. It's a life where "in everything God works for good with those who love him, who are called according to his purpose" (Rom. 8:28)! Right now when Jesus brings us out of our emotional deadlocks, others are helped to know the priceless treasure. Right now when Christ restores our broken relationships, the glory of his love is reflected into other lives. Right now his life shown in our illness, pain, and loss can inspire faith and hope in others who suffer. Right now, when by the persuasion of the Holy Spirit we keep on working toward the impossible goals or "lost" causes of justice and of love, the life of Christ works life in other people.

Pentecost people are a miracle of God that he produces through Baptism and faith. Because of Jesus' resurrection and the gift of the Holy Spirit, Christians receive the priceless treasure; they see themselves as servants and clay pots; they live by power not their own. In them the life of the risen Christ is openly shown and works in the lives of others.

Come! Join us! Let us consecrate ourselves and our limitations, our hardships and our hopes, to the glory of God and to the salvation of all people.

We are of good cheer! Christ has overcome the world.

REYNOLD N. JOHNSON
St. Mark's Lutheran Church
Minneapolis, Minnesota

WHAT WE BELIEVE, WE SPEAK!

Third Sunday after Pentecost
2 Corinthians 4:13-18

"Since we have the same spirit of faith as he had who wrote, 'I believed, and so I spoke,' we too believe, and so we speak, . . ." What do you believe? In whom do you believe? What would you give up everything—including your life—for? The answer to those questions, Paul says here, becomes clear when you look at what you talk about.

What do you talk about in your family, with your friends, neighbors and associates? What did you talk about at home this morning or when you first greeted your brothers and sisters here at church? The weather? Your job? The government? The stockmarket? Unemployment? Fashions? Your vacation? Your golf game? Your teachers? Or Jesus Christ as Lord of all. What you talk about is what you believe in, says Paul.

Paul had one topic above everything. I'm sure he talked about the weather the night his ship was caught in a storm and in danger of sinking. But he also talked to, and about, his Lord. He probably talked about jobs, fashions, the government, and so forth, at various times. But most of all he talked and wrote about Jesus Christ.

Because he believed in him. He really believed that Jesus was Lord. And he believed it so firmly that he gave up everything for him. And he did that because in Jesus Christ he found everything he'd been looking for—the forgiveness of sins, the power and presence of God, the purpose for his whole existence.

Because he knew and talked of a living Lord worth giving up everything for, there was excitement and life wherever he went. There were healings, signs, and wonders. There was the sense of the presence of the living God. And people who were sick or troubled or dying came because they found something real there.

It was the same with Jesus' ministry—only more so. The Gospel for today tells us that "the crowd came together again, so that they could not even eat." Why? Not to hear someone talk about a budget or about how to organize to drive out the Romans, or about the weather, or their golf game, or even to give a talk about God. They came because he spoke with authority. They came because they knew he knew what he was talking about. They came because they knew he could heal them. They came to him finally, again, because in him they found something real.

A Crisis of Faith

We hear and read a fair amount today about the crisis in the institutional church. People are not really flocking in. Some few churches grow. Most barely stay afloat. A few slip under the waves. We hear many explanations for the crisis. We live in a post-Christian era; we live in a day so saturated with materialism, secularism, and science that people cannot hear the Word of God. And so on. But if I hear this word rightly, God would disagree. He would say that if there is a crisis, it is a crisis of faith, of your faith and mine. Because what we believe, we speak. And if we're speaking God's Word, as did Jesus and Paul and many others, people will come just as they did when Jesus and Paul walked the earth.

Such Speaking Provokes Hostility

Not that such speaking is always easy. Paul speaks of his "outer nature wasting away," which is a rather indirect way of describing his life as one of suffering and persecution. That was the story of his life, beginning almost immediately in Damascus and never really changing. You know the long list of sufferings in the 11th chapter of this letter. And the tradition is that he was finally beheaded for his speaking.

It was the same for Jesus. The incident referred to in the Gospel happened fairly early in his ministry. His own family thought he was "beside himself." The people officially in charge of religion in those parts accused him of being in league with the devil himself. And you know the end of his life.

Which is all very strange! Because Paul's purpose—and surely Jesus'—was in the words of this text "to extend grace to more and more people, to increase thanksgiving to the glory of God." Wouldn't you think people would want that? To feel so great that they couldn't help giving thanks? To receive grace? For grace is the amazing nature of God; that even when we're hurting and broken and running as fast as we can to get away from him, he still reaches out to heal us. That's why Jesus came. That's why Paul spoke in Jesus' name. And yet, strangely, even though people flocked to hear, many ended up hating them. And Jesus said we should expect the same.

Imagine! If you found a cure for cancer, which might give people an extra 20, 30, or 40 years, you could name your price. People would literally come from the ends of the earth and give you everything they had. But if you tell them about Jesus Christ and his cure, which literally erases death forever, many of them will hate you.

The Old Testament Lesson tells you why. Because the Word of God uncovers the sin and nakedness of our souls which we so carefully try to hide. And when that Word gets too close to the tender spots in people's lives, they try to defend themselves, either as in this Old Testament Lesson by blaming someone else —their wife, their parents, the environment, God, anything—or by turning on the bearer of that Word.

But Paul spoke it anyway. As did Jesus. And as have countless numbers since then. Why? Because they knew it was life. Jesus, of course, because he knew God's life was in himself as well as through the gift of the Spirit at his Baptism. And Paul and others because in Jesus they had found everything.

We Need Healing

That's what we need. I know I do. And we need it, not just to find something to talk about or to witness to or to see others come to hear. We need healing ourselves for our own sake. We need to find that still today Jesus is alive and through his promised Holy Spirit still giving everything.

Because when you know he is alive and can give you everything, you will believe in him. You will trust him. You will be filled with him and, like Paul, you will speak because you believe. Like Peter and John you'll find yourself saying to those who might not approve of what you're saying, "If you don't like this word, you'll have to handle it as best you can. But we simply must talk about what we have seen and heard."

And so we've come full circle. We believe and so we speak. We talk about what we believe it.

How to Believe

But there's one last very important item. How do you believe? There have been hints about that in this sermon but we must yet hear Paul's beautiful and simple description of the source of his faith and life. He says it so plainly, ". . . because we look not to the things that are seen but to the things that are unseen; for the things that are seen are transient, but the things that are unseen are eternal."

Now, on the face of it, my friends, that's the most logical, clear and irrefutable word you'll ever hear. Don't look to and trust what won't last very long—which happens to be everything you can see. Good sense? Certainly. If it doesn't last, it's a poor place to pin your hopes or to look for meaning.

And what are those things you can see? Anything and everything. Look around you right now. What of anything you can see will be here after a hundred years? Us? This building? Those trees? Our cars? Probably none of them.

And yet they can seem so important. People. When you're around them, they loom so big. "What will they think of me; will they like me?" we ask. But where will they be in a hundred years? Or the house you live in? Or the piece of paper that says you can spend so many dollars for the next half month. That latter one, of course, has the shortest life of them all.

So the first secret of faith—of being whole, of finding what you're looking for and what you'd give your life for—is not to look at what you can see. Forget it. Cross it off. Leave it behind.

But there's a second item which really makes the first possible. And that is to look at what you can't see. For Paul that had to be Jesus Christ. Because it was when Jesus Christ revealed himself to Paul on that road to Damascus that Paul's life began. And so it will for you. It is in Jesus Christ and only in him that there is life.

Because, you see, Jesus Christ is the eternal God who became your brother. He loved you so much that he said to the Father, "I'll become responsible for their sins and I'll do battle with all their enemies so that they can be free to belong only to you." And that's exactly what he did. He took our place to shed his blood and die for us and for our sins. He did battle with our every enemy so that we might be set free.

And he rose again as the One who destroyed every enemy, including death—to show us his victory and to share it with us. He lives today to give us everything—to fill us with his Holy Spirit and all his gifts.

Two things then: We need to look at him as that unseen One —see him as the One for us. And we need to turn our eyes from everything we can see. In a word, we need to repent. That's what it means to repent—to change your direction, to become new and different. In this case, to take your eyes off and to give up everything we can see and to fasten them only on Jesus Christ.

In that kind of look is the faith which heals and satisfies our own deepest needs and longings. And in that kind of look is the faith which cannot but speak what it has seen and heard.

ROBERT G. HECKMANN
Our Redeemer Lutheran Church
Newark, Delaware

WHAT IF I DIE?

Fourth Sunday after Pentecost
2 Corinthians 5:1-10

Oh take my hand, dear Father,
And lead thou me,
Till at my journey's ending

I dwell with thee.
Alone, I cannot wander, one single day,
So do thou guide my footsteps
On life's rough way.

What if I die?
How many times has each of us asked that question!?
What if I die?
Yet, as Peter Marshall said in one of his great sermons on that question from Job of old, "How strange to say 'if.' There is no 'if!' *When* I die, shall I live again?"
But still we wonder. What's it going to be like for us after we die? What will happen to us when we die?

Is Life Over at Death?

Which of us, in weaker moments has not wondered: are those words from the Bible and the church really true? Are we going to live again? Or will the silent ground quietly cover us and return us to itself from whence we came, and that's it?
Raymond Moody, in a recent book titled, *Life After Life,* tells the story of scores of people who were pronounced dead, but were medically restored to life. They tell of experiencing bright lights, and ringing sounds, and, above all, a profound feeling of peace. Person after person said those few moments of bliss have given them new vitality to live. Yet how strange, that Lazarus returned, and our Lord himself returned from death, and left no such record. So how do we know?
In our text, St. Paul also faced this question of what happens to us after death. At the beginning of this chapter, he said, "If the earthly tent we live in is destroyed, we have a building from God, a house not made with hands (one that is), eternal in the heavens."
Several summers ago, when we were on a backpacking trip with our Leaguers in the Bighorn Mountains, one night we had all fallen into a delightful, heavy sleep when suddenly the tent came down around our heads, folding over us like a wet dishrag. At first we thought it was some silly prankster, but peeking out we found all the tents down from a sudden heavy snowstorm. With our tents down in the spine-chilling cold, we longed to be back here in our homes, safe and warm once more. And we could begin to understand Paul when he says, "While we are still in this tent, we sigh with anxiety . . . to be further clothed . . . that the mortal may be swallowed up by life." And he quickly points out that this is not some vain *hope,* some philosophy made up by dream-

ers on a starry night. He who has many mansions waiting, who has gone on before to prepare everything for us, Paul says, is God, who has given us the Spirit as a guarantee. He's made the down payment for us, to hold our home until we get there.

I have a friend who is from Ecuador. He has a wife from here, a job, a house, a car, and likes it here very much. But you talk of Ecuador and his eyes begin to sparkle. You ask him where home is and he shoots back, "Ecuador." He has a house here. But home is Ecuador.

Where our Friend, our Brother, our Savior is, there, for us, is home. We have a house here. But home is there!

So, Paul says . . . therefore . . . because we *know* that, beyond a shadow of doubt . . . since we know where our home is *we are always of good courage.*

No matter what happens, what life may bring, or how death may come, we know that we have a home to come to, and a homecoming awaiting us, and he in whose hands it all rests is true and to be trusted. He is Lord of all.

In the meantime, we walk by faith, not by sight. "Faith," as C. K. Barrett *(Commentary on Second Corinthians)* put it, is "believing in life when nothing is visible but death."

Luther said, "In this life we are pilgrims and wanderers." Our age has forced into our lives another word: refugees—those whose home is in one place but who suddenly find themselves having to live in another place. They live there, but it isn't home to them. So the apostle says in the midst of this troubled life we find ourselves here in the body, but we would rather be at home with the Lord.

What Shall Live On?

Unlike some other religions, our faith is *not* to get rid of our body, as a thing that drags us down, so that our soul can be free and fly away like some super Jonathan Livingston Seagull of the heavens. Our faith is rather that this very body will be made over, bettered, renewed, redressed to fit eternal styles.

With this talk of clothing, the Bible speaks of what will happen to us when we die. It says that when we die, this body shall one day be raised from the dead. And this will happen to all people, believers and unbelievers, the just and the unjust. As Luther puts it in the Third Article, "He will raise up me and *all* the dead. . . ."

But what stark contrasts meet our eyes here. For we see that the non-believers shall also be clothed, but their clothing shall be unacceptable. Like the man in Jesus' parable about the wedding, they shall be thrown out of the Father's house. As one writer put it, "Those not covered with the mantle of righteousness through Christ, who are wearing instead their own mantle of . . . selfish reliance on their own deeds, will be cast into outer darkness. While living here, their clothing looks alright, like that of the believers, and here all pass inspection, but in the resurrection they will be found out and separated out with the goats" (W. Kelly, *Commentary on Second Corinthians*).

> Blessed indeed are they who have put on Christ's robe.
> Are you one of them?
> If you are, then you need not fear death!

Paul would say to us, how beautiful to know that when we are born again, when God has accepted us into his family in Baptism, we don't have to be nervous anymore. Then we are no longer visitors in the house. We no longer have to be on edge, but like our family at home, we can relax.

Thus in death as in life, we put our trust in him. Someone said, "The world trusts where it ought to mistrust, and so is cheated. People do not trust Christ and so cheat themselves, and then they trust religious fakes and so cheat themselves once more" (R. C. H. Lenski, *Commentary on Second Corinthians*). But, in death, as in life, the Bible would tell us to trust the God who has redeemed us with the cross of his only Son and now stands ready to complete in us the work that he began there.

Because of that one lonely cross, and because God raised *Jesus* from the dead, St. Paul could say a second time within the span of three verses, "So . . . therefore . . . since this is so . . . since we know this, now we do our best to live our lives pleasing to Christ." Since we will lay down our tents anytime now, we want to clean up, to do everything to please the Lord. We want to look like he expects us to.

How many wives have gone to the hospital to have a baby, and for three, four, five days the husband doesn't do the dishes or clean up the house? But the morning before she comes home, he works like crazy to get it all shined up. Why? Not because she told him he had to, but because he wants to please her. He's glad for the baby she's borne, and now he wants to make her glad.

Thus Paul can say, whether we die now, or a while from now, in the meantime we try to live as he wants us to. The thing that keeps us going, even if we fail miserably, is what God has already done for us. So we face death with quiet confidence; not brashly as one marching dumbly into the jaws of disaster, but as those who know the battle has been fought and the victory already won.

That could make John Calvin say, "Believers desire death and yet do not try to hasten the day the Lord has fixed for it; for they willingly battle on at their earthly post for as long as the Lord thinks fit; preferring to live to the glory of Christ rather than die for their own profit."

"The thought, then, that his future is in the hands of God does not lull the Christian into false security but makes him the more determined to be obedient" (C. K. Barrett).

Knowing we are family, we want to live in a way that brings honor to the family name. We don't sit around like spoiled rich kids just spending our father's money. And we know our Father won't kick us out if we don't do everything just like he asks. But still we are eager to make our family reputation even brighter, for above all we know what our family's name has cost our Father and our elder Brother.

So we face death not with confidence in the deeds we may have done, but knowing full well, as George Forrell has put it, "I'm not OK, and you're not OK. But that's OK." We come to death confident that Christ's death was not in vain; that his mercy and grace are waiting for us there in that awesome moment as they were here in this life; that forgiveness is ours in death as in life; that our Baptism and the Supper of the Lord will be our robe of righteousness forever.

Shall I be Judged?

Then our text adds a curious note: after we die, and before we are taken home, we will "all have to appear before the judgment seat of Christ so that each one may receive good or evil, according to what he has done in the body." Is Paul here saying something different than he holds everywhere else? Is he saying we are indeed saved by our works?

Not at all. Paul well knew Christ's word: "He who believes in me *has* eternal life; he does not come into judgment but has passed from death to life" (John 5:24). Paul means that in the judgment it will be made known to all the world whether we truly trusted God's grace and gave ourselves into his hands with all our faults and sins, or whether we were religious phonies who dressed right and spoke right and acted right, but our clothes were only imitation-Christian and not the real thing.

If you've ever walked in the hush of England's magnificent Westminster Abbey and seen the hundreds upon hundreds of burial vaults for kings and queens, lords and ladies, artists, poets, statesmen, think of all these people suddenly rustling forth from their vaults and standing there—now you get the feeling for this great day.

And notice who the judge will be: none other than he, whom John says, is "faithful and just to forgive us our sins and to cleanse us from all unrighteousness" (1 John 1:9). No wonder Paul could say elsewhere, "for me to live is Christ, to die is gain!" And we can join him with that old spiritual that grew out of the anguish of slavery: "All my trials, Lord, soon be over."

What if I die? All my trials, Lord, soon be over!

MILTON OST
Grace Lutheran Church
Albert Lea, Minnesota

WHAT IS A CHRISTIAN?
Fifth Sunday after Pentecost
2 Corinthians 5:14-21

What is a Christian? It is a disturbing question! It is a disturbing question to the newcomer to faith who is seeking to find his way. It is a disturbing question to the seeker who yearns to believe. It is a disturbing question to the stumbler who feels lost and alone. It is the disturbing question raised by the mocker: "How come one can't tell Christians from those who are not?"

What is a Christian? It is a disturbing question because within the Christian tradition there are many answers. Out of the cataphony of voices we hear:

> To be a Christian is to run the great race.
> To be a Christian is to fight the great battle.
> To be a Christian is to live a righteous life.

What is a Christian? In his Second Epistle to the church of Corinth, Paul gives us a concise and clear picture. A Christian is a new creation, a person with a new point of view and new motivation.

A New Creation

This new creation is not just the best of the old creation. Nor does the new creation come through the intensification of the finest human wisdom and energy. The source of the new creation is the same creative action which brought all reality into existence. The same God whose Spirit moved over the chaos in the beginning, the same God who brought reality into being, the same God who made everything out of nothing, is the source of the new creation.

This creative power is present in the Gospel for this day. Jesus, sleeping in peace and calmness in the turmoil of the storm, is contrasted to the trembling disciples fearing their destruction by the elements. Jesus, at the disciples' frantic request, speaks and the winds cease; the disciples stand in awe unable to comprehend the creative presence of the new creation. The source of this new creation is also the power of God which comes to Job. It sustains him in the hours of his loss of family, fortune, and health. It is God's prevailing presence wrestling with him in his moment of anguish, enabling him to face himself and to endure the testing and temptations. The source of the new creation is the multi-faceted functioning of God in the world.

This creative action of God which brings the new creation, focuses in the death and resurrection of Christ. In the Old Testament Israel is called to represent the world. The remnant is called to represent Israel and finally in the fulfillment of prophecy Jesus Christ is called to represent the remnant. In Jesus the Christ the whole world is gathered together and made new. As Jesus Christ dies and is resurrected, the world dies and is resurrected. The focus of our new creation is the life and death of Jesus the Christ who died for us and with whom you and I died and live again. The new creation continues to make its way into the world as we announce the good news: "In Jesus Christ the old has died and the new has come."

What then are the realities of this new creation? First, the old creation with its distortion, its decay, its disease, its despair, and its death is passing away. Therefore even though these things are still with us they are not everlasting. Even as our bodies grow older, decay, and ultimately die, so the old creation, the old reality is passing away and it too will die. In its place God will continue to create a whole new reality. In the midst of the old, like leaven in a loaf the new creation makes its silent, hidden, mysterious, but pervasive, presence known. We see its signs all around us. We see it in the growing pains of a little child. We see it in truth of Scripture experienced and lived in the consciences and lives of those who stand for faith and justice in Russia, China, Africa, Washington, and in your city and mine. We see it bring wholeness.

She came one day with ashen face and broken spirit. She was 40, but looked 80. Out of the guilt of an affair in her youth which had devastated her life, she sought healing for her spirit from medical doctors and psychiatrists. The healing did not come. The night before she had attempted suicide. Now in the early morning hour, we read from the Psalms. Psalms 32, 38, 51. As we read her spirit began to lift, quietly she changed. We prayed and she left. The next day she slipped an envelope under my door. She had penned these words: O the comfort, the inexpressible comfort of being deeply understood, to pour out all words, good and bad together, trusting that a faithful hand will keep that which would be worth keeping, and with a breath of kindness blow the rest away. The new creation is present in healing, in forgiveness, in liberation and in hope. Even now God's future reaches into our present. As you and I live the old passes and the new comes. The new creation is the good news that you and I shall not die with our bodies. In Jesus Christ we have already died. In Jesus Christ we have risen again. With Jesus Christ this day is the first day of the rest of an existence that goes on forever.

A New Perspective

The reality of the new creation announced to us, present in us, gives us a new perspective. The disciples experienced this new perspective in the contrasting manner in which they viewed Jesus. While on earth they saw in him a potential rescuer from their bondage to Rome. Caught up in the expectations of their time they saw a new king, the one who would bring new hope to Zion. When he was crucified as an insurrectionist, hailed by many as a lunatic, by others as a heretic, they were crushed. Then came his resurrection! In the light of that event they saw Jesus with new eyes. He was no longer the one whose failure had smashed both their hopes and spirit. Out of the resurrection they saw him as the living spirit and presence of God. He was alive, pervasively touching the spirit of those in the Christian community! Now they professed him as Lord! Out of this new perspective they saw life in a new way and set forth with boldness to announce to the world the coming of the kingdom of God. His message took on a new dimension; God was now with them, within them and through them, reconciling the world unto himself.

The new perspective experienced in the life of the disciples belongs to us—as Christ's death and resurrection is announced to us; as through it the passing of the old creation is made known; as we experience the signs of his coming; as we celebrate our new future that goes on forever we too, see our own time with new eyes. People are no longer competitors but companions.

People cease to be objects; they become persons with needs, yearnings and desires that throb within our own spirit. In the stranger; in the hungry; in those who are prisoners; in the alienated; we see not someone to be despised and feared, but we see instead the face of Christ. Rather than problems and despair, there come possibilities and hope.

In a certain African tribe the young chief was to choose his bride from among the women of the village. He astounded everyone by choosing a woman the villagers considered one of the plainest, most common women of the tribe. As was tradition, after the wedding the young chief and his bride left the tribe to live alone for a period of celebration before they returned to leadership in the village. When the couple returned to the village, the young bride had changed. There was a new radiance in her face and new confidence in her voice. She was strong and beautiful. The chief had seen in the young woman what others could not see. Out of his discovery the woman had become more of what God had designed her to be.

So it is as we live under the love of Jesus Christ. Affirmed, forgiven, and encouraged we experience our unique value as the sons and daughters of the king. Freed by his love we too become more of what he has intended us to be. In this transformation we begin to see one another through different eyes. We see the new creation among the old. Through us the new perspective moves out into the world transforming people, moods, events, and institutions.

A New Motivation

The new perspective brings new motivation. Rather than seized by the passions of the old creation, the Christian is seized by the love of Christ. Motivation in the old creation manifests itself in searching for security and self-aggrandizement. The new motivation arises as we receive what we have long sought. This motivation develops out of the awareness and celebration of our liberation from the captivity of distortion, decay, disease, despair, and death. The man had been an Olympic swimmer; he was 72 years old and recuperating from a heart attack. His recuperation meant long walks along the harbor. One day as he was walking, a pleasure craft with a young family aboard was swamped accidentally by the wave of a large boat. The family's two young children were washed overboard into the icy water. In a moment the old man was in the water and pulled one of the young boys to safety. The other drowned. The old man and the boy were rushed to the hospital where it soon was apparent that in his weakened condition the old man would die. One day the young boy asked to see the old man; quietly he tiptoed up to the dying man's bed and said, "Sir, how can I thank you for saving my life?" Staring at him through the veil of death, the old man replied: "You can live your life so others might be saved." Today up and down the coast of New England there are a series of rescue stations founded by a young man who saw life through new eyes and was motivated by the awareness that someone had given his life for him.

What is a Christian? It is a disturbing question and it will continue to be. But in the letter to the church at Corinth we have a clear, concise picture of a Christian as a new creation, with a new perspective and a new motivation. You are invited into the world to live in the new beginning which God has launched for you in Jesus Christ.

ROLAND MARTINSON
Luther-Northwestern Seminaries
St. Paul, Minnesota

BLESSED TO BE A BLESSING

Sixth Sunday after Pentecost
2 Corinthians 8:1-9, 13-14

There once was a man who had a very unique relationship with God. The relationship began, not because of anything the man had done, but because of something God did. God intersected the man's life and chose him for a particular task which, in turn, has affected humankind down to the present age. The man's name was Abram, and what God did is summed up for us in the twelfth chapter of Genesis: "And the Lord said to Abram, 'I will bless you . . . and in you all the families of the earth shall be blessed.' " (Gen. 12:1-3). God blessed Abram so that Abram could be a blessing. God gave to Abram so that Abram could give to others.

Blessed to be a blessing. That is the story of the Christian life. We may often think of ourselves as blessed by God, but rarely do we consider *why* we have been blessed. The biblical witness cuts to the heart of the matter: we have been blessed by God in order that God might bless others through us. Like the water of Baptism and like the bread and wine of Holy Communion, we Christians are, in a very real sense, a means of grace—we are

168

tangible ways through which God touches the lives of the people around us.

The Apostle Paul picks up on the theme of "blessed to be a blessing" in our lesson for today. He is writing to the Corinthians, and we can best understand what he says and why he says it if we grasp the background against which he is writing. You will recall that almost from the beginning, the Christian church was divided. Denominations are not new. Following Pentecost, it did not take long for two branches of Christendom to develop. There were the Jewish Christians based in Jerusalem under the leadership of Peter, James and John; and there were the Gentile Christians based in Antioch under the leadership of Paul and Barnabas. There were obvious ethnic and theological differences. There was also a commonality in the Lord Jesus Christ. Somewhere in-between these two poles was their economic status. While neither group was well-to-do, the Jewish Christians in Jerusalem were in dire poverty, so much so, that when Paul left Jerusalem in A.D. 49 to carry the gospel throughout the Roman Empire, the Jewish leaders begged Paul not to forget them but to remember the poor, which Paul was eager to do. He made it a point to carry on a stewardship program throughout his churches. Without pledge cards and offering envelopes he received benevolent offerings which were sent back to Jerusalem to aid the saints there. Throughout the Gentile churches, the people of God had been blessed. Why? To be a blessing to others.

We Don't Need Much

Blessed to be a blessing. Paul appeals to the Corinthians to come to grips with this biblical theme and act upon it. He does so first by using the Macedonian Christians as an example. They were under persecution and extremely poor, he writes, but they gave generously to the saints in Jerusalem. In fact, they begged to give. They sensed they had been blessed by God and they wanted to bless others with what they had been given, regardless of how meager it may have been.

Their action is more than just interesting. It is profound. They made no apologies for not having enough to share but got excited about sharing what they did have. How often have we heard people say they have no talent, there is nothing of importance they can do. "I can't sing, I can't teach, I can't speak, I can't paint." Perhaps that's what the Corinthian Christians were saying, too. "We don't have very much. How can we give it away?" We need to realize what our forefathers of the faith in Macedonia knew so well: even the smallest gift is a blessing given to us in order to bless others. It's not how much we have or do not have that matters; what counts is what we do with what we have. Blessed to be a blessing. That's you and me.

A story from the Gospels comes to mind. One day Jesus sat down opposite the Temple treasury and watched people put in their offerings. Many wealthy people came and gave generously out of their abundance. Then came a woman who was very poor. Her contribution was only a penny, but then it was all she had. Jesus responded to that by saying the woman had put in more with her penny than all the wealthy people combined. They had given out of abundance; she, out of poverty. Jesus is here not chastizing the rich. He is simply lifting up the fact that the woman did not complain about what she did not have, but gave what she did have. She sensed she had been blessed—however meagerly it may have been—but she had been blessed to be a blessing (Mark 12:41-44).

One day the ushers found a note in the offering plate. It read, "Don't have a penny to give—but thank you, Lord, for thinking about me. I'm alive and doing fine." A thank you may not seem like much, but when that's all you've got, then that's something.

Paul appeals to the Corinthians to give what they have. His appeal stretches over the centuries to us. Give what money you have. Give what time you have. Regardless of how much or how little we have been given, it has not been given us to hoard but to give away. You and I have been blessed—to be a blessing.

What Prompts Us

Paul then suggests to the Corinthians that the motivation for their blessing others ought not be based upon a command from Paul, but as a response to what Christ has done, who, though he was rich, yet for our sake became poor so that by his poverty, we might become rich. The apostle here reflects upon Christ's decision to leave his heavenly home, take on the garb of human flesh and live as a servant, even unto death. Such Christ-sacrifice has not made us monetarily rich, but rich in love, grace and mercy. Paul thus reminds the Corinthians that they have been blessed by God's grace, and it is upon that foundation, and that foundation alone, that they are to bless others.

That is good news for those who often give out of a sense of guilt. It is such guilt that prompts us to say yes when deep down we want to say no. The telephone rings. You answer it only to discover your pastor is on the other end. The first thought that races through your mind is, "Oh, no, what does he want this time? What is he going to ask me to do?" It doesn't take long for you to find out! Whether an immediate answer is needed or not, the process is the same. You agonize inside. You want to say no but if you do, you'll feel guilty because you believe you will let your pastor down, let the church down, or fail God. And so you say, yes, not because you want to, but because your yes is really a no to your feelings of guilt. That is no way to run a life or a church. That is no way to be a blessing to others either.

We are blessings, that is, God uses us to touch the lives of others, as we respond to him because of the grace he has shown us in Jesus Christ. Prince Vladimir was the first Christian ruler in Russia. Prior to his Baptism in A.D. 989, his life had been brutal, bloodthirsty, and lacking in moral restraint. After he became a follower of Jesus Christ, he was not the ideal ruler, but because of how this Christ of God had changed his life, Vladimir responded to the grace of God by offering kindness towards criminals; he responded to the generosity of Christ by giving to the poor; he responded to the comfort of Christ by supporting Greek missionaries in his country. Vladimir was blessed and through him, God blessed others whose lives Vladimir touched. Vladimir did not act out of guilt but out of grace. When the blessed are blessing others, the grace of God is at work.

We Can Give Only What We Receive

Blessed to be a blessing. Paul, at the end of our text, reminds the Corinthian Christians that as they bless others they need not do so to the point of having nothing left to give. Paul says they do not need to become poor so that others can become rich. That would only serve to perpetuate the cycle of poverty. If the Corinthians gave away all they had been given then someone else would have to give in order to support them. Paul appeals for equality, for fairness.

In our day and age, Paul's writing has something to say to us about the blessed blessing others to the point where the blessed are burned out, to the point when people give so much, they are exhausted and have nothing left to give.

J. Russell Hale has just published a study on *Who Are the Unchurched?* After six months of listening to unchurched people in the six most unchurched counties in America, Hale has cataloged twelve different types of unchurched persons based upon the reasons they gave for being unchurched. One of these groups was the "burned-out," people who felt that the church had consumed all of their energy; people who felt used, exploited, manipulated. Now it is true they may have felt that way because of their own inability to say no, as we mentioned earlier, or because they expected too much from themselves or from the church. But the fact remains that many people in the church get burned out because they try to give more than they have been given. It is thus necessary for the Christian to keep in tension the blessings received and the blessings given. On the one hand it is not at all biblical to hoard the things with which we have been blessed and not bless others. The consequences of that are described for us in Jesus' parable of the man who built more barns to store what he was hoarding. His heart was not in the right place and death consumed him (Luke 12:13-21). But on the other hand, neither can we give more than we have received.

God does not demand from us more than he has given to us. It is obvious he does not expect me to paint like da Vinci or sing like Robert Merrill if I have not been blessed with such gifts. What is not so obvious is that neither does he expect me to be super-pastor or you to be super-church member. This does not mean that we can settle for mediocrity. It does mean he only asks us to be faithful with what we have been given. Pastors and laypersons alike need to remember that.

Blessed to be a blessing. This is the story of Christian life. Whether in want or in plenty, we are called upon to give as we have received; not more, not less. It was that way with Abram and with Paul. So it is also with you and me. Blessed to be a blessing.

WILLIAM S. WAXENBERG
St. Luke Lutheran Church
Spokane, Washington

OVERCOMING FRUSTRATION
Seventh Sunday after Pentecost
2 Corinthians 12:7-10

Introduction

Once again we raise the age-old question: Why does God allow suffering? One may be reminded of the grim humor which appeared some time back in the Peanuts comic strip where Snoopy with his broken leg is shown in a despondent mood musing to himself: "Today I get my cast off. These have been the longest six weeks of my life. . . . Of course, an accident like this makes you think. It forces you to take a closer look at your own life. . . . It makes you want to ask questions: like *why Me?*"

Why me? We can tell others to grin and bear it, or we can claim that suffering produces endurance and patience and has a positive side, but what if it strikes me: Then it's more difficult to remain composed or content oneself with the thought that every affliction must somehow, under the dispensation of God, work out for our final good.

Another Peanuts episode once showed Charlie Brown telling Lucy: "I've never felt more low in all my life. I don't seem to fit in anywhere! I don't seem to belong. Everything I try is a disaster." Lucy, the amateur child psychiatrist, responds by saying: "Well, try looking at life this way. . . . People are like decks of cards. . . . We're all part of the deck. . . . Some are aces, others are tens or nines or twos. . . We can't all be face cards, can we? We can't all be kings and queens?" To this Charlie answers: "No, I guess not." Then Lucy lowers the boom by suggesting: "Maybe you're the two of clubs, Charlie Brown." Unconvinced and unhelped Charlie retorts: "I doubt it . . . even the two of clubs takes a trick now and then."

For anyone who feels that much of a failure, for anyone who is frustrated by curbed ambitions or abandoned hope it may be salutary and uplifting to turn to a consideration of the plight which confronted the greatest of the apostles.

I

St. Paul was an extraordinary figure whose experiences have never been fully duplicated in the career of any other person. His life was full of contrasts in mood and temperment ranging from bitter disappointment to the most jubilant elation. He had his ups and downs. From the depths of near-despair he could rise to the heights of unexcelled achievement. In his second letter to the church at Corinth he relates that he was privileged to enjoy numerous visions and revelations. At one point he even claims that he was permitted a glimpse into celestial glory—he was "caught up into Paradise—whether in the body or out of the body" he could not be sure. But the ecstatic delight was so intense that it was inexpressible in human language.

Considering his special relationship to God, the apostolic authority which had been conferred on him, and the special gifts of the Holy Spirit which he exercised, it would be easy to understand that Paul could have become egotistical and boastful. To keep his spiritual life on an even keel, to prevent him "from being too elated by the abundance of revelations," he explains to the Corinthians that he was afflicted with a thorn in the flesh. This "messenger of Satan," as he labels it, harassed him and kept him from flaunting his own superiority. So instead of bragging about his strong characteristics, the apostle extols his weaknesses. And therein lies the lesson we need to learn. God does not meet us exclusively in our successes—in our hours of triumph—but also amid defeats, letdowns and vexations. In describing his own personal affliction and how it assisted rather than retarded his life with God, Paul shows us how we can overcome our frustrations and turn apparent evil into actual good.

Biblical interpreters have offered many guesses as to what Paul meant by his thorn in the flesh. Usually it is assumed that it was a physical illness of some kind, whether epilepsy, eye trouble, malarial fever or whatever. The English preacher Leslie Weatherhead assumed that the affliction was nervous exhaustion superimposed on some bodily ailment. In any case, it is clear that this thorn (as he called it) drained his vitality and seemed to interfere with his missionary objectives. Three times, evidently with earnest and prolonged prayer, he asked God to remove it.

Observe that there was no morbid sentimentality in Paul's attitude toward disease. He saw it as an ugly and deplorable thing—a device which Satan used to assault him. It was natural and it was proper for Paul to seek divine healing in eradicating this bane, (this irritant, this obstacle) to his welfare! Disease is always a blight on God's good creation. Curing disease is part of God's redemptive work, especially as we find it exhibited in the healing ministry of Jesus Christ. To reduce our maladies, to improve our health—whether it be by medical skill or the power of prayer (or most likely a combination of the two) is in accord with the good and gracious will of God. Whenever and wherever possible we should avail ourselves of the means provided to nurture our physical strength and to minimize illness.

Yet, sickness, distress, or tragedy may strike us. And when it does we must cope with it realistically. Theologically speaking, we say God is not to be blamed for the evil which befalls us or surrounds us (it is a consequence of human sinfulness). Nonetheless, sickness does not come without God's permission. Paul says it was given to him; and implies that there is a loving will behind it. Jesus had to drink the bitter cup but God used this act to restore a fallen world. Even though we are unable to solve completely the problem of the origin of human suffering we find it comforting to know that however it has entered into our lives, we may take it from the loving hands of God as a burden he calls us to bear, assured that it can be used by him for our good. We are not the victims of blind fate, but we are always upheld by the God who created us and who sent his son into the world to suffer and to die for us. This is what Paul recognized and this is why he could rejoice in the midst of his woes.

A major benefit which the apostle detected in his own plight was the conquest of spiritual pride. He repeats the phrase "to keep me from being too elated." If anyone in the Christian community could have a right to boast it would have been Paul. He gained more converts than anyone else. His adventures had been more exciting and his escapes from perils on land and sea had been more miraculous than those of any other leaders. He was the major theologian of the early church. In the practice of charismatic gifts like speaking in tongues or prophesying he could outdo all others. More than anyone else he was granted insight into divine mysteries and was the recipient of supernatural revelations and sublime visions. But the thorn in the flesh which God decreed should not be removed kept him humble—fully aware that his fame and brilliance and achievement were undeserved for without the illuminating power of the Holy Spirit he would be nothing.

All pride is dangerous. Dante put it first in his list of the seven deadly sins, because it is the worst form of self-love. Pride of success, of money, of popularity, of intellect, of physical prowess or beauty or whatever it may be is evil because it is a form of self-worship and isolates us from other people and from the authentic source of our being. But the pride that comes from the contemplation of our moral virtues or religious wisdom is the worst of all because it feeds on that which should make us humble—God's mercy and grace. Paul knew that danger; it was from this pit that he had been rescued, his feet set on the rock of utter dependence on God.

II

This text on Paul's thorn in the flesh, I would submit, can be of immense help to Christ's followers today. For one thing, it can offer us guidance in our response to frustration. In varying degrees and in different ways frustration is an inescapable part of our day-by-day experience; everyone has some project to complete which never seems to get done or some ideal to be fulfilled which remains elusive. The most common reaction to such frustration is to try to escape from it. Some seek escape in cynicism or vindictiveness toward others. Some are driven by frustration to excessive drinking or the abuse of drugs.

Edgar Allan Poe was brought up by foster parents in Richmond, Virginia. When he entered the University of Virginia at Charlottesville, he was not given much spending money, and this put him at a disadvantage in relation to his many classmates who, as the sons of wealthy planters, had plenty to spend. Poe gambled to recoup his losses; but instead went further into debt. In his frustration he took to drink and became an alcoholic—his literary genius marred and his life span cut short. . . . In extreme instances people seek escape from frustration in suicide. An increasing number of people are being overwhelmed by their disappointments and become so despondent that they deliberately take their own lives. . . . Some sceptics have decided to reject God entirely. One might point to a person described by Heather Robertson in her book *Grass Roots*. John Sarvas, a successful cattle farmer near Biggar, Saskatchewan, who founded the Society of Prairie Atheists in 1970, was embittered by the violence and indignity of life. And so he snarled at God: "If He's gonna be a God," Sarvas complains, "why couldn't He be a good God?"

The Christian response to frustration, however, is not to run away from it, nor attempt to escape it, nor to blame God nor to become an agnostic. It is, rather, to accept it, and by the grace of God to make the most and the best of it. This is what Paul did with his thorn in the flesh; and this is how Christian people in every age have responded.

Paul's endurance of his thorn in the flesh gives guidance to the Christian understanding of unanswered prayer. Often it may seem that our own prayers are ineffective or that God is declining our requests. Nothing seems to happen. Nothing seems to change. Remember, however, that if God is saying no to us it is never a blank refusal. It may appear to be so; but that only means his answer is either delayed or is unrecognized. In one way or another the Lord may be telling us, "My grace is sufficient for you. What you have your mind set on is unnecessary or undesirable. What I am willing to give you is what is most crucial for your welfare."

George Meredith once wrote, "Who rises from prayer a better man, his prayer is answered." This is not the only answer, but it is a good answer. A Christian will be content with it. Whenever he asks for temporal blessings it will be with the reservation that it be in accord with God's will and higher wisdom. If he asks for material help—a better job, economic progress, a happier marriage, even recovery from physical disabilities—it will not be as an end in itself but for the better fulfillment of God's purpose.

Adoniram Judson, a pioneer missionary from North America to Asia a century and a half ago, claimed that no prayer of his had gone unanswered. But he had prayed to be sent to India and he had to settle for Burma. When his wife took sick he prayed that her life might be spared, but she died. He was imprisoned by one of the Burmese leaders and languished in confinement. Although he prayed for release, it did not come for months. All the time, however, the great prayer of his life was being answered; for through his work and witness and sufferings the Christian Gospel was penetrating Burma in many vital ways.

Paul feared that his infirmity would hinder his effectiveness. He had to learn that nothing could separate him from God's love in Christ Jesus. There are divine compensations for every handicap in life. In prayer, in worship, in Holy Communion we have spiritual resources that can enable us to overcome any shortcoming. Moses had a stammering tongue and yet became the Great Emancipator of his people from Egyptian slavery. Jeremiah was dismayed by a consciousness of his own deficiencies and yet became one of the most courageous of the prophets. Again and again through faith in the all-sufficient sacrifice of Jesus Christ a defect has been transformed into a stimulus. The struggle to overcome a weakness can develop capacities in us that might otherwise lie dormant. Sometimes the mathematics of God is paradoxical: when he adds he subtracts; when he subtracts he adds. As Paul says, "When I am weak, then I am strong." As Robert Browning once defined God:

> God the strong, God the beneficent,
> God ever mindful in all strife and strait,
> Who, for our own good, makes the need extreme,
> Till at the last He puts forth might and saves.

Conclusion

The power that counts is that which comes from the indwelling Christ supplying us with the fruits of the Spirit, especially peace, love and joy. Mishaps, injuries, reverses may serve to deepen this indwelling by throwing us more completely on God. What seem like difficult circumstances may be God's way of answering our prayers. We pray for courage, and God leads us by roads that expose us to danger. We pray for patience, and we get a disagreeable neighbor. We pray for love, and we are compelled to come into contact with people who are irksome and repulsive. We pray for humility and events pierce our pride. Always we can hear the Lord telling us, "My grace is sufficient for you, for my power is made perfect in your weakness."

RALPH L. MOELLERING
Gloria Dei Lutheran Church
Edmonton, Alberta

A GOSPEL PANEGYRIC

Eighth Sunday after Pentecost
Ephesians 1:3-14

Never at a loss for words—that's St. Paul. We might, however, feel lost in words at times when we read him. "Wordiness" is one of Paul's main characteristics—not the blah-blah kind, but wordiness born of the need to express the Gospel of Christ out of his deep faith and profound mind.

This text—half the first chapter of Ephesians—is a single sentence in the original language of the New Testament. The words and phrases pile up in our minds and spread out before us. The ideas tumble out one after another. The concepts surround us and close in upon us.

What to call this divine wordiness? Take the word *panegyric* —an oration, a song of exultation, a statement of fulsome praise. This text for the Pentecost season is "A Gospel Panegyric."

Blessed Be God—He Has Chosen Us!

The text begins and ends with praise to God. In between we can detect a chain of ideas which link the first and last lines together in this Gospel panegyric.

The first link is to praise God because he has chosen us. "Blessed be God . . . who has blessed us . . . with every spiritual blessing." (As we said before, the words pile up!) Paul writes to the Ephesian Christians to glorify Christ in their life as a community of the faithful. Set in a first-century world of assorted cults and mystery religions, the church is to be a witness that Christ is both starting point and fulfillment of all human life. So it's something to praise God about that we are part of this faithful community. *He has chosen us.*

Chosen—the word is rich in meaning, though often misunderstood in Christian piety. When we say that God has chosen us, that is to say that it's rooted in his good will and pleasure for us; *God wants us* for his own. He chooses us not to go our own way but to go his way. Notice how the writer puts it here: God chose us "in him" (that is, in Christ) . . . "before the foundation of the world" . . . so that we may be "holy and blameless before him."

What's Paul getting at here? We can believe that God's choosing of his people—of us—is not merely (a) chance, (b) luck, (c) afterthought, (d) accident. No, none of the above. We don't just happen to believe in Christ. We don't stumble onto the Gospel. We don't pick and choose to favor God with our willingness to join his team. No, the Gospel tells us that God chooses us, he welcomes us, he offers us his kingdom. It's by design of God, claims the New Testament.

The New English Bible includes the word "dedicated" here. It reinforces the "chosen" idea. God's choice of us is a call to dedicated commitment to him—responsibility, not privilege; that commitment is our response to his choosing.

As if he hasn't used enough words, Paul adds more to drive home the point. God "destined us in love to be his sons (daughters) through Jesus Christ." That may be another risky word—destined. We can avoid the confusion of "predestination" by keeping to the biblical outlook: It's God's good will to choose us, to make us his children.

All that is cause for praise. No wonder Paul says "Blessed be God . . . to the praise of his glorious grace." Blessed be God—he has chosen us!

He Has Chosen Us—His Will Is Revealed!

The second link in the chain of words in this Gospel panegyric is one that emphasizes God's will. It runs through the text: "according to the purpose of his will" . . . "the mystery of his will" . . . "his purpose which he set forth in Christ" . . . "a plan for the fullness of time" . . . "according to the purpose" . . . "according to the counsel of his will."

It may seem too bold of us to speak of knowing God's will. After all, we reason, he is God and we are just people. It may be too presumptuous, too daring, for us lowly humans to claim access to the knowledge of God's will and purpose. Maybe Paul could do it, but he was special. I have seen sincere church people hold back and become almost immobilized for fear of saying they are trying to do the will of God, as though by doing so they would be treading where they don't belong. That blocks risky and creative endeavor in the kingdom. In worship, in education, in theological wrestling, in social action and in other arenas of life we might be tempted to retreat by saying "But who can say that it's God's will for us to do such and so?"

The fear isn't there for Paul. No problem is it for the New Testament writers. It doesn't hold them back. The Gospel panegyric lilts along with confidence and assurance that God's will is plainly active in the life of the community of faithful believers. The difference, if we look carefully, is in discerning the will of God in a broad view, not in isolated decisions detached from each other. The significant thing is that God wants us for his own and wants us to live in ways that testify to our identity. We've said it many times: He chooses us, we don't choose him. So if the initiative and action are his, that's a fundamental clue to his will at work in our lives.

Thus, where do we discover the will of God? In ourselves! In our call to faith, in our fellowship as his people, in the simple yet glorious title of "children of God." Let that sink into our hearts: God wants to be our Father and wants us to be his children. From that profound truth we can step boldly into life talking about his will for us in the circles of church and world where we daily encounter decisions about what to do in accord with his purpose.

The flowing and flowering phrases of the text seek to say it: "In him we have redemption through his blood, the forgiveness of sins, according to the riches of his grace which he lavished upon us." Again: "We have been destined and appointed to live for the praise of his glory." And more: "He has made known to us in all wisdom and insight the mystery of his will."

The Gospel enjoins us to make what may seem like a preposterous claim: He has chosen us—his will is revealed.

His Will Is Revealed—It's a New World!

Paul's Gospel oration moves to the third link; it has to do with the whole universe. God's gift of choosing according to his will is offered for the good of all creation. All wisdom and insight into the depths of his will are set forth in Christ "as a plan for the fullness of time, to unite all things in him, things in heaven and things on earth." When God's will is revealed, this is a new world in which we live.

We have to catch the cosmic scope of the Gospel here. It's an echo of the first chapter of Colossians, another panegyric that encompasses all things in Christ. This Gospel is no mere cultic exercise dealing with sacrifices and rituals and morals alone. It's a cosmic grasp of all forces, movements, heavenly bodies, earthly inhabitants—"all things" in the biblical term.

In Christ, the Gospel seems to say, everything hangs together and fits in place and honors God and evokes our faith and mirrors God's will. *That's* a new world!

The new world can be seen from three angles in this text. First, as existing in the *fullness of time*. It's a crucial New Testament thought. It's a way of saying that when we see God's will in Christ, that's what all history and all of mankind's seeking is aiming for—for some kind of end-point that ties everything together. History's progress is filled up, completed, and moves on—in a fullness of time.

Second, the new world is viewed as having *all things united*. Heaven and earth (whatever that meant for the first-century mind) were united and fulfilled in God's will shown in Christ. "All things"—and we can take that term in all of its vast literal meaning—come into unity and harmony under God's rule. It harks back to creation itself, the goodness and harmony that Genesis exalts as God's doing. That unity broken by sin is restored in Christ.

Third, the new world is seen as *people under Christ*. A couple key phrases attract us: "we who first hoped in Christ" and "you also, who have heard the word of truth." Paul speaks of himself and others who "first hoped"—the covenant people whose hope is described in the biblical story of the Old Testament. And he speaks of others who heard of Christ and received the Holy Spirit, fulfilling the biblical note that the hope was for all nations.

To be specific, this is another way of saying that both Jew and Gentile are in the kingdom of God. Both the "first hopers" and the "later hearers" are united in Christ. You and I are among those late hearers; we're in league with the biblical folk who held fast to the promise of redemption. Together we're evidence of a new world that comes about when God's will is revealed.

It's a New World—Blessed Be God!

One more link in the Gospel panegyric brings us back to God's praise. The new world, the new *cosmos* under Christ is upon us. That provokes thanks and praise, as well as a certain expectation. There's more to come in a final fulfillment. The Holy Spirit's seal upon us is called "the guarantee of our inheritance until we acquire possession of it, to the praise of his glory." The new world calls forth a vision of God's glory, and we can say "Blessed be God."

There's a symbol of this new world in today's Gospel reading from St. Mark, the account of Jesus sending out his disciples. When the word goes out to the world to repent, to take the invitation to a new life, to be healed of its sickness and demons, all of that is the surging movement toward a new world under the lordship of Christ. And later on the disciples came back to report to Jesus, and their response was one of praise. They must have glimpsed a new world.

The new world is a place of blessing. Where the kingdom of God is, there is his praise and glory. "The only thing that counts is new creation," says the apostle in another place (Galatians 6).

One of the best places where we find this sense of a new world mixed with praise of God is in the Psalms. Because it is not just people that praise; the world itself is called to join in. All people are invited to dance in honor of God . . . but so also there is a call for all things to praise him—heaven and earth, seas and sea monsters, fields and their growing grains, fire and hail, snow and frost, mountains and trees. On and on it goes. Only a new world can praise this way.

The new world in miniature (or, to use a good word for it, the new world in microcosm) is right here in the worshiping community which we constitute. Here it is that we catch hold of the vision of new world and praise. Our gathering is the repeating and the remembering of God's gracious choice of us. When we hear the word of promise and fulfillment, the new world is spread before our eyes again.

That's what word and sacrament are all about. Baptism keeps reminding us of the new creation within the people of God. Eucharist keeps reminding us of our place in the new creation; the communion becomes our praise and thanks for new life in mother church. Around the font and the table we are affirming: It's a new world—blessed be God!

Feel free to be lost in words today, in this Gospel panegyric. It's an oration that overflows with words which have to be spoken. Let it sink in and soak into our consciousness. Sum it up with some words from today's liturgy: "Surely his salvation is at hand for those who fear him, that glory may dwell in our land."

ROBERT J. BROWN
Madison, Wisconsin

JESUS CHRIST, HARD HAT

Ninth Sunday after Pentecost

Ephesians 2:13-22

If gophers are tunnel diggers, we human beings are wall builders. We are persistent wall builders, and we do a good job. Think of New York's beautiful skyline. Its walls gleam in the bright sun, glow a soft red as the last rays of day strike them, and sparkle like jewels at night. These city structures are living monuments of our wall-building capacity.

We also build more humble walls to protect ourselves from the cold and rain. We set divider walls on our highways to prevent head-on collisions. We build flood walls to safeguard low-lying towns. There are fences to keep farm animals from straying. And there are certain necessary personal boundaries which Robert Frost celebrates when he declares that good walls make good friends.

Here a Wall, There a Wall

The trouble is, however, we take a good thing too far. We begin with walls, but we end up with mazes. Look at the Berlin Wall. How would something like that ever get built? Yet, there it is. Or, who could ever construct a wall between father and son? Impossible. Yet, only too real; only too common. And there are race walls. There are ethnic walls. Walls between members of the very same Christian congregation. Incredible; but only too real; only too common. Here a wall, there a wall; everywhere a wall. Like the greeting card company, we have a wall for every occasion. And they are not all as attractive as those which crowd the skyline of New York.

A Fine Religious Wall

A particularly significant structure is the famous religious wall described by the ancient Jewish historian Josephus. In front of the holy temple in Jerusalem there was a large courtyard where the people of God gathered. Around this courtyard ran a very special wall with a very special purpose. Namely, the intention of this wall was to keep pagans from entering the courtyard of God's people. And no intelligent pagan could miss this intention, for all along the wall the warning was repeated that any Gentile who trespassed the boundary would be killed.

Now this is an exceptionally fine wall. In the physical sense, as both Josephus and archeological remains attest, it was solidly and attractively constructed. More important, in the spiritual sense it served a most excellent purpose. That is, it preserved the ritual purity of the people of God from the contamination which contact with the pagans might bring. At the same time, of course, this wall also held the pagans at a healthy distance from God's temple. And the justification for the wall was God's very own Law, which was itself a kind of wall separating the people of God from the godless nations. So this is, indeed, a very fine structure. Its foundation is the sacred Law of God, and its purpose is the preservation of the holiness of God's own people. You shall not beat that for a good wall with an excellent purpose!

The Middle Wall of Hatred

It is just at this point, however, that Ephesians 2:13-22 begins to raise serious questions for us wall-builders. We have just described *the* wall par excellence. It has everything going for it; everything to commend itself to us. It is a noble structure. It smacks of divinity. And yet, what does our Ephesians text say concerning it?

> Jesus is our peace. He makes the people of God and the pagans to be one people. *He knocks down the middle wall of hatred.* In his flesh, he abolishes the Law.

As fine a wall between persons as ever was built, a structure justified if ever there was a justified structure, a truly spiritual monument to our endeavors, and what does Jesus do? He knocks the thing down. He knocks down the middle wall of hatred. Not Joshua at Jericho, but Jesus in Jerusalem: And the walls come tumbling down.

And the Walls Come Tumbling Down

We think of Jesus in many different ways. We call him the Good Shepherd, Son of God, King, and many other such names. But who ever heard of calling Jesus the Demolitionist? We can picture him with a shepherd's staff; we can picture him at the throne of God; we can picture him with the crown of David upon his head. But who ever heard of Jesus wearing a hard hat? It is only by means of the title "Demolitionist" and the hard hat crown, however, that we are able to do justice to our Lord as he comes before us today in our Ephesians text.

We stand before that wall of walls in the temple court, that noble structure, that dividing boundary, that instrument of holiness. We marvel at its foundation—God's own Law. We admire its purpose—the separation of the holy. And we expect Jesus to come with the blue ribbon prize for our wall of walls. But instead, he comes on a bulldozer! And the walls come tumbling down. The most noble wall of all between persons, built of the finest religious stuff, set to preserve the purity of God's people, of God's temple, perhaps even of God himself, and the walls come tumbling down.

The Demolitionist

Christ the Demolitionist. Specifically, Christ the *wall* demolisher. Now if Jesus had concentrated his act of destruction on tunnels that would be cause of alarm only to gophers. But, when he starts attacking walls, he is trespassing on our favorite turf. The real difficulty which our text poses for us is that in it Jesus has singled out the very *best* of walls between persons and has destroyed it. If he will not allow even this wall to stand, what chance then does the far less noble wall of race have? What chance does the wall between parent and child have? Or the wall between neighbors? Or between husband and wife? Or between members of the church? Oh yes, we love to build walls. Our whole human tendency is to build them. We want to place them where there were none before. We want to cover the social landscape with our beautiful partitions. But, the one whom we call Lord turns out to be the Demolitionist.

And not without good reason. We possess a genius for the construction of walls; but somehow this genius takes possession of us. It runs wild. We know how to begin, and cannot stop. And out of our landscape rise really hideous structures. The wall of race is so well built in South Africa, that black and white Christians kill one another across it. The political wall has been so cleverly constructed in Germany, that German Christians shoot German Christians over it. The ethnic wall in our own cities stands so firm, that Spanish Christians and English Christians fear to greet each other through it. All this is wall-building madness; and Jesus comes to us today as the Demolitionist.

And there are plenty more such ugly structures. Can you imagine a Christian household with a wall right down the middle of it? A wall between father and son, or husband and wife? Unfortunately, we can imagine this only too well! But can you make sense of it? Can you explain why the wall should be there? Who would ever want such an ugly thing? And yet, there it stands, a fine momento of our wall-building gone wild. Today, Jesus comes as the Demolitionist.

8

Or what of that amazing wall between members of the same Christian congregation? Two persons pray together, sing together, serve together. Yet, their eyes never dare meet across the wall. How can this be? To what can we attribute such a wall, except to our wall-building gone absolutely haywire. Here too, Jesus comes as the Demolitionist.

There was never a finer wall of separation between persons than that ancient middle wall of partition which separated the pagans from the people of God in the Jerusalem temple court. But, as fine a wall as it was, the Lord Jesus came to demolish it. If that wall came tumbling down, our lesser structures do not have a chance.

H. DIXON SLINGERLAND
St. Jacobi Ev. Lutheran Church
Brooklyn, New York

good!

THE IMPOSSIBLE DREAM

Tenth Sunday after Pentecost
Ephesians 4:1-7, 11-16

No two of us are totally agreed on everything. We have our differences. Some of them, of course, are built-in differences, for God in his creation never used the same mold twice. He is a God of infinite variety and rich diversity. Each of us has been endowed with a uniquely different set of genes, equipped with different pounds and talents: no two of us identical.

Some of our differences have been accumulated on the way. Each of us grew up in a unique environment, developed one way or another with the training of the home, the influence of peers, and personal choices that became ingredients of character. We developed our peculiarities, our idiosyncracies and habits. And sometimes we have difficulty understanding others who are different from ourselves.

We Have Our Differences

No two of us are totally agreed on everything. We have our differences, and we intend to cherish them. We resist the trend of a computerized society that seeks to blend us all together in one globby mess, a world where everybody looks alike and acts alike and thinks alike and where one cannot tell the players without a program. But often when we focus on our differences our vision is distorted and the molehills and the mountains come out looking much the same in size. We become cantankerous about the molehills that divide us, the differences that separate us from the crowd, and we can blow them into mountain ranges that defy the boldest challenge of the mountain climber. We can be crotchety, embittered, and divided when we do not see eye to eye with one another, until at length we make a lie of our confession, deny forbearance, brotherly affection and forgiveness, and in fact deny the name of Christ. We separate ourselves from others with haughty, arrogant disdain, insisting on a generous allowance for our differences, but making no allowance for the differences of others. We become one-level people who will tolerate no likes or dislikes, tastes or preferences that might be different from our own.

Humanity Is Torn to Shreds

This is a divided world. Humanity is torn to shreds. Our differences of national origin, political affiliation, color, language, culture and religion are the fences that divide us. Throw in economic status as the biggest barrier of all! Even the diversity that God intended in creation as a blessing has become a judgment. And even in the company of Christ we choose up sides around such noted figures as Anita Bryant, Corrie ten Boom and Pat Boone, if not with Presbyterians, Episcopalians, or Missouri Lutherans. The difference and diversity in God's creation that once existed in great harmonies of praise to the Creator have become the discord of humanity. The walls that separate us have destroyed the ties that bind us. "Human relations" has become a household word that signals trouble.

The Impossible Dream

Dare we dream the impossible dream? Dare we dream of a point where the discord of division can again become the harmony and unity of God's variety, where the rifts are healed and people can be one again? This is the burden of the apostolic Word today—a blueprint from the drawing boards of God himself for a model city he alone establishes. It's the humanly impossible dream— the unity of the Spirit and the bond of peace—one Lord, one faith, one Baptism, one father of us all, one family of God!

St. Paul knew something of the discord and contention and division that has torn the human family in shreds, and that often slashes through the fellowship of faith. The discord is as old in history as the barricaded gates of Eden since the day that sin first scattered people to the winds of discontent. There was an urban crisis in the days of Paul in Ephesus when silversmiths decided that a temper tantrum was in order because the man of God disturbed their profits. Christians were the main dish on the smorgasbord for lions near the palace of the emperor in Rome. The church at Corinth knew contention and divisiveness. Crotchety believers, evangelical hypocrites, and peevish liturgical specialists will always be with us to walk as becometh their version of sainthood. You know how it is—the pettiness of people who disturb the peace with piddle and create a major crisis out of every crackpot gripe and distort the church's mission into a people-pleasing farce which only Satan could consider comedy. There is little reason to expect that with a few adjustments or with several cute maneuvers we can eliminate the discord and achieve a Pollyanna world.

The Discord Is a Symptom

But the discord the apostle saw just as the discord we so often see was not the problem really, nor did it cause the problem. The discord was the symptom of a deeper problem, the fallen state of people. When man forfeited his trust in God for admiration of his personal achievements, when he destroyed his unity with God in favor of his hiding places, when he banished God to take the throne himself—at that point he also forfeited community with others, became a separatist, and lost the tie that binds men to each other. So we witness now the spectacle of shattered marriages and broken families and assertive children turning on their parents, friendships turned to anger, hatred, bitterness, man's conspiracy against his fellowman, dead bolts on the doors to lock out undesirables, and people isolated from society in fear, crushed spirit and self-pity. The rifts will not be healed, the barriers will not be broken down, no brave new world will be constructed out of any of our cleverly concocted schemes for the general improvement of conditions.

Unity Is a Gift

For unity is given—it is not achieved. And that's the gist of St. Paul's letter to the church at Ephesus, and particularly of this apostolic paragraph today. In the first three chapters of the letter the apostle lays it out for us—the grace of God in Jesus Christ that broke the barriers and called us from our several hiding places to be one again—in Christ and with each other. In those three chapters Paul spreads out the saving act of God with all its implications—that we who had been dead have now been made alive in Christ, we who had been divided have been reunited in one family. In those three chapters Paul spells out forgiveness—forgiveness for each one of us and through us for each other. And then he comes to this, "I beg you, brothers, sisters, to lead a life that's worthy of your calling, in lowliness and meekness, forbearing one another in love, eager to maintain the unity of the Spirit in the bond of peace." In Jesus Christ and through his eyes I see my neighbor as my brother and my sister. In him I begin to understand that we are children of one Father in the family of believers. The impossible dream takes shape, trust replaces fear, love resolves hatred, and our diversity becomes a symphony of praise.

It Works

Do you mean to say it works? Does this unity exist? Does the fellowship of faith, the church of Christ, remove dividing walls and bind the hearts of people into one again? Or shall we list St. Paul among the idle dreamers along with Jesus Christ who prayed the night before his cross that we might all be one, as the Father and the Son and Spirit are all one? As surely as our Lord was crucified and raised again, the unity of the Spirit and the bond of peace has been established. As surely as we have been called by one Spirit through one Baptism to one faith and one confession that Jesus Christ is Lord, we are a part of that community of faith. As surely as the holy Gospel of the Scriptures is no static list of dogmas to be swallowed but the power of salvation to be reckoned with, that power brings hostilities to a screeching halt.

Sometimes We Are Failures

Sometimes, of course, we have been failures in our witness to the unity that God has given us in Christ and by his Holy Spirit. We are failures when our personal likes and dislikes, our resentments and our pride refuse to exercise forbearance, love, forgiveness, and consideration for a brother's likes and dislikes. We are failures in our witness to the unity of faith when we do not extend a heart and hand of love to others. We are failures when we slander with loose labels hastily slapped on to everyone with whom we don't agree in each detail. We are failures when we pray for unity and then deny God's answer to our prayer because the answer threatens our denominational securities. We are failures in our witness to the unity of faith when we permit our churches to become brick fortresses of purity, arrogant truth claims to ourselves, become competitive and triumphalist. We are failures when we practice rugged individualism that seeks only a direct dial access on a private wire to God, and finds no fellowship with all those other oddballs in the church.

Grow!

We carry in our flesh the evidences of our fallen nature, the marks of our divisiveness. We who have been called to fellowship and to the unity of faith still have a lot of room to grow. They did at Ephesus, and that's why Paul appealed to them to live a life worthy of the calling as the called-out people of the living God. And so do we. We have one Lord—just one! We have one faith—just one! We have one God and Father and the Father has one family—just one! We have been initiated into that one family by one Baptism—just one! But there is room to grow—to maturity and to the measure of the stature of the fullness of Christ. And for that growth and for that ministry and for that witness, our ascended Lord dispenses gifts to nurture and to nourish with the Gospel of his cross and resurrection until the nursing grows to manhood and the weak become the strong and the fearful become the fearless.

If you were traveling in a foreign country and a foreign culture and among a people of another color or another language, and suddenly, perhaps while riding on a city bus you noted someone wearing the familiar symbol of the cross, you would immediately recognize that you and he had more in common to unite you than the differences that might divide you. You would understand instinctively that in your common faith you were united to each other, and you would speak to one another and perhaps become good friends because the both of you discover one another as a fellow child of God. But what is even more significant, others on that bus would note your sudden friendship, hear your animated conversation, and observe your witness to your common faith and fellowship. And the dream that you had always thought impossible would then afford a glimpse of its reality.

Got the Point?

To maintain the unity of the Spirit in the bond of peace is not an option. To recognize it when God gives it and to act on it

190

becomes a central duty. We who confess Christ's holy name within the circle of this congregation are a family of faith—each one of us a personality unique, but all of us are members of Christ's body. Walk worthy of your calling to the faith among your brothers and your sisters in the Lord . . . in lowliness and meekness and with patience, forbearing one another in love. That's the oil that lubricates the heart and eliminates the friction. And with that oil God is at work today to build his church, extend the fellowship, establish the community, and gather in his people, and watching him at work, even though at times we suffer a satanic setback, is probably the most exciting story of this century. I hope and pray that you are in on it, even to the day of glory that remains beyond the cross when the impossible dream becomes complete reality.

ALTON F. WEDEL
Mt. Olive Lutheran Church
Minneapolis, Minnesota

THE NEW LIFE IN CONDUCT
Eleventh Sunday after Pentecost
Ephesians 4:17-24

The Problem of Conduct

Most of us, I suppose, grew up in communities where certain standards of personal conduct were taken for granted. Everyone knew the standards, and those who engaged in "unacceptable" actions were readily identified and criticized. Today, however, through exposure to television as well as to different systems of values in an increasingly intercultural society, these past standards—once presumed to be binding on everyone—no longer gain unquestioning allegiance throughout a community.

Yet all of us are faced with the need for guidelines to help us determine our conduct. Should I do this or that? What will be the effect of a present decision on a later situation? Or, how will my decision affect others? We all need a moral code by which to guide our actions.

And everyone does have a moral code! The differences among persons is the manner in which each one ranks the various values. Even an "immoral" person has a moral code in this sense.

As Christians, we frequently need to reexamine the basis of our conduct. We need to ask whether our actions express adequately the life of Christ in us. And our text today helps us in this review.

191

Old Conduct

Paul is contrasting two types of conduct—which we might call old conduct and new conduct. The new conduct is appropriate for a Christian; the old is a denial of Christ.

Listen again to the sharpness of Paul's words:

> In the Lord's name I warn you: do not continue to live like the heathen, whose thoughts are worthless and whose minds are in the dark. They have no part in the life that God gives, for they are completely ignorant and stubborn. They have lost all feelings of shame; they give themselves over to vice and do all sorts of indecent things without restraint. That was not what you learned about Christ (vv. 17-20; TEV).

These are strong words. Pointedly, they indicate that guides for conduct based on our self-interest or our impulses or instincts are inadequate. More than that, when we live and act in these ways our thoughts are "worthless," our minds are "in the dark." Such, Paul says, "have no part in the life that God gives." Loss of shame, vice and indecency are the result.

Lest we too easily take comfort in a suspicion that this warning does not concern us, conflicting values *do* influence our values today. Some persons are strongly motivated by a *pragmatic ethic*, where one can do anything one can get by with. If I don't get caught, it's okay. Others are more directed by a *hedonist ethic*, where the search is for instant gratification of the desires of the moment. Whatever satisfies sexually, whatever reduces boredom, whatever appears to be immediately relevant—these become the guides. Still others are bound more to a *cultural ethic*, where the prevailing accepted patterns serve as guides to right and wrong. Others seem to respond to a *withdrawal ethic*, where complacency or lack of involvement become prized virtues.

We know ourselves well enough to recognize that all of these value patterns compete for our attention, and that we are sometimes influenced by one, sometimes by another. The old conduct is still very much with us.

New Conduct

Over against this old conduct, however, Paul points to a new conduct. It is not based on any test of whether it works, or satisfies, or has majority approval, or eliminates risks. It doesn't stem from self-interest. Rather, the new conduct comes from the life of Christ within us.

The new conduct takes the values of the Ten Commandments seriously. It looks to the Beatitudes in the Sermon on the Mount for a description of the kind of character that is suitable for kingdom-living. The new conduct reflects the fruit of the Spirit in us—love, joy, peace, patience, kindness, goodness, faithfulness, humility, and self-control (Gal. 5:22-23). These are the qualities of life appropriate for the Christian.

Listen again to Paul:

> You certainly heard about Christ, and as his followers you were taught in the truth that is in Jesus. So get rid of your old self, which made you live as you used to—the old self that was being destroyed by its deceitful desires. Your hearts and minds must be made completely new, and you must put on the new self, which is created in God's likeness and reveals itself in the true life that is upright and holy (vv. 21-24).

Paul's overriding concern is that everything about our lives, including our conduct, should reflect what God has done and is doing in us. Against those who say that a Christian's belief is more important than conduct, Paul says conduct cannot be separated from belief. Against those who suggest that motive is the primary factor, Paul says that our specific actions count. Our actions, our conduct, he notes, are the outward appearances of our true inner nature. Conduct is important precisely because it shows what's inside of us—whether we honor Christ or dishonor him. Our thoughts and feelings and actions reflect the quality of our life *before God*.

New Conduct from New Life—Already Given

But we are not left simply with an *appeal* for new conduct. The text is gospel—good news—because it reminds us of what God has already done and is now doing which makes it possible for our conduct actually to change!

In his Letter to the Ephesians, Paul carefully emphasizes both the *proclamation* of what God has and is accomplishing in Christ —our forgiveness and freedom—and *instruction* or a word of encouragement that our lives should reflect God's work. The first chapter describes the divine plan of love. It notes the will of the Father "to bring all creation together, everything in heaven and on earth" (v. 10), his choice of us "to be his own people" (v. 11). The instrument for accomplishing the plan was and is Christ (vv. 4, 9, 11, 20-23), and the Spirit serves both as the guarantee that the plan shall finally be completed (v. 14) and as the present power for our transformation (vv. 17-19).

The second chapter dramatically contrasts the meaning of God's action in our life—a shift from death to life, from being condemned by God to being set free by him, the giving of new life. The rest of Ephesians shows the meaning of this new life in several areas of life: in the church (4:1-16), in conduct and attitudes (the focus today) (4:17—5:20), and in interpersonal and social relations (5:21—6:9). In these areas Paul encourages our attention to "sanctification," the changes in our life which are to follow from God's gracious action.

So the warning in the text today, the admonition for a new type of conduct, is given because God has already acted in such a way as to make the changes possible. We don't have to change in order to merit God's favor; we are to live in such a way as to reflect the favor that *he has already conferred* on us. The stranglehold of old conduct was broken in the crucifixion and resurrection of Jesus. *And in our Baptism we have access to resurrection power—the Holy Spirit—to create new patterns of conduct in our life.* God has acted—this is possible! This is the great fact behind Paul's urging to "get rid of your old self."

The Shaping of Christian Conduct

The shaping of Christian conduct does not happen overnight, however. It is a lifelong process—a daily struggle between the Spirit of Christ in us and our unrelenting weakness for self-interest, which spawns the old conduct. We never fully arrive in the building of the Christian life. The effort ends only when we pass into the Lord's future on the day of our physical death.

The process of moral formation—the shaping of a new conduct—parallels an inner transformation of our heart and mind and will. Paul says our "hearts and minds must be made completely new" (v. 23). The Holy Spirit changes us from the inside out. Our conduct reflects the state of our inner submission to the Spirit. As Christ gains more complete control over us, he is able to direct our outward life accordingly.

From experience we realize that our own best efforts cannot achieve lasting change in conduct. The old conduct keeps coming out. Only God can accomplish our re-making—and he does!—as we allow him to shape us. This is the process of sanctification, the changes in our lives brought about by the Spirit's transforming work within.

The growth of Christian character proceeds from regular attention to the practices of prayer and meditation, the study of God's Word, and worship and fellowship with the faithful. It is nourished by the example of other mature Christians and by correction given in love. The renewed mind gives a sensitivity to the conscience, an awareness to ethical reflection, and "intuition" concerning guidelines for new action.

All of which is to say that the conduct of a Christian is a *gift from God*—a reflection of the life of Christ within. It is bread from heaven given a disciple in the daily exodus from slavery on the way to the promised land (First Lesson). It is possible because Jesus is that bread of life which quenches hunger and thirst (Gospel). So "put on the new self" (v. 24).

Let the Lord continue his miracle in you!

BYRON L. SCHMID
Our Saviour's Lutheran Church
Lincoln, Nebraska

THE ART IN CHRISTIAN UNITY
Twelfth Sunday after Pentecost
Ephesians 4:30—5:2

Early in the fall of 1976, Northern California became the setting for a unique and ambitious art event. The actual object of art lasted only two weeks and is remembered as Christo's Running Fence. A shimmering construction of nylon, slung between steel posts, Running Fence rose from the sea on the rugged California coast. Then it rushed over 24½ miles up hill and down vale, revealing and concealing itself over public roads, through dozens of farms and several small towns. For an artwork it also consumed a staggering amount of time, people power and materials: 300 students, 2050 posts, 165,000 yards of materials and miles of wire. There were also 17 public hearings and 3 sessions of the California Supreme Court before permission was won for construction. Controversy continued, even after Christo's Running Fence was completed. One critic called it the most artistic rip-off of the decade. Another poetically observed, "It is as if nature has taken on a spine." But Christo, the artist himself, gave the project its most lasting meaning. As he reflected on the impact of his fence, he carefully included, as a part of the art, every person involved, every decision made and every obstacle over- come.

What remains now is the memory of a bold project that joined together thousands of people from all walks of life around a common enterprise dedicated to beauty. The art of Christo's Running Fence was the vision and the experience it created of human unity.

Our text focuses on the same theme. The Epistle to the Ephe- sians is an art treasure of the church. It is regarded by many as the finest of all the writings of Paul. Some scholars suggest it is a summary of the Apostle's theology and the chief means by which his thought has influenced the church. Yet the real art of Ephesians is the vision, yes, and the experience the reader can have of human and cosmic unity. It is in this Epistle to the Ephesians that the Apostle discloses the essential nature of the church as the body of Christ in the world, and its central mission to unite all races and nations in a single communion of worship and love. But it is only as we relate the three sentences of the text to this grand scope of the whole art piece that we begin to see how each sentence contributes some particular insights to the driving theme of unity that characterizes the Epistle.

The word "and" at the very beginning of the text serves notice that we are breaking into the middle of the Apostle's thought.

And do not grieve the Holy Spirit of God in whom you are sealed for the day of Redemption.

Paul has already announced in the first chapter of his letter that he regards all his readers who have heard the word of truth and believed in him to be "sealed with the power of the Holy Spirit," probably in Baptism, the act by which their hearing and be- lieving is made public. Likewise, the Apostle has already con- nected the gift of the Holy Spirit with unity, begging everyone, as he puts it, "to maintain the unity of the Spirit in the bond of peace."

The "and" carries us back to all this; then Paul adds,

Don't Grieve the Holy Spirit of God

It's an interesting idea isn't it? In a sense, this is one of those quaint ways the Bible has of turning a phrase that takes us off balance and makes us think through the language in a totally new way. How in the world could you or I grieve the Holy Spirit of God? The answer of Ephesians is, we grieve God's Holy Spirit

196

by not grieving over the disunity of humanity and especially of the church.

It is so easy to forget this commanding universal vision of the mission of Christ's church on earth stretched out in Ephesians. We get locked into our own doctrines and our own denominational distractions and directions and let them substitute for the universal mission of unity. It is actually rare to encounter a person who really does grieve over the brokenness of Christ's body in the world, but there are some!

Following a seminary communion service at the end of the octave of prayer for Christian unity, a retired professor noted that the celebrants had not observed the occasion. His study and passion for 40 years has been aimed at demonstrating the essential oneness of the church. He addressed the students with tears in his eyes, pleading for their prayers and concern on behalf of Christian unity. Such grieving is rare among us.

Yet, when we allow this Epistle to speak to us and hear again its claim that the great design of God is to gather into one all things and all people in Christ, our imaginations are fired, our faith is focused on a goal and our sense of significance is stirred. God sends his church to be the agent of Christian, human and even cosmic unity in Christ.

Biblical visions are not left without a witness. That is the promise. Now and then, some of us, I believe on behalf of all of us, are given experiences which ratify the goal. I believe such an experience was mine in Tanzania two years ago. I was there with a study seminar on a five-week trip to Africa. One of those weeks was spent in a village in the Pare Mountains, a fairly remote section of the country. The Tanzanian pastor invited me to preach on Sunday and to baptize the eight people who had been readied for the sacrament. When I indicated that I did not want to usurp his pastoral role he quickly indicated that the people would expect a visitor from afar to officiate as a sign that Baptism is the mark of our unity in Christ. So on that Sunday, in a small mud chapel, with worshipers jamming the aisles, hanging in the windows and emptying out on the road in front of the church, I said the ancient words and with water and the Holy Spirit eight Africans were made members of the body of Christ. But in me, that event aroused and excited the vision of our essential oneness in the church and our universal mission.

Making the Spirit Glad

If we can grieve God's Holy Spirit by our indifference, I trust we can likewise make the same Spirit glad, today or any day, when we recall and recommit ourselves in prayer with passion to the vision of unity in Christ.

The second sentence of the text admonishes us to change our behavior. It tells us to do away with such things as bitterness, hatred, anger, conflict and slander and to practice graciousness and forgiveness with each other. At first it sounds like one of those many do's and don'ts passages that pop up frequently in the Bible and from which Lutherans often shy away. Sentences like this smack of human works and we have a particular stake in proclaiming salvation only through the free gift of grace through faith. Still the do's and don'ts keep coming. It is clear that the New Testament writers (as well as the Lutheran reformers) expect that the behavior of those sealed in Baptism will be transformed from things that divide to things that unite. Again, it is not for personal piety, certainly not for salvation's sake that the Ephesians writer advises good works. It is for the larger and all-consuming sake of unity. Here too we have abundant evidence in the church of how the power of graciousness, kindness and forgiveness do work toward unity.

A student at our seminary developed cancer. He was flown to a city four hundred miles away for surgery. When I visited him before his second operation his room was literally papered from floor to ceiling with cards and letters mostly from other students. Calls came regularly from all over the country and most of the flowers delivered had to be stored in another room. Such attention might make some people sicker but in this case it was the right medicine. Kindness, graciousness and forgiveness kept this very troubled young man from alienation and isolation. His unity in and with the body of believers was enhanced through illness. And the effects spilled over to work the work of unity in others. One nurse at the hospital, a church drop-out for some years, saw her own life by comparison as separated and estranged and gave this seminarian a chance to minister to her through his illness. She became aware through the gracious behavior of believers how much she wanted to be included in the body of Christ.

"The sense of being prayed for" was the title of a sermon I heard long ago that spoke of this gracious behavior that we are called by the Apostle to extend to each other, especially within the body. Much is done, and much more could be done to build up the bond of prayer, peace, good will, and forgiveness within the body. One feels a sense of shame and disgrace at the failure of so many congregations and communions to achieve this behavior change that demonstrates our unity. Pursuing the admonition is

198

well worth the effort. For in a practical and pragmatic way, gracious behavior among us and toward others does become one of those outward signs of the inward claim that grace through faith has made upon us.

Imitators of God

But the text reserves the biggest surprise for last. The third sentence instructs us to be imitators of God. I would guess that few people can pass that expression over with indifference. The phrase is striking, even unique. Centuries ago Thomas a'Kempis wrote a devotional classic entitled *Imitations of Christ*. American protestants are used to being admonished to imitate Jesus or asking, "What would Jesus do?" But it is something of a shock to be called to imitate God. Yet this is the more characteristic stance of the New Testament. In the post-resurrection stories and in the books of Acts through Revelations, it is not Christ whom we are admonished to imitate as some sort of ethic-hero. It is rather the God who gave us Jesus in the first place, who made him our Christ and our Savior, whose love and sacrifice Jesus demonstrates, who we are called to imitate. With this astounding disclosure, the Apostle plunges us to the depth of his insight and also introduces a distinctive emphasis in his letter.

Here in Ephesians, even Christ's death and resurrection are seen in relationship to human unity. The more traditional emphasis of his passion as payment for our sins is passed over. Here Christ's cross and empty tomb are the vital key to the unifying of all humanity into "one new person." "He is our peace," says the Apostle, "who has made us both one and has broken down the dividing wall of hostility." "Therefore be imitators of God" is a call from the Apostle that moves us to the love of all people. "To walk in love" is the Bible's way of talking about a life-style that reaches out beyond the circle of those who love us and that shows us to be "children of the Most High," as Luke puts it, "for he is kind to the ungrateful and the selfish." With us such love is impossible, but with God's Spirit sealed in us through Baptism and empowering the vision and vitality of the church, we confess that all things are indeed possible.

These three sentences of the text touch on both the magnificence and the manageability of the mission, as the whole book of Ephesians sketches it out. On the one hand, the Apostle sees in a new and exciting way, even for our day, that Jews and Gentiles, (we can read all humankind) are the objects of God's love and care and the audience for his unifying Gospel. At one point he calls us "joint heirs, members of the same body and partakers of the promise in Christ." God has been at work spinning out his unifying plan since the very beginning. What was a mystery before has become plain to all who have heard and believed the Gospel. Precisely how it will all come about is still a mystery to most of us. But the faith of Ephesians says that "the power at work in us is able to do far more than we ask." Perhaps the best response to the magnificence of this Epistle's vision is simply to stand back and enjoy the view.

On the other hand this vision of unity is made manageable in Ephesians. In parallel sentences the Apostle lays the magnificence and the mission side by side. He breaks it down into manageable bites, encouraging us to practice graciousness among ourselves and others, to be aware and to be concerned and to grow in our passion for the wholeness and reunion of the church, to reach outward and to build unity with those who are most different and farthest away. And with great artistic care he weaves together these things we can manage, with the magnificent vision of unity God himself is bringing about.

Like Christo's Running Fence, the sheer magnitude of the vision draws us out a bit to take a look. And before we know it, it becomes clear that we have already done some small things that form a part of God's grand plan to make all creation one. Who knows, perhaps some day we will do much!

WILLIAM E. LESHER
Lutheran School of Theology
Chicago, Illinois

BUYING UP EACH OPPORTUNITY

Thirteenth Sunday after Pentecost
Ephesians 5:15-20

Opportunity knocks but once! When we think something is really important we spare no effort to get it. So some stand in line for hours waiting for an early-bird sale. Others will pile their shopping carts sky high to buy up things which are reported in short supply. When we really want something we spare no effort to get it. What about the precious gift of time? How careless we are about time! It so easily slips away, unused for lasting blessing.

God's Chosen Ones

The Apostle has just rehearsed the eternal blessings of Christ's love. His words ring with excitement and praise, "Blessed be the God and Father of our Lord Jesus Christ, who has blessed us in Christ with every spiritual blessing in the heavenly places, even as he chose us in him before the foundation of the world that we should be holy and blameless before him. He destined us in love to be his sons through Jesus Christ according to the purpose of his will to the praise of his glorious grace which he freely bestowed on us in the Beloved. In him we have redemption through his blood, the forgiveness of our trespasses, according to the riches of his grace which he lavished upon us (1:3-8). Then he points out how God's people were rescued from spiritual death and made alive in Christ for faith and good works. They are united in one body through one Spirit, one hope, one Lord, one faith and one Baptism. Their calling is to live out their life in Christ in the world. As God's chosen people they are "to make the most of time" (5:16).

Time Is Precious

Here is a metaphor from business, and it means literally, "buy up the time." We are to use fully the opportunities of life. We are not to escape from it. We are to live it up and out. We catch the impact and urgency of this divine admonition as we look at various translations: KJV, "redeeming the time"; RSV, "making the most of the time"; PHILLIPS, "make the best use of your time"; NEB, "use the present opportunity to the full"; TEV, "make good use of every opportunity"; AMPLIFIED, "making the most of the time, buying up each opportunity." Whether at work or at play, at home or at school, wherever we are, we are to buy up each opportunity taking it away from evil, and using it for God and for good. In a clothing store for needy families, sponsored by Christians, volunteers are greeted with this sign, "Work hard for the Lord. The pay is not so good, but the retirement plan is out of this world."

Someone once said there are two ways of dealing with time. We handle opportunities much like we regard water. For some, water is something to play in like children frolicking under a sprinkler or beach lovers dashing into the surf. For others, straining under the burden of deadly fever or hopelessly stranded in the desert, water is life. Time is life. Buy up each opportunity before it slips away. How?

Look Carefully

How do you buy up opportunity? Most people would probably say you have to watch for the big sale, get the best deal, wait for something to break. God's answer is much more sober, much more real, much more day-to-day. We are to use each opportunity to take a careful look how we walk through life. "Look carefully then how you walk, not as unwise but as wise, making the most of the time because the days are evil" (5:15). The Old Testament Lesson reminds us, "walk in the way of insight" (Prov. 9:6). Be alert. Don't hide your head in the sand. Have your eyes wide open. Know what's going on and what you are doing. Watch out for the trouble spots. Have a kind of field vision so you know where the opponents are. What are our opponents? Secularism, materialism, pessimism in a thousand different masks. The days are evil. Evil also has its eyes on time. It shops twenty-four hours a day, buying up the opportunities. So we must buy them up at all cost. Practical day-to-day decisions must be made, recognizing that we are in the world but not of it. The lowering of moral and religious standards in the world may be an excuse for some to lower theirs, but for someone who looks carefully in this Christian walk and buys up each opportunity, living according to God's will provides the greatest challenge and fulfillment.

The Will of the Lord

If each opportunity is important, then we will not only apply our own best judgment but also seek the will of God. "Therefore do not be foolish but understand what the will of the Lord is" (5:17). Foolishness is a lack of practical judgment, making decisions without God, knowing the theory but not following through. When "the fool says in his heart, 'There is no God'" (Ps. 14:1), he is saying God doesn't really matter. There may be a God but his being gives no direction to my life. We are not to be that kind of fool. We are to seek in each case what the will of the Lord is. Each opportunity is also an invitation to ask God's guidance. Although it is God's will that we are his people and that we should be "holy and blameless before him" (1:4), we are not told precisely how we can know God's will in every situation.

There is no magic formula. The emphasis is on taking the time to seek and understand God's will. Taking time to seek God's will through the Word of God and prayer, through the fellowship of believers, we also will learn and understand his will in the concrete situations of life. In the Psalm for today, God promises, "Those who seek the Lord lack no good thing" (Ps. 34:10). Jesus said, "Ask and it will be given you, seek and you will find, knock and it will be opened to you" (Matt. 7:7). Perhaps, as we begin each day we can remember this simple prayer of Thomas a' Kempis, "O Lord, in the simplicity of my heart, I offer myself to you today, to be your servant forever, to obey you and to be a sacrifice of perpetual praise."

Filled with the Spirit

Furthermore, use each opportunity to be filled with the Spirit. "Do not get drunk with wine for that is debauchery, but be filled with the Spirit" (5:18). Let the most profound experiences of life be Spirit-filled. In Bible times, too, as in ours, wine sometimes was used to excess, and in pagan cultures, devotees would seek communion with their gods through intoxication. Even today people look for "highs" to free them from the humdrum of daily routine, for escape into another world. So drugs, beer, wine, and whiskey are best sellers. St. Paul says that kind of living is "debauchery," the same word used in Luke's Gospel to describe the life-style of the prodigal son who "squandered his property in loose living" (Luke 15:13). That kind of living is a waste of time. It is opportunity lost. We cannot escape from life. We must face it realistically, buying up each opportunity. This is best done when we are filled with the Spirit. The prohibition not to get drunk with wine doesn't help unless it is replaced by something positive. The spirits of wine must be replaced by the Spirit of God. In the words of St. Augustine, "Thou hast made us for Thyself, and our hearts are restless until they rest in Thee."

The Apostle assumes that the Spirit is already effective in people who claim Jesus as their Savior and Lord, who said of himself in today's Gospel, "I am the living bread which came down from heaven. If anyone eats of this bread he will live forever" (John 6:51), and who promised, "I will pray the Father and he will give you another Counselor, to be with you forever, even the Spirit of truth, whom the world cannot receive, because it neither sees him or knows him; you know him, because he dwells in you and will be with you" (John 14:16-17). With faith in Jesus, the Spirit is already in us. What we are to do is ask for an increase of the Spirit's blessing, resulting in living the Christian life day by day, buying up each opportunity. In the words of an ancient hymn *Veni, Creator Spiritus:*

Come, Holy Ghost, Creator blest,
Vouchsafe within our souls to rest;
Come with Thy grace and heav'nly aid
And fill the hearts which Thou hast made.

Encouraging One Another

St. Paul then tells us how the Spirit-filled life works. We are to encourage one another, "addressing one another in psalms and hymns and spiritual songs, singing and making melody in your heart to the Lord with all your heart" (5:19). The Spirit's presence reaches out to others. It is never satisfied with private euphoria. Words spoken to others harmonize with hearts filled with the Spirit. They are psalms, hymns, spiritual songs, words about God's Word, his demands and promises, reaching out in judgment and mercy for all. That the words are sung emphasizes the joy and devotion of the believer. The Word of God to be shared is too captivating just to be spoken. It must be sung. It has been said that "He who sings, prays twice." We are told that the early church got on its way singing.

Those who are Spirit-filled gather together. They pray, they sing, they worship. In this they also buy up each opportunity. Like Jesus who went into the synagogue on the Sabbath as was his custom (Luke 4:16), like the early Christians who "devoted themselves to the apostles' teaching and fellowship, to the breaking of bread and the prayers" (Acts 2:42), so we gather today in our churches and other places of worship for mutual encouragement and support in the faith. This is an important part of buying up each opportunity. As we read in Hebrews (10:23-25), "Let us hold fast the confession of our hope without wavering, for he who promised is faithful. Let us consider how to stir up one another to love and good works, not neglecting to meet together as the habit of some is, but encouraging one another, and all the more as you see the Day drawing near." As God's people walk hand in hand over the slippery ice of a cold and heartless world, those who fall are lifted up by the gentle love of those who have not lost their footing, keeping in mind that those who stand today may fall tomorrow and those who fall today may stand tomorrow. Let us use each opportunity to encourage one another.

Giving Thanks

Finally, we use each opportunity to give thanks, "always and for everything giving thanks in the name of our Lord Jesus Christ to God the Father" (5:20). Earlier, St. Paul had expressed his ceaseless thanksgiving for the faith and love of his people, but now his admonition becomes much more comprehensive. We are to give thanks always and for everything, reminding ourselves of the importance of every opportunity. Bad things, as well as good, are opportunities for giving thanks because we have a loving Father, who gave his Son into death that we might

204

find salvation and life. We are God's by his choice not by ours. His love is so great that it is unbelievable. We need God's own power to comprehend its breadth and depth and length and height (3:18). Nothing can separate us from his love. As we give thanks always and for everything we are mindful that the final outcome of life is already assured by the precious death of Christ and his glorious resurrection. Our lost opportunities have been found by him, forgiven and restored, so that in everything God works for good with those who love him (Rom. 8:28). His power within us can do far more than we ask or think (3:20).

The Time Is Now

So buy up each opportunity. Time is precious. Don't waste it. Use it constructively. Don't let opportunities slip past you. The time is now. In Thomas Carlyle's diary from the day he visited his wife's grave, we find these words: "Cherish what is dearest while we have it near you, and wait not till it is far away. Blind and deaf that we are; think if thou yet love anybody living, wait not till death sweep down . . . and all be at last so mournfully clear and beautiful when it is too late."

A tourist recalls his visit to the Strasburg Cathedral with its great and renowned clock. At the hour of noon, statues of the twelve apostles process before the figure of Christ who lifts his hand in blessing while the cock flaps his wings and crows three times. At the center there are four figures representing the four ages of life: Childhood, Youth, Manhood, Old Age. At the first quarter of the hour, happy Childhood strikes the bell; then rosy Youth comes forth, then robust Manhood, and finally feeble Old Age lifts his hand to strike the bell. In the midst of the four figures is Death who strikes the bell on the hour. Some who stand watching the clock belong to happy childhood, some to rosy youth, some to robust manhood, some to feeble old age. And one can see that before long, death will lift his hammer and strike the bell. And as one puts himself in one of the four groups, one wonders how much time is left. What have I done with my life? What am I doing with it now?

That's the question of today. God's answer, "Buy up each opportunity."

LESTER E. ZEITLER
Pilgrim Lutheran Church
Bethesda, Maryland

DO YOU KNOW THAT I LOVE YOU?
Fourteenth Sunday after Pentecost
Ephesians 5:21-31

The other day a young Marine came into my office to see the chaplain. He was dressed in an expensive three-piece suit, with jewelry and wearing a large cross on a chain. He wanted help, he said, to get out of the Marine Corps. He had found the Lord, he wanted to witness to his fellow Marines in his work section, and the sergeants would not allow it. So he wanted out, in order to study for the ministry.

I questioned him further, to find out more about this man's situation. What chapel on base, or what church in town was he attending? None, he said, he'll do that when he gets out. Why wasn't he in uniform on this working day? He wouldn't wear the uniform, for it was the devil's uniform. And he whipped out his New Testament and showed me why I was a sinner, and why he was right.

I listened to him for awhile, then asked why he couldn't minister while being a good Marine, on his own time, and named several others who were effectively doing just that. But he wouldn't accept that. He wanted no connection with the military. He went on, and his anger at those senior to him and his hostility toward those who didn't agree with him surfaced. Finally, when he stopped to see if his arguments had had their desired effect, I asked him, "But those people to whom you want to tell about the Lord, do they know that you love them?" He looked stunned at my question, and answered "No."

A few minutes later, he left. He was still angry, and now also at me, for failing to help him get out of the Marine Corps.

Greater Love Has No Man . . .

Countless memorial services for soldiers and Marines have included the famous verse from John's Gospel: "greater love has no man than this, that he lay down his life for his friends." These words evoke the reminder of noble, even heroic sacrifice in the face of death, that one man should risk, should offer up, his life for the sake of his buddies. These words have commemorated the act of a soldier in Viet Nam who sees the incoming grenade in his foxhole and muffles the explosion with his own body. It calls to mind the tradition that the wounded are never left on the battlefield, and it has been acted out hundreds of times in the corpsman who has died pulling a man back to the safety of his friends. It is commemorated by the courage and sacrifices at Chosin Reservoir in Korea as the Marines fought their way out of the frozen wasteland, bringing their wounded with them.

Human beings commemorate heroic deeds. We name ships after heroes, write songs in their honor, kneel in prayer at their graves. But why do these actions evoke such feelings, and what motivates a man like Fr. Capodanno, who won the Congressional Medal of Honor in Viet Nam, dying to help a wounded Marine? I'm sure it was not the hope of the Medal. That wasn't what motivated him to plead for an extension of his tour so that he might share the hope of the Christmas message with the troops with whom he had shared so much. Rather, if you had talked with Fr. Capodanno, you would have heard that he drew his strength and courage from his Master, from the Christ who gave himself on the cross. For, as Paul says, "Christ loved the church and gave himself for it." The sacrifice of our Lord on the cross was because of his great love for us. How many times have we easily passed over the first part of John's famous statement on the gospel: "For God so *loved* the world that he gave his only Son." Without God's great love the sacrifice would not have been made. And so Fr. Capodanno tried to be like his Master, and give himself for God's people.

But it might be easy to dismiss Fr. Capodanno's statement, for after all, he was a priest, one who had been trained to see himself in his role as an embodiment of the Christ for his people. It might be very well for him to interpret what he does as acting out what God has first shown, but what about the eighteen-year-old Marine? He won't tell you his friend gave himself as an attempt to follow more closely the actions of his Christ. No, he won't say that at all. He may talk about how it happened, and if you are patient and understanding he may tell you what it was like, out there with his buddy, waiting for the medics to arrive in time, and being afraid his friend was dying. He may talk about how scared he was when his buddy was gone and he was alone. No, he probably won't talk about his love for his buddy, but he may have a better understanding of the Christ story, for he has been a recipient of that same kind of love that gives without stopping to weigh costs. There may never have been any discussion of faith between the two of them, but there for a brief time, the buddy may have acted as a Christ figure, and if that is articulated to the young Marine, he may begin to have a glimmer of understanding of the tremendous love which is found in the cross of the Lord.

Christ Loved the Church and Gave Himself for It

This verse from Ephesians is a complete statement of the gospel message. It contains the two dynamics which are at the heart of the Christian community: That Christ gave himself for the sake of the church. That Christ loved the church.

The first statement explains the nature of the redemption God effected for us through his Son. Christ gave himself totally—gave himself in a way that cost him his life—gave himself without question, without weighing the odds, without trying to evade his purpose. And that is what he sees as the self-chosen designation of his ministry. "The Son of Man came not to be served, but to serve."

And the second statement is to be held in tension with the first. Christ loved the church. The gospels say of our Lord that "he had compassion on them." "Compassion" is a word that has lost its force with us. A contemporary meaning might be "his heart went out to them." A compassion that was real, and that was understood by those with whom he had contact: The leper who returned, the blind man who was healed, the disciple who was redeemed after denying his Lord, the woman who was a sinner—all of these *knew* that Jesus loved them, that he had compassion on them. Christ gave himself freely, in love, for the church.

In our text, Paul uses the marriage relationship to illustrate his two-fold point. But that relationship causes us problems, and many of us would reject it, especially where it says, "wives, be subject to your husbands . . . husbands love your wives." We hear the words "be subject to," and it grates on our ears, for it goes contrary to almost everything we hear in our daily lives concerning mutually fulfilling roles in marriage. But perhaps we read into the text something which isn't there. For us "subjection" is a confrontive word, a word representing power. After all, the winner has power to compel the loser to submit, and the loser has no choice. But that is completely incorrect. Submission which is compelled by another is oppression, and not at all what Paul intended. The verse at the beginning of the lesson says "be subject one to another." The subjection Paul is speaking of is self chosen. The early hymn says, "Christ did not count equality with God a thing to be grasped, but emptied himself, taking the form of a servant." A submission Christ freely chose out of love. That's the kind of submission Paul is advocating, not the powerlessness of the vanquished. There is no possibility of exercising power in a win/lose struggle if love is basic. How can a husband really love his wife and compel her to submit? And if one loves, one will even choose the lesser role for the happiness and well-being of the other. In a relationship truly founded on love, both husband and wife will freely choose to let the other be dominant, for the best interest of them both.

Those who truly minister to others are those who do so in love, as Christ loved. Perhaps that is why so many young Marines were attracted to Fr. Capodanno, for they sensed that he loved them. Maybe that's why the death of a buddy has such an effect. And perhaps that's ultimately why heroic stories are remembered and passed on, since, in a small way, they are acting out of the gospel—they are each a sacrifice of one person's life, freely chosen, for the sake of others, and the others sense an act of love.

Do You Know that I Love You?

"It's all very well," you might say, "to talk about heroic act in battle, yet I will never be faced with that choice. So what relevance does all this have for me?" But of course, heroic acts are not limited to the battlefield. Heroic acts occur all around us every day. Many are unsung, like those who minister to the unwanted in our mental hospitals and homes for the handicapped. Others have sought out places in this country and abroad where they live quietly, sharing their hope and strength and love with those who are their neighbors. The size of the act doesn't matter, either. The smallest act of self-giving done in love for my neighbor is heroic in that it is following our Lord's example. A simple act like the parent who sits up all night with a sick child, is heroic if done in love, while the most dramatic act, one which may even cost a life, if done without love, is worthless.

And that's ultimately what the young Marine who came to my office did not understand. In his zeal to do what the Lord wanted, he thought that all he had to do was present the word, and his job was done. But he did not act out of love, and those around him were quick to pick up on that, and they were not about to hear what he had to say.

As you and I seek to share our faith with others and to serve our neighbors, perhaps we should provide check on our motives. We need to ask ourselves as we encounter others, "Do you know that I love you?" If the answer is "no," then somewhere we need to make some changes. If the answer is "yes," then we can rejoice that we are doing as our Lord has shown.

"Christ loved the church and gave himself for it." If in our Baptism we are called to be like him, we can do no less for our neighbor.

CHRISTINE MILLER
Naval Education and Training Center
Newport, Rhode Island

THE FUTILE BATTLE

Fifteenth Sunday after Pentecost
Ephesians 6:10-20

The Struggle

Have you ever felt as though the whole world were against you? We speak of "one of those days" when everything seems determined to cross up our best intentions. And who doesn't have "those days" with some degree of frequency?

The feeling that we are oppressed under a strange and foreign force is neither new nor unique to our times. It is grounded firmly in the thought of the Scripture, and our text for today puts the thought very forthrightly: "For we are not contending against flesh and blood, but against the principalities, against the powers, against the world rulers of this present darkness, against the spiritual hosts of wickedness in the heavenly places" (Eph. 6:12). Our forefathers from of old had this sense of being opposed by demonic powers that would hinder and deter all the good possibilities of life. So if you feel that such powers are set loose around your life, you needn't feel surprised!

All too frequently in our more "sophisticated" age we explain these forces that oppose us in terms of psychoses and neuroses and inner problems of mental health. Goodness knows that we have enough to contend with there, even if there were no external forces oppressing us! Our selfishness and our greeds, our self-love and judgmental attitudes, our lovelessness in the face of need around us and our willingness to use our neighbor to our own advantage . . . all of these things afflict us in our daily life. We can certainly explain more than we care to explain of the troubles that surround our life in terms of our own failure to control the urges and desires and lusts that spring up from within. The Gospel for today reminds us of them with force: "For from within, out of the heart of man, come evil thoughts, fornication, theft, murder, adultery, coveting, wickedness, deceit, licentiousness, envy, slander, pride, foolishness. All these evil things come from within and they defile a man" (Mark 7:21-23).

It is enough to crush us simply to think of what forces lie within us that we are supposed to curb and control. Knowing their power and experiencing our literal slavery to them, we hardly want to hear about other forces that oppress us.

But our text for today, the Second Lesson, turns our attention to those enemies that swirl about our very being with every evil intent. It is not that we ever see them nor even that we hear them speak to us directly. Yet their force is felt daily. Paul envisioned us and the world as being surrounded by an army of powerful enemies. And Luther picked up this kind of an image when he wrote his Reformation anthem, "A Mighty Fortress Is Our God." He said:

> Tho' devils all the world should fill,
> All eager to devour us. . . .

He, too, sensed the nearness of the enemy, the tempter who confronts us with doubt and unbelief, who lures us from faith sometimes with powerful temptations and sometimes with subtle temptations. It is the principalities and powers at work trying to convert us to the notion through newspaper and TV advertising and friends speaking and business associates trying to convince us that what really counts is a good home, three automobiles, a hefty bank account and a wet bar in the family room. There's nothing wrong with that, is there? And when the question is put like that, of course there is nothing wrong with that! But if the question implies that everything is *right* with that, then we have been lured into an idolatry and we set our hearts on it. The principalities and powers have had their way through the people and things who surround us with "The Great Lie" even while they are disguised as our friends persuading us we should believe in "The Great Truth"!

If we need an example of the power of these forces around us and how they work, we need but to look to our Lord, himself. From the very beginning of his ministry Jesus regularly had to confront and deal with the powers that assaulted him on the right and on the left. His forty days in the wilderness after his baptism were days of confronting the great questions of what his task was to be, and the "wiles of the devil" (to use the words of our text) were his constant companion. "Why the cross?" the devil asked Jesus. "Merely sign with a token gesture that you want the world from my hand and I'll give it to you for the asking!" Win it with powerful miracles and great displays of divine power. Anything but the cross . . . anything but the servant role . . . anything but salvation through humility! "Take your power and turn it to your own advantage," the tempter urged Jesus. "Don't go to Jerusalem where you will be killed" came the voice of the tempter through Jesus' close companion Peter. From friends and foes, in the private moments and in the public moments Jesus was beset before and behind with the voices of the principalities and the powers and the rulers of the present darkness, the spiritual hosts of wickedness in the heavenly places. The struggle was fierce for him, and it is no less fierce for us!

The Futility of the Struggle

Were it a struggle that we could wage with reasonable expectation of success, then we might engage in it with some hope. And on occasion the very wiles of the evil one even lets us win a battle or two in order to get us to put our guard down. After all, there is a march that goes two steps forward, one step backward, two steps forward, one step backward, to illustrate that in giving a little here and there one may still make great progress. How gladly the evil one concedes a skirmish or two in order to put us at ease, to convince us that we can resist with a little struggle . . . or sometimes even with very little struggle! How we can be set up for the great fall!

Paul knows that and warns us: "Keep alert with all perseverance, making supplication for all the saints" (Eph. 6:18). Don't for a moment let down your guard. Don't for a moment think that the battle can be won with your own strength. It is a futile battle if you fight it alone, and one moment left unguarded can be our undoing. Again Luther said it so well:

> With might of ours can naught be done,
> Soon were our loss effected.

"Pray at all times in the Spirit, with all prayer and supplication . . . making supplication for all the saints." Jesus had taught the disciples to pray thus: "Lead us not into temptation, but deliver us from evil" (Matt. 6:13). As someone has said so well, this is not a simple or easy prayer. It is the prayer of a desperate person, one who knows the futility of the battle in which he is engaged and who knows that the battle will be lost unless a force bigger and stronger than the one assaulting him enters the fray. "Protect me from this one who would gladly devour my very being," would be a paraphrase of the prayer Jesus taught. Paul, Luther, Jesus . . . and any human who has ever entered the battlefield where the principalities and powers hold their banners high, know very well the fury and the strength that ride into the assaults they launch.

The Hope in the Struggle

Against such odds there would seem to be no hope. And out of the depths of this futile effort rises a David to meet the Goliath. Who will engage such forces and destroy their power? Can a boy defeat a giant? Can a man stand up to the principalities and the powers and the rulers of this present darkness? Is a child born of a virgin and soon chased to Egypt in order to save his life against a mere flesh and blood enemy capable of taking on the spiritual hosts of wickedness in the heavenly places? Surely the battle seems uneven. But since nobody else can, is it not at least worth our while to consider the possibility?

One can only stand by and watch as this man mounts his campaign. He beats back blindness and lameness, raises the sick from their bed and commands nature itself, and finally restores to life the son of the widow of Nain, Jairus' daughter, and his good friend Lazarus. The people—and we—stand in awe of him. Surely he is an extraordinary man. He is a good man, a just and merciful man. But what can he do against the principalities and powers when they assault him? With what fury they infest a whole crowd that cries, "Crucify him!" The very citadel of the faith condemns him to death. The wiles of the devil have won over the very hearts of those who supposedly were closest to the secrets of God! The powers of the religion that named God and the powers of the state are enlisted by the principalities and powers to do away with this man! And he stands helpless with a crown of thorns before a jeering crowd. Lifted to a cross, submitted as public example number one of the powerlessness of man against the strength of the world rulers of this present darkness, Jesus dies! Goliath has laughed at David and come out with sword gleaming!

The Victor in the Struggle

At first the death of death could hardly be seen. Like the pebble hurtling swiftly from David's little slingshot, hardly noticed in that split second between laughter and death, Jesus' death seemed the end of it all while it was really the beginning of it all! Risen from the dead, the shout suddenly went up. The mighty Goliath lay beheaded before the very eyes of those who only moments

before had despaired! Death is undone! What seemed impossible
has become reality!

> We tremble not, we fear no ill,
> They shall not overpow'r us.
> This world's prince may still
> Scowl fierce as he will,
> He can harm us none,
> He's judged; the deed is done;
> One little word can fell him.

In this way Luther described the end of the powers exercised over
us by the spiritual hosts of wickedness in the heavenly places.

> But for us fights the Valiant One,
> Whom God Himself elected.
> Ask ye, Who is this?
> Jesus Christ it is.

The battle is over . . . and yet, of course, it goes on. It goes on
between the principalities and the powers who rule this present
darkness and us, who are the children of light. The fight is still
futile if we try to engage in it on our own strength. But to "put
on Christ" as the Scriptures so regularly instruct us, is to "take
the whole armor of God, that you may be able to withstand in the
evil days, and having done all, to stand" (Eph. 6:13). To examine
the description of that armor is to find what it means to have
Christ as the One who defends us in the hour of peril.

The Struggle Aggressively Waged

Nor is it enough to wear the armor of defense. In our hand
is placed "the sword of the Spirit, which is the word of God"
(Eph. 6:17). This is the sword Paul was using when "utterance
was given him in opening his mouth boldly to proclaim the mystery of the gospel" (v. 19). It is the sword given to us as we
are sent not merely to defend ourselves against the principalities
and the powers, but to move aggressively against them. With
Word and sacrament both as our sustenance and as our strength,
we are sent alongside Paul to proclaim the good news to all the
world that the oppressor has lost the right to say the last word.

He still has a word, to be sure—a strong and powerful and
subtle and frequently deceiving word. The fact that he has lost
the *last* word by no means indicates that he has no word at all
or that we can let down our guard.

But there is another Word over and above the spiritual hosts of wickedness. And we are sent to assault the fortresses of darkness with the light of Jesus Christ, to proclaim to all the world the faith that the futility of the struggle has now been reversed . . . it is not *our* struggle that is futile, but it is the struggle of the principalities and the powers to regain the world that is futile! They who have lost are struggling to regain that which was torn from their hands by the man who set his foot toward Calvary and came away from the grave alive.

To the man or woman who walks with this Jesus, the battle is won even while it is being waged! For he who wears the armor of God will surely win the battle, no matter how furiously the war goes on around him!

HUBERT BECK
University Lutheran Chapel
Texas A & M University
College Station, Texas

JAMES: STRAIGHT-UP RELIGION

Sixteenth Sunday after Pentecost
James 1:17-22 (23-25), 26-27

Straight-Up Religion

The adult baptisms and the wedding of Rick and Rita were very different because he was a member of the Bushmasters motorcycle gang. I baptized them in the little chapel of our congregation after their wedding rehearsal. I married them the next day. About thirty members of the gang arrived on "choppers" which they parked in the church parking lot. They were dressed in black jackets, black pants, and black boots. They wore "shades" over their eyes and German helmets on their heads. The wedding reception was at the union hall behind the Burger Chef. The bride and groom had changed from their rented formal attire to the traditional motorcycle gang outing shirts, bib overalls, and stocking caps.

Rick took me around the room to meet the other members of the gang. When he came to one fellow, his comment was, "Hey, man, why did you leave your hat on in the church? That's a straight-up church!"

I haven't figured out for sure what the young Bushmaster motorcyclist meant by a "straight-up church," but I think I know! I think Rick was describing what James was saying in 1:27: ". . . What God the Father considers to be pure and genuine religion is this: to take care of orphans and widows in their sufferings and to keep oneself from being corrupted by the world." Rick, when he talked about a "straight-up church," was talking about what was to him "pure and genuine religion."

Genuine Religion

James, the writer of the New Testament epistle, and Rick, of the Bushmasters motorcycle gang, want us to take a few minutes to consider if what we do is genuine. Because they both know that a congregation can lose its genuineness, it can become phony, it can appear to the community as neither real nor legitimate. Both James and Rick realized the danger of our kind of liturgical worship. We are constantly in danger of becoming aloof and exclusive in our desire for beauty and perfection in art, music, and the worship liturgy. They knew how easy it was to fall into a rut of comfortable worship which often has nothing at all to do with the way we live our lives the rest of the week.

I heard the story a long time ago of two Moslems who were feuding. The one had drawn his knife and was chasing the other down the city street trying to kill him. At that time, from one of the minarets in that town, there came the call for Moslems to worship. Both stopped, got their little prayer rugs, knelt down and bowed to Mecca, and said their prayers. When the prayer time was over, they folded up their rugs, and continued the chase down the street. This is often the way our religion works in our lives—a brief moment of prayer and pause about God, and then go on our merry chase through life with little thought as to the significance about what took place in that worship.

James must have known the Lutherans! He said for us to watch out about the way we carry out our worship. He gave us a warning. Genuine religion, according to James, is not dependent upon the things we so often feel are important, but upon a simple and sincere devotion to God, demonstrated by a compassionate relationship with other people.

Dr. Karl Menninger was asked at a forum, what one should do if he felt a nervous breakdown coming. The famous psychiatrist said, "If you feel a nervous breakdown coming on, lock up your house, go across the railroad tracks, find someone in need, and do something for him." That also can be true of a congregation as well as an individual! If and when we are quarreling among ourselves, disagreeing over the business of the church, worrying about insignificant worship practices, let's lock the doors, go across the tracks in our town, and help.

216

Booker T. Washington said, "I think I began learning long ago that those who were happiest are those who do most for others." That certainly must be why Jesus promised joy with our kind of religion.

Our Concern for the Poor

Micah, long before Rick of the motorcycle gang or James, author of the epistle, had put it in a similar way: ". . . the Lord has told us what is good. What he requires of us is this: to do what is just, show constant love, and to live in humble fellowship with our God" (6:8).

This definition of religion which is "straight-up" is so simple that many of us just cannot believe that it's good enough, but James' way of practicing the faith is so difficult that we prefer instead to go about our ceremonies with their complicated elaboration and find that easier to offer to God instead.

It's less demanding on us to worry about whether we like the hymns we sing than it is to be concerned about the warmth of the children who live within a few blocks of our church building. We would rather press out the wrinkles in the dossal curtain than see to it that God's love and concern is given in concrete acts to the disgusting, old widow who lives in loneliness and whose water was shut off by the city. We often ignore the minorities, the alcoholics, the drug users, the welfare cheats, the prisoners in our local jails, and other classifications of unlovely human beings in our community while we spend great amounts of religious energy on the niceties of sacrament and worship. It's much more complicated to get involved with those locked up and guilty in our community than it is to introduce a new service book and hymnal! The money for a new roof on our church building will come in easier than that same amount for the treatment of delinquent teen-agers at the treatment center sponsored by our synod.

Rick of the Bushmasters motorcycle gang claimed that we were a "straight-up" church. James said, "What God the Father considers to be pure and genuine religion is this: to take care of orphans and widows in their suffering."

Worship and Service

Let's look carefully at what James says here. The Good News Bible translates it, "What God the Father considers to be pure and genuine religion is this: . . ." According to William Barclay, "the word translated religion is *threskeia* and its meaning is not so much religion, as the outward expression of religion in ritual and liturgy and ceremony. It is worship in the sense of which we speak of the worship part of the service; it is worship in the sense of which we speak of the different kinds of worship which are found in different churches." (*Daily Study Bible*, 71.)

What James is saying is that the finest and purest and most genuine response to God's gift of grace is in service to the poor and personal purity. Today's Epistle began by saying that "every good gift and every perfect present comes from heaven; it comes down from God." Now a genuine, "straight-up" response to that, according to James, is not so much in magnificent liturgy or great church buildings or elaborate vestments—but in practical service of people and in our own personal purity of life-style.

If we sing, "O, Brother Man, fold to thy heart thy brother," and go from this place and hate in subtle ways, by reinforced prejudice and lack of accurate information, if we pray, "God help all those less fortunate than we are," and ignore a plea for help at the local settlement house, if we, as God's family, buy new beautiful altar paraments, and can't afford our social ministry budget, James says that's not what God calls genuine religion. That's not what Rick of the motorcycle gang calls a "straight-up" church, either! It is very possible for a church to be so wrapped up in its buildings and beautiful liturgy, that it neglects the time and money for practical Christian service. And James says that's not genuine religion. God wants the orphans cared for, the widows considered, and keeping oneself from corruption of the world.

What James gives us here is not a new idea. He was scolding and pleading and warning just like the prophets had done before. His Bible said: "God, who lives in his sacred temple, cares for orphans and protects widows. He gives the lonely a home to live in and leads prisoners out into happy freedom . . ." (Psalm 68:5-6). Zechariah scolded the people for ". . . closed minds and hearts as hard as rocks," and he pleaded with them to "see that justice is done, and . . . show mercy to one another." He continues to say: "Do not oppress widows, orphans, foreigners who live among you, or anyone else in need. And do not plan ways of harming one another" (Zech. 9 & 10). Micah complained that "all ritual sacrifices are worthless, if we didn't do what was right, show constant love, and to live in the right kind of fellowship with God" (6:8).

Julia Ward Howe was talking to the old fire-eater Charles Sumner about another person needing help. The senator replied,

"I've become too busy to concern myself with individuals." "That's remarkable. Even God has not reached that stage yet," snapped Mrs. Howe. There's something drastically wrong with the kind of concern that bleeds for mankind, yet can't focus on a person.

Ritual or Sacrifice

Down through the years, we have often yielded to temptation to make ritual and liturgy a substitute for sacrifice and service. We can fall into the trap of making our religion splendid within this church at the expense of neglecting it outside our building.

Tradition has it that Pope Innocent IV and Thomas Aquinas were standing watching bags of gold being carried into the Vatican. "You see," said the Pope, "the day is past when the church has to say, 'Silver and gold have I none.'" "Yes," replied Thomas, "and the day is also past when she could say to a lame man, 'rise up and walk.'"

This doesn't mean that it is wrong to try to offer the very finest worship to God within these walls; but, it is to say that all this beautiful worship is empty and phony unless it *sends* us out to love God by loving all of God's people; and unless it also sends us to walk in a pure way amidst the tempting ways of the world. No single definition of religion is perfect and James' definition isn't either. But no definition can be true to the Old Testament prophets and to Christ unless the two essentials which James underlines are prominent: First, compassion toward our neighbors and others, and second, keeping from being corrupted by the world.

There is a tradition that St. Francis was praying in an ancient church which was badly in need of repair when he heard a voice from the crucifix over the altar say, "Francis, go and repair my church, which you see is falling in ruins." Francis went to get his tools, but soon realized that the voice meant the state of the people, and not the building. If we have thought of the church as brick and mortar and councils and committees and liturgies and vestments, then Jesus Christ says again to us today from his cross, "Repair my church."

To "be merciful just as your Father is merciful" (Luke 6:36), is to be genuine in your religion.

Rick of the motorcycle gang said of his new church, "Hey, man, that's a straight-up church, and you should take your hat off." The member of the gang to whom Rick was speaking slowly raised his hand to the top of his head and felt for his hat. "Hey, man, I didn't know I had my hat on!"

It's probably true that as we are caught up in the beauty of this worship service, in the proclamation of this good news, in the singing of this music and the art forms that are expressed here, we simply don't realize that we may have allowed this wonderful experience to become our total religious practice. James asked us to remember that this experience should be to provide the tools for us to go out into the world and to care for all the suffering. James wrote it down for us this way; "What God the father considers to be pure and genuine religion is this: to take care of orphans and widows in their suffering and keep oneself from being corrupted by the world."

JERRY L. SCHMALENBERGER
First English Lutheran Church
Mansfield, Ohio

GOD'S POWER AND LIGHT COMPANY
Seventeenth Sunday after Pentecost
James 2:1-5, 8-10, 14-18

Here in the Pacific Northwest we are very much aware of water. It falls to earth as rain or snow and we welcome it as a basic element of life. It falls as a gift of God on the hills and mountains and follows relentlessly its nature and destiny down the valleys to the sea. We have learned to count on that and have made of it a major source of power and a faithful servant which we respect.

Sometimes water turns to ice as in the glaciers but even then it is persistent as it makes its way down the mountains where it melts and flows in rivers to the ocean. So we have built dams to hold back the water until its power can be harnessed to drive the enormous turbines which produce power and light for our cities and countryside. We enjoy these benefits by joining together in companies both public and private. Water is turned into light and power because together we harness the energy inherent in it.

Today's Lesson helps us recognize the place of faith and works. What is the place of faith in the lives of God's people and how does it relate to the good works we can do? If it is true that the people of God are to be a beacon in the world and to be the power that does God's will, is it by our faith that we accomplish this, or by our works? Is James really raising the question whether it is better to do good works rather than to have faith?

The Meaning of Faith

First we should understand something of the meaning of faith. If faith means that we believe that Michelangelo painted the ceiling of the Sistine Chapel, we are not talking about biblical faith. Neither is it faith to believe that the corn will grow, the marriage will work out or the weather will change.

Faith in the biblical sense is not something you and I can do, it is not a human accomplishment. It is not a sort of religious experience nor a state of mind. Rather, faith is a gift of God which comes to those who hear God's Word. When we respond to God's saving act in Jesus Christ we simply acknowledge his total claim on us and we surrender every trace of self-reliance to him.

God creates faith in an infant through the water of Baptism. That faith is perfect because it is received without prejudice as a pure gift of grace. But it is not meant to be static or frozen in that child. It is meant to grow by the hearing of God's Word until it sets the course of that person's life. Christian faith is a commitment to go where Christ leads, to follow him whatever the risk. For example, suppose you had made the down payment to NASA and were scheduled to be on the first civilian flight into outer space. You are in Cape Kennedy ready for takeoff. You are on board the aircraft 'piggy-back' on the 747, the elaborate system has been set and the engines have started. Now there is no turning back. If there is no malfunction you will soon be in orbit. So it is when by faith you go with Christ: "If any person would be my disciple let him deny himself, take up his cross and follow me." If that is what you mean when you say you believe in Christ, you are speaking about biblical faith. Your course of action will follow his. You will pick up your cross as he carried his. You will think little of your personal rights and much about God's will. You will discount the importance of your personal ambitions, your money and property and your self-interest because your mind and heart are set in him.

Does this sound like a description of your faith? Or are you wondering now whether you really believe at all?

In today's Gospel, Peter's faith is examined. To Jesus' question, "Who do you say that I am?" he answers, "You are the Christ." That was just fine! But that faith is fickle. Mark's arrangement of the text points to this when in the next paragraph he has Peter denying that Jesus would suffer and die. Then Jesus says to him, "Get behind me, Satan, for you are not on the side of God but of men."

Peter's faith, as yours and mine, was ephemeral. His faith and ours is short-lived, isn't it? I think you will agree that my faith or yours will never be the "beacon-light in all the land." Where then is there such a light and such a power? Where is the faith that will batter down the gates of hell?

A Faith that Works

God in Christ has taken care of that. Like raindrops falling on the mountains "morning by morning" God daily gives his gift of faith to all people everywhere. Wherever his Word is preached and taught there is that precious water of life. As he brings together the little drops of faith into one body there is built an enormous reservoir of faith.

As individuals our faith will never impel the turbines. Alone we are helpless. The lights of the city would go out if they depended upon you or me alone. But our Father has made you and me members of his holy family, the people through whom his Spirit shines as a light to the world, the company of divine power to a dying humanity.

It should be noted that the turbines are dependent upon the body of water and not the other way around. Without the impelling force of a virtual torrent of water relentlessly seeking its destiny in the ocean, the good work would never be done. The turbines would be inert. But on the other hand, without the turbines the reservoir would be useless. James is not only right but also understandable: "Faith by itself, if it has no works, is dead." Without works, faith is dead.

But it is also true that without faith there would be no good works. As Jesus said, "Without me you can do nothing." So God has given faith, not to Peter alone, not to you or me alone, but to his holy church. It is in the company of God's people, created by the gift of faith that the works of power and light are made known to the world.

What then is the essence of that power and light? What is the will of God for his faithful people? His command is that we should love one another as he has loved us. Or, as Jesus told the inquisitive disciples of John, "Tell him what you see. The blind receive their sight, the lame walk, the lepers are cleansed, the deaf hear, the dead are raised and the poor have good news preached to them." He could have told them plainly that he was indeed the Messiah but he chose rather to show his divine power and godliness in his works of mercy and justice. And above all, he demonstrated his true identity in his suffering and death upon the cross. There his love was complete and perfect. And from that act, God's incomprehensible love is perfected in and through

222

us to the healing of the whole world. We cannot atone for the sin of the world but with the help of God we can announce God's forgiveness and treat one another in mercy, justice and love.

The works that you and I do will never justify us. Only God's supreme act of love in Jesus can do that. Only his gift of faith can convince us to throw ourselves upon his grace and mercy. But that same gift of faith, however insignificant it may seem to us, becomes the very power that gives light to those who walk in darkness. That is our destiny. We are indeed, God's Power and Light Company.

ERLING C. THOMPSON
Trinity Lutheran Church
Tacoma, Washington

THE DIFFERENCE TRUE WISDOM MAKES

Eighteenth Sunday after Pentecost
James 3:16—4:6

While walking down the street minding your business, a voice cries out, "Hey there, wise guy." You stop. Dare you turn? You wonder, "Did I do something foolish or stupid? They must be calling someone else." You hope! It is not very desirable to be called a "wise guy."

Again, you are walking down the same street. A person runs up to you and says, "Wise person, may I speak with you?" Ah, quite a different feeling now. To be thought wise is a very high compliment indeed.

It is easy to see that we use the word "wise" in two very different ways. While the height of compliment on the one hand, it can be downright insulting on the other.

In the text for today, James makes a similar distinction in his discussion of wisdom. There is a kind of wisdom that deserves compliment, while another so-called wisdom receives only criticism. So James gives a warning to the early Christian church concerning the self-styled preachers who were gaining in reputation and following among the people. The preachers claimed to speak from a vast storehouse of wisdom and so impressed their hearers. But theirs was a false wisdom, indeed not wisdom at all. In one way, these preachers appeared to be wise, but they worked from a base of intellect and knowledge which was founded on self. The results of their "wisdom" were quite the opposite of what should be expected in a family circle of believers. So James calls on his readers, and upon us, too, to seek rather the true wisdom which is founded on God and his love.

James' warning is applicable for us today. We, too, are easily attracted and impressed by the claims of false wisdom. The church must always be on its guard against the false guides in its calling to maintain the truth of the Gospel.

But there is a more personal application. Each one of us as individuals is tempted to become one of the false teachers imposing our self-styled wisdom upon others. We set ourselves above another. We seek to defeat another, or at least put him in his proper place—below us. We often encourage dissension and dispute, exercising both loudly, at the expense of the other. We strive for victory through argument seeking to win and thereby exalting ourselves above the other.

When and where does this happen? Surely not in the Christian community? Certainly not in the Christian home? But we all know the old saying, "You only hurt the ones you love" is all too true. Listen to the language sometime. Hear the very words you say to another. "I told you so." "You're not so smart." "Now you listen to me." "And I don't want to hear another word about it." "Period!"

Not so wise, says James. And we can agree. So what is the alternative? James says that the really wise life is so because it is founded upon God. It is an alternative worth considering. It has some very practical offerings for the richness and wonder of life.

What Is Wisdom Anyway?

Wisdom is not a hard word to say. But what does it mean really? Is the wise old owl a good example of a life of wisdom? One might question that in light of his habit of staying up all night, and screwing his head around so it looks like it might fall off. We call our four last teeth "wisdom teeth." So wisdom comes with age. But what of the over-thirties who have never cut these teeth? No wisdom? I hope not! Wise guys don't appear to have wisdom at all. And did the wise men display wisdom when they risked life and limb, even reputation to follow a star just to see a baby? What is wisdom anyway?

When I was a child, my grandfather spoke often of "horse sense." Now I knew that horses were a lot smarter than cows, pigs, and sheep. But it seemed, on closer observation, that "horse sense" most often described the actions of people, and not horses at all.

So wisdom has to do with action. It has to do with choices

made in life. Right decisions came from "horse sense," while wrong ones had not used it at all. "Horse sense" became synonomous with "common sense" and for most purposes that meant "wisdom."

It is true that wisdom has to do with decisions. It is the determining factor in choices we do or do not make. Wisdom has much to do with quality of life as it is lived out in real everyday terms. It is like a reference point. Though traditions and mores may vary from people to people, it is wisdom that motivates us to do that which is proper, effective, and acceptable.

Wisdom is not an accumulation of knowledge. It is not determined by one's I.Q. A very learned person may be lacking in wisdom. Wisdom is application of one's knowledge and intellect to life as it is lived. A person may have many degrees from institutions of learning, but may still flunk life.

Wisdom Is the Fear of the Lord

The Word of God speaks of wisdom in terms of relationships. It begins with the fear of the Lord, writes the author of Proverbs (Prov. 9:10). The Psalmist echoes this thought in Psalm 111:10. The New English Bible translates this in a footnote, "The main part of wisdom, is the fear of the Lord."

So wisdom then is based on a relationship with God himself. Wisdom is to know who God is, to seek his will, to honour and praise him. Wisdom is a faith relationship with the Father. It is coloured by his Word, will and plan. Wisdom is to say with Joshua, "As for me and my house we will serve the Lord." It is a relationship to be sought.

But more than this, it is a relationship made possible by God himself. He becomes our God by his own initiation. Our relationship is restored through his loving activity seen in Jesus Christ our Lord. It comes as his free gift. No wonder it is of such great value. Life that begins within God is indeed rich and full. He sees to that on our behalf. This great gift is richer by comparison than all the weapons of war. It is of more value than jewels, pearls, even gold. Though there are references in the Scriptures to wisdom, in most instances it is spoken of as being a faith relationship with God, his plan, and his Word.

Life lived outside this relationship with God, is simply unwise. It is foolishness. The attractions to this unwise life may well be appealing and tempting, but life offered cannot be as full. Jesus clearly shows this in the familiar parable of the two houses built by two men. The one on the strong foundation stood through storms of high intensity. The other soon toppled and fell crashing to the ground. Our lives are the same. Grounded on world "wisdom" nothing lasts. Founded upon God, life is solid, strong, and rich.

It is this very distinction that James writes about. As both "wisdoms" beckon to us, seeking our allegiance, James asks us a question: "Which is to be the starting point of your life?" A choice is called for.

The wisdom which we choose becomes a life-style, even a confession, and a commitment. The truly wise life, based on the fear, love and trust of God, moves out in a life of agape. We live a life of self-giving love. St. Paul beautifully illustrates this in 1 Corinthians 13. False wisdom might claim, "If I had prophetic powers and understand all mysteries. . . ." Now this may well be commendable, even desirable. But it is not wisdom. ". . . if I have no love I am nothing. True wisdom displays love, the kind of love shown by our Lord. It is a love that needs no deserving. We deserved none of his. It is a love that sets us free and motivates us to free others. Moved by his love, we actively live out our response with praise and worship at the same time that we care for another. Begun by God, love is lived out in his people. This is a life of wisdom.

Fruits Visible in Lives

James becomes very practical in verse 18 of our text. He shows that a life from the wrong base can get mighty mixed up and lead to difficulties. How real his words are for a society that seems determined to isolate, separate, and even destroy relationships. We need not look far to see these fruits. Nations, neighborhoods, families are increasingly torn. There is little care, little concern and little communion left. Our intellectual skills and scientific knowledge seem to say we can do anything, but we cannot get along with our friends. We push down. Disorder, disturbance, tumult, revolution, even anarchy are the fruits of the false friend. Injustice grows.

James asks, "Is this the world you want?" Then James shares the results of a wise life founded on the fear of God. He gives us seven fruits of true wisdom. He portrays the ideal, the potential for the wise in the Lord.

The Seven Tasty Fruits

The seven fruits are as practical as morning. They work in the nuclear family and in the global village. Here are fruits that restore, comfort, bring peace. This is a love life that binds wounds, heals diseases, frees oppressed. Justice is established. Wrongs are made right. Let us hear the question again, "Is this the kind of world you want?"

First, *wisdom is pure*. That is, it is solely dedicated to the Lord and his will. It follows no other masters. This is not a percentage life. It is a call from him to lose our lives, to die. What a gift for a family, for one to seek first life for the other. The potential is fantastic. Like a little child so engrossed in a game that even hot dogs can't lure him home, so is a wisdom that seeks only love for the other.

Wisdom is peace-loving. This is a matter of initiation. It is not only praying for peace, but actively working for it. It is opening up self to forgive, repent, discuss with the other. It is not insisting on one's own way. It is found in giving in, lowering the voice. Peace-loving is no definition. It is action.

Gentleness is a fruit of wisdom. The New English Bible translates this word "considerate." Wisdom does not stand on its own rights. It does not fly off the handle at the drop of a hat. It does not mope around after losing an argument. It may not even argue. It says, "let's try your way," rather than a grumbled, "Have it your own way." There is a gentle difference.

Wisdom can be entreated. This is simply to say that the wise one can be reasoned with. Wisdom has ears. It can listen. It is slow to speak. The one who listens performs a very wise service to another. How welcome to hear someone say, "I'll listen," when someone else says, "Let's talk."

Wisdom enlarges life for others. It is contagious as a child's giggle. It may be but a smile, a song, a slap on the back, a tear, a nod, but it counts for the other. It makes a better day for the other one. Like salt and light, wisdom brings new views and new flavours to someone else.

Wisdom is straightforward and sincere. It wears no masks. It needs none. Here is trust and truth. There is no hypocrisy or pretence. A wise person can be met and dealt with where he is because he can say, "You can know me. I will not run and hide."

Finally, *wisdom acts in mercy*. It comes from the same base as God, and that is who or what God is. God is love. From that point and knowledge we have our being. Wisdom does not count yesterday's errors and mistakes, nor does it anticipate tomorrow's blunders. Rather, it lives in the acceptance of today. How freeing that kind of love can be for all. It realizes potential. It removes weights. It allows another to come fully alive, which is in truth the glory of God. Merciful wisdom says without attaching string, "I forgive you, and I love you."

What are these fruits? They are gifts from our Lord, begun in us and continued for us today. He asks us to carry on his work, and promises wonderful results. Again we might ask the question, "Is this what you want for your world?"

To ground our lives totally on God and his word is wisdom. It is following a star of promise like the one followed many years ago. If we follow his star it is bound to make a difference in our lives. Christina Rosseti writes in a poem, "The wise may bring their learning. . . ." She asks, "What can we bring?" Are we able to bring anything at all? She continues, ". . . I give my heart." Let us add, "To God and to one another." That is the wisest life of all.

DAVID KAISER
Lutheran Collegiate Bible Institute
Outlook, Saskatchewan

JOGGING WITH JESUS
Nineteenth Sunday after Pentecost
James 4:7-12 (13—5:6)

Twenty million joggers and runners in the United States! Isn't that amazing? I suppose that's probably one of the most revolutionary exercise programs that's happened in any country. It's a part of the "conditioning" thinking, I believe, that is sweeping through much of the country. And you know it's funny to see people running, isn't it? We see them running in snow and in the rain. At the place I run, I even see people with tee shirts on entitled, "Plumbing Under Repair." I couldn't understand that and I asked somebody one time, "What does that mean?" It turns out these people have either had cardiacs, or open heart surgery and they are getting back in shape. Something that's really taken hold, I believe, the concern for conditioning, the concern for jogging.

The Bible talks about jogging and running a great deal, too. St. Paul says, for example, "I have fought the good fight, I have kept the faith, I have run the race." The anonymous writer of the Book of Hebrews says that now we're surrounded by a great crowd of witnesses, and they're in the stands cheering us on. (It's something like the Drake Relays; the people who have victoriously run the race before us, are saying, "You can do it, you can do it!") The writer of the Book of Hebrews says, "Let us also run the race that is set before us looking to Jesus." We are meant to be people conditioned. We are meant to be people in shape. We are meant to be people, if you will, *jogging with Jesus.*

Our older brother, James, says there are several things that happen to us if we jog with Jesus, if we allow our lives to be put in shape by our loving Lord Jesus Christ. One thing that happens if we jog with Jesus, if we allow him to condition our lives is that, we are put into shape with God.

We Are Put into Shape with God

Isn't it great to be in shape—in a relationship with God, who even has the hairs of our heads numbered? But that's what James says happens to us. We're put into shape with God through Jesus Christ.

I know this business of training and discipline is in opposition to a whole lot of American thinking. The three-car garage is in. "Enjoy" is the key word. "If it feels good, do it." My goodness, how many material things we assume. I found that out this week. My doctor wasn't allowing me to jog yet, and so I thought I'd walk a little way. I walked six miles. I found out that I was assuming a car. It was a very good gift and I had been assuming it all along. You see, we're meant to be put in condition in a different way. Jogging with Jesus means several things, our brother, James, says.

It means that we're to be subordinate to God. Now, subordinated isn't a very good American word, is it? We don't like to be subordinated to anybody. The big number one—first place. Those who are first are where it's at! Anything else is not where it's at! Yet, it becomes a great word, if we allow our thinking to be converted to Jesus Christ. Our thinking being converted to him means that subordinated is made into a great word, because we're thrown back to Number One. We're put back to our "roots" and our "roots" are that Jesus Christ is Lord; that God is our maker, and through Jesus Christ we're put back to him. That's what it means to be conditioned. That's what our brother John says, in Jesus' high-priestly prayer, when Jesus prays this way for you and me. He says, "this is eternal life, that they know thee, the only true God, and Jesus Christ, whom thou hast sent." Knowing him!! I hold in my hands 14 themes from 14 young confirmands entitled, "My Faith Story." A part of these stories says, "here is how God has led me to know him. I know my roots in Jesus Christ." Isn't that a joyous day? They are back home with him; they are conditioned.

But James says we're also to be people put in shape to resist the devil. "Oppose the devil and he'll flee from you." But it's not that of the self-made American person who is strong enough to resist the devil. Nobody who does that wins. Instead, it's the judo style. Satan comes at us with all his power, and we remember the style of Jesus who said when he was tempted, "It is written." Three times he announced that to Satan with calmness and with assurance, and Satan had to get away from him, just like he has to get away from us when we say, "It is written. In the name of Jesus Christ of Nazareth, Satan, you are only number two."

Today these 14 young people will be asked: "Do you renounce the devil, and all his works, and all his ways?" What a frightening question! Do you renounce the devil? By ourselves we cannot do that. But as Jesus did saying in the words of Scripture, "It is written," they, too, can boldly make that promise and you can remake that promise to your Savior too.

Being in shape—Jogging with Jesus—means that we draw near to God. The equipment, says St. John, is all ours. All the equipment is ours. We could paraphrase what Jesus prays in his prayer from John 17, "Father, I'm coming back to you now. But you know what I did: I announced your word to these people. You know what they did with your word? They allowed it to come into their hearts. And you know what? I promise that they have eternal life *now* and it's going to blossom out in heaven forever."

These themes of these young people, announce to the church council, to this congregation, to the entire radio audience, and indeed, to the world, that there are 14 young people that believe that Jesus Christ is their Lord and Savior. That is good news!

Draw near to God, and he will draw near to you! I'm a part of a congregation. In this congregation there are people who believe that. It's a part of their bloodstream. I found out, when I got out of the hospital a few weeks ago, that there were people who had actually organized a prayer vigil for me. They didn't even need a pastor to organize it! They did it themselves and they prayed 24 hours for me! What love! They drew near to God and he drew near to them and to me.

Our brother, St. James, says, "Be cleansed." A part of being conditioned is to be cleansed. How much of our life is distorted and twisted because we fail to be honest with God. That doesn't mean that church is for good little people who come before God and say, "look at how nice and polished my halo is." But rather, we are sinful people. That's a part of us. That's not a put-down, that's the way it is. So we come before God and say, "God—I can be honest with you." We can go through exercises and say, "Who have I hurt this week? How have I hurt them? How do I feel? Do I still feel mad and hateful? What are *you* going to do about it?" And he is the one that can come in in that kind of an honest situation, and heal us.

Jogging with Jesus Means that We Know Him

When we jog with Jesus, we're put into shape with other people. We're never converted to God without also being converted to other people. Our brother James says there is something destructive about slander. There's something destructive about speaking against somebody. It's sort of an anesthesia. It stops us from a real relationship, from going to the person and being reconciled.

So to jog with Jesus, to run with him, means to be put into condition, to be one with our neighbor. And who among us doesn't need to hear words of comfort, hope, and forgiveness, because only in the power of God can we refrain from slandering our neighbor.

There is a story about four pastors who were out fishing. Now fishing is bad enough (my personal prejudice says). But they were telling stories, kind of doing a confession to one another at night. One pastor confessed his sins to the other three. He confessed that sexually he had been indiscreet several times in his life. The others listened. The second pastor said he had a real weakness toward booze. He told about some sins that he had done there, and the other pastors listened. The third pastor told about his sins of overeating. The potluck was too much for him and he told about his sins of doing that, and the other pastors listened. Finally, the fourth one—what would he say? The sin that he had a problem with, he said, was *gossip!* Boy, were the other three in trouble! Wait till he gets home!

And we laugh about it! That's good that we can laugh about it because we dare to laugh in the face of Satan! We dare to laugh! But we also are to be people put in shape with God enough to face that head on, and say, "Father into your hands I commit my spirit, and I want to be clothed in your righteousness because I can't solve that tongue problem by myself. I know that you can."

Jesus says, "*I* am praying for you!" Jesus is praying for you. What is he praying? "Holy Father, keep them in thy name."

You who are confirming your faith today, Jesus is praying, "Keep them in thy name." You who have been walking with Jesus, jogging with him for a lifetime, Jesus is praying, "Holy Father today I pray that they may be kept in your name." And the thing that happens—what is it? Jesus says, "that they may be one, even as we, Father, you and I, are one." You see, Jesus Christ is praying that you may be in shape with your neighbors. That you may experience that oneness with them.

Conclusion

Jogging With Jesus—put in shape with God. It means health with God and with our neighbors. Not a direction book that our Lord just gives to us, but his very self. He gives himself to us that we may be in shape.

GENE H. HERMEIER
Zion Lutheran Church
Des Moines, Iowa

O.K, illus?

WITH GLORY AND HONOR

Twentieth Sunday after Pentecost
Hebrews 2:9-11

One of the best compliments we preachers can receive is to hear one of our own members say something like this: "You know, pastor, I just feel real close to you. You're so down to earth, so human, so easy to relate to." The implication, of course, in such a compliment is that some clergymen are rather aloof, detached, even distant, and others seem to have that unfortunate habit of separating themselves from people, even their own parishioners. Indeed, it seems some pastors don't want their people to know just how human they really are, and so they go about almost denying their humanity and alienating their people in the process. The church hungers for pastors we can "feel close to."

But it's important for all of us to be able to identify with others and to have others able to identify with us. At the heart of a real marriage, as our Old Testament Lesson today reminds us, there's a oneness between the man and the woman, with each one trying to help the other, and with real identification and understanding one for the other, "bone of my bones and flesh of my flesh!" So too in the relationships between children and parents.

How often a father will pour out his heart and say of his child: "I just can't seem to relate to him or to her." And how equally often our youth today will say of their parents: "They just don't understand me . . . they can't really identify with my situation." Identification is vitally important in all human relationships.

And this is why it's such a relief sometimes (when we're in a close-knit relationship with a friend, or when we're in a sharing situation, like away on a church retreat), it's such a relief to suddenly learn that we're not the only one with problems, and that indeed, everyone in the group has a number of them; in fact, some may have the very same difficulty or concern in life that we have. That's identification, and, boy, we can really relate to these people—we can understand one another!

Isn't that why Alcoholics Anonymous works? For when you get down to it, alcoholics are really the only ones who can identify fully with someone afflicted by the disease. Or again, when someone contracts cancer and is facing an operation, who can better answer that person's questions or alleviate his fears than someone else who has already gone through the same ordeal. That's identification!

Jesus Identified with Us

And that's the good news the writer of Hebrews is emphasizing in our text. Jesus Christ fully identified himself with all of us! "For a little while he was made lower than the angels . . ." (v. 9). "He is not ashamed to call them brethren" (v. 11). He becomes, therefore, fully one with us, like in a good marriage! Or as Paul so beautifully pictures it in his "hymn" in Philippians 2:6ff:

> Who, though he was in the form of God, did not count equality with God a thing to be grasped, but emptied himself, taking the form of a servant, being born in the likeness of men.

William Barclay has said that the basis of the Greek idea of God was detachment; the basis of the Christian idea is identity. And how beautifully Christ identified with us.

Note also the interesting relationship here between this Hebrews passage and Psalm 8, which the writer quotes in verse 6. The point being made is that God, in the very beginning, created us in his image, making *us* a "little lower than the angels," giving us dominion over the earth and all other creatures. God created us, then, to be "crowned with honor and glory." But, of course, mankind "blew" all this, as the events in the garden of Eden make abundantly clear. Adam and Eve's story is our own, and the result is, as we well know, that we just aren't what we were created to be! And that's putting it mildly! We become our own worst enemies, and we end up frustrating both ourselves and our creator with our prodigal ways, our sinfulness and self-ishness. And thus, we who were created to be "crowned with glory and honor," and have dominion over everything, can't even control ourselves or our passions. To paraphrase Paul, the good we want to do, we don't do at all; and the evil we don't want to do, we end up doing! "O wretched man that I am!"

But the good news—the grace and love of it—is that it's pre-cisely into this sad state of affairs that Christ Jesus, our "brother," comes! He who shared in the very creation of the world, now is himself "made lower than the angels" as he iden-tifies fully with us in our plight. Theologians refer to this, of course, as Christ's humiliation. He assumed our very human na-ture and circumstance. He enters our state of defeat, as Paul writes the Corinthians (2 Cor. 8:9): "For you know the grace of our Lord Jesus Christ, that though he was rich, yet for your sake he became poor, so that by his poverty you might become rich!"

He Suffered for Us

And that leads to another great lesson in this passage from Hebrews, namely, Christ not only identified *with* us, but also suffered *for* us. So the writer refers to "the suffering of death" and says that it was "by the grace of God" that Christ "might taste death for everyone."

It's one thing for someone to identify himself with our needs, our suffering and our death. It's quite another thing for that someone to take our place and to suffer and die for us! Here then, is the Good Shepherd, who not only identifies with and lives with his sheep, but who actually lays down his life for them, for *us*!

The whole concept of a *suffering* messiah is emphasized here, and those Jewish Christians, reading this letter, probably found it hard to accept. This just wasn't the Messiah of their dreams! And yet, this is precisely the Messiah often described by the Old Testament prophets. Listen to Isaiah 53:9ff:

> Surely he has borne our griefs and carried our sorrows;
> yet we esteemed him stricken, smitten by God and af-
> flicted. But he was wounded for our transgressions, he
> was bruised for our iniquities; upon him was the chas-

tisement that made us whole, and with his stripes we are healed.

The great high priest, as the writer of Hebrews is to refer to Christ (v. 17), comes, and tastes death as *our* substitute, becoming an expiation for our sins. He is indeed, as John pointed out, "the lamb of God, taking away the sins of the world." He not only identifies with us. He also dies for us, to make us what God had created us to be!

He Is Exalted, and So Are We!

And that's the other great message in this text, that as Christ is exalted, so are we! He met our sorrows head on . . . he faced our temptations . . . he suffered and died. This was his humiliation. But there was also an exaltation. For he "who for a little while was made lower than the angels," is now "crowned with glory and honor because of the suffering of death." As Paul says in Philippians 2:9ff:

> Therefore God has highly exalted him and bestowed on him the name which is above every name, that at the name of Jesus every knee shall bow, in heaven and on earth and under the earth, and every tongue confess that "Jesus Christ is Lord" to the glory of God the Father.

But there's more! For what is even more wonderful for us is that along with this exaltation that Christ receives because of his suffering and death, he also brings "many sons to glory." And that means us all! We too are freely given honor and victory; indeed, the full and beautiful glory, intended by the Father for us from the beginning of creation, is now finally secured for us, once and for all, by Christ!

He stooped down to become one with us in order that God could bring us, his "many sons," to glory. That's how much he loves us! And we now share the exaltation and the glory that Christ wins for himself. He makes us more than conquerors as he heals us of our brokenness, forgives us of our sinfulness, and restores our lost glory and honor as children, "brethren," of a gracious and loving Father!

ROBERT L. HOCK
St. John Lutheran Church
Winter Park, Florida

IT'S TIME TO BUILD

Twenty-first Sunday after Pentecost
Hebrews 3:1-6

The great biblical pessimist, the writer of the book of Ecclesiastes, has an unforgettable statement on "appropriateness" in his third chapter. Lines are often quoted from his enumeration of the appropriate time for a great range of human endeavors from kissing to death.

In one phrase he says that there is a time for tearing down and a time for building. That idea concerns us today as we look at our text. Ecclesiastes makes clear that all times are set by God who gives and withholds opportunity.

We have surely passed through a time of tearing down from the 1960s until now. The tumult and convulsion have threatened the fabric of American life. But it seems we have recently entered a time for building.

Then let us build.

Some attitudes, institutions and habits needed tearing down. In our own country racism was so strong it was often reenforced by law. That racism needed tearing down. Corporations and political institutions were placing property and power ahead of people, and that value-structure needed attack. Too many men and women were smoking too much, and that habit needed to be called into question.

But, as Jesus once pointed out, to drive out demons and leave a vacuum results in the return of other, fiercer demons, so we dare not only tear down what is weak or evil, we must build good things in its place.

To state a truism: Houses must be built. They do not simply appear. Our text uses the figure of houses to say something about building for God.

When I see a deserted house, wherever it may be but especially a lonely, deserted farmhouse along an interstate highway, I am stirred to all kinds of reflections. Among them is a feeling of sadness as I think how happy and proud someone was when that house was first built and lived in. For it had to be built by someone and for someone.

That observation, that every house is built by someone, is included in our text. From that obvious premise the writer of Hebrews leaps over several intermediary conditions to the grand aside: God is the one who has built all things. But grand as it is, it is in this instance merely an aside. His main point is that God's house—by which he means people—needs faithful care by persons as great as Moses and Jesus and as ordinary as you and I. Therefore, think about this:

It's Time to Build

"Think of Jesus," is the first instruction of the author of Hebrews to those who are called by God. This time he urges reflection on Jesus as the High Priest who established God's house (that is, his people) in exemplary fashion. For God chose him to do just that.

Priests had a vital, if somewhat ordinary role, in the Old Testament process for working out a relationship between God and his people. Seldom were priests dramatic figures like the prophets, God's shock-troops who burned out like flaming meteors. Only when the office of priest combined with the work of the prophet in one person were their lives extraordinary.

Otherwise priests taught, supervised sacrifices, performed rituals and tended the sacred properties. Jesus fulfilled one of those roles so exceptionally, the sacrificial one—by offering up himself for the sins of all—that he can only be called the great high priest.

The Book of Hebrews contains in its seventh chapter (vv. 26-27 TEV) a further elaboration of this idea.

There we read: "Jesus, then, is the High Priest that meets our needs. He is holy; he has no fault or sin in him; he has been set apart from sinners and raised above the heavens. He is not like other high priests; he does not need to offer sacrifices every day for his own sins first and then for the sins of the people. He offered one sacrifice, once and for all, when he offered himself."

Moses, on the other hand, who is also cited in the text as an exemplary worker in God's house, was not really a priest at all but a prophet and a political leader of his people. He performed priestly functions, however, even though his brother, Aaron, became the first official high priest of the covenant people.

What Moses did faithfully in tending God's house was, of course, far less than what Jesus did. For Moses only tended God's house, that is, the covenant people; Jesus, on the other hand, is the basis of God's eternal covenant and the foundation of God's house, his called-out people, the *ekklesia*.

What the writer of Hebrews gives us in this text is a complex picture of God and his church with implied intricacies that need unfolding. Though the picture is intricate and complex, the point is simple: "We are God's house if we keep up our courage and our confidence in what we hope for."

We Can Build

Our self-assurance that we can build stems not only from the resources of mind or material which we command but also, and even primarily, from the recognition that God has chosen us to build.

There is a time for building as there is a time for tearing down, and God himself has opened up opportunities to build his house. The opportunity is here now to begin to restore the moral and spiritual capital on which we have drawn and which has been gradually dissipated. In no way is this dissipation more evident than in the lack of moral consensus which ordinarily undergirds a stable society.

Apparently we cannot agree on what good conduct is in human relationships, in family life, and even in personal habits. Nor is this true only of minor differences; it is also apparent in major areas of moral concern like honesty, responsibility, and decency.

It is time painstakingly to build a climate of moral values so that young and old are not caught in the morass of mere whim or of driving human desire. We need to stress again the molding of conscience, the development of good order and the creation of discipline that comes from definable social and personal goals.

We can build, too, the very undergirding of moral values, namely, a steadfast faith in God which springs from the proclamation of God's saving love for us. Our faithfulness at a congregation's worship services and our interest in the meaningful development of those services to glorify God and help people are ways to build. But so are the words and actions by which we communicate our concern for human justice, our emphasis on mercy and our efforts to walk humbly with God.

Out of the biblical evidence we draw the message which builds human lives and human society in a pattern God has set: love the Lord God with all your heart, soul and mind and your neighbor as yourself. To move toward the completion of that kind of house we must ourselves be established in the new hope God gives us through Jesus Christ, who reconciled us with God by his death and resurrection.

The Emphasis Is Simple

The emphasis in the final sentence of our text is clear and simple: as people who are God's "house," we need courage and we must have confidence in what we hope for.

When we look at characteristics of people with living Christian faith we seldom point to courage. We may speak of strong faith or good self-control or exceptional kindness but somehow courage is not often enumerated in the list of Christian virtues.

For a time of building, however, courage is vital. The courage we need is the courage to risk something in the name of Jesus. Perhaps there is no better recent example of visible Christian courage than that which was shown by those who, out of Christian conviction, marched and worked for racial justice in the 1960s. The scenes of Selma and Montgomery will not soon be forgotten. Or we might call up once more the image of Dr. Albert Schweitzer who summoned Christian courage to leave success in several careers to go to serve a very evident and desperate need.

It takes courage, too, to go on with jobs that seem unrewarding personally but from which we cannot escape. To continue there faithfully and with a cheerful heart takes courage which comes from our relationship to God who gives meaning to life. It takes courage to risk misunderstanding and ill will because we defend the friendless, admonish the wayward, or protect the weak. It takes courage to give for Christ's cause until it helps, to accept roles of responsibility in church and community, or simply to endure pain when we are called to suffer.

Coupled with the simple and clear emphasis on courage by God's strength is the encouragement to maintain confidence in our Christian hope. That hope is beautifully defined in 1 Peter 1:3-4 (TEV): "Let us give thanks to the God and Father of our Lord Jesus Christ! Because of his great mercy he gave us new life by raising Jesus Christ from death. This fills us with a living hope, and so we look forward to possessing the rich blessings that God keeps for his people."

If we keep alive the confident hope that heaven awaits us, that the greatest salvation is still to be revealed when this world ends and Jesus comes again, then we faithfully show that we are God's house.

Now is the time to build, whether that be in the ordinary and inconspicuous way of simply tending God's house by helping people in his name or whether some more spectacular prophetic role of risk shall be our lot, let us keep up our courage and our confident hope in God. Also in our building it will be God himself who works through us if we do it faithfully.

OMAR STUENKEL
Lutheran Church of the Covenant
Maple Heights, Ohio

ON ESCAPING GOD'S WORD
Twenty-second Sunday after Pentecost
Hebrews 4:9-16

A magazine publisher gets religion and announces that the image of his magazine will change from pornography to something more socially uplifting, and thereby joins former Black Panther and Watergate hatchetman as the latest examples of the fact that God's word has power—the power to change lives.

Now certainly famous converts are nothing new. You can trace them back through history all the way to the Apostle Paul. The fact that God's word has the power to change lives has been proven again and again. And not just through dramatic conversions, but also in your life and mine. Not one of us would be here this morning had not God in some way or another touched our lives and made some changes. Maybe not in such a dramatic way as with certain well-known people, but since the day of our Baptism, in one way and another, God has been touching our lives, changing and molding, forgiving and cleansing, directing and guiding. God's word has power.

Proclaiming the Power

That God's word has power should not surprise us, for our text says, "For the word of God is living and active, sharper than any two-edged sword, piercing to the division of soul and spirit, of joints and marrow, and discerning the thoughts and intentions of the heart. And before him no creature is hidden, but all are open and laid bare to the eyes of him with whom we have to do." Whether the word of which the author speaks is the Word Incarnate, Jesus Christ, or the written word, the Scriptures, or any other way that God may choose to speak to us, that word comes to us with power and with force. The text piles four statements about that word, one upon the other, moving from the general to the specific, from the word itself to what that word does to you and to me.

The word of God is first of all, *living*. His word is not just some ancient writing, of interest only to scholars who deal in antiquities. It is not just a word spoken long ago that brought a world into being, but now lost in the echoes of time. It is as modern as tomorrow. It has to do with our living of each day.

Second, it is *active*, powerful, effective. It is able to accomplish what it says. When God speaks, things happen. It is not just something to be read, or heard, or even studied. It is something to be lived and done.

240

Third, it *penetrates*. It is sharper than any two-edged sword. It gets inside. It really cuts. It cuts so deep that it pierces "to the division of soul and spirit, of joints and marrow." It tests our body and soul, bringing both under the scrutiny of God. Whatever a person does and whatever a person thinks and whatever a person is, all are exposed to the testing of God's word.

And finally, it *discerns* "the thoughts and intentions of the heart." That's the whole point of it. It is not just a word that is living and active in some impersonal way or in some other person's life. It discerns *my* thoughts. It exposes *my* intentions. It points its finger directly at me. God's word has power—not just some power in general, but power applied directly to me. Power to expose my sin. Power to expose my life. Power to bring me to my knees in repentance and faith.

I Defend Myself Against that Power

Certainly what has been said is true, but in all honesty I have to ask myself, "How often does this happen? How often does the word of God actually do that to me?" Certainly I agree that God's word is living and active. Certainly there have been times when that word has really cut me and exposed me. Certainly there have been times when I have felt like David of old, with the finger pointing directly at me, hearing the words, "Thou art the man." Certainly there have been times when the thoughts of my heart have been so revealed that I have been driven to my knees in repentance. But when was the last time that happened? How often does it happen?

When the Scriptures were read from the lectern this morning I didn't notice anyone squirming in their seats as though some accusing finger were being pointed directly at them, or notice any winces of pain as though some sword had pierced them, dividing soul and spirit, joints and marrow. And I must confess that when I read these words the first time to prepare this sermon, I didn't feel any stab of pain as that sword cut into me. Certainly there have been times when I have felt that way, but I admit that that is not my most common experience with the word. Much of the time I read God's word, and for the effect it has on me I could just as well be reading the comic strip. But why should this be so? How do I manage to keep that sharp two-edged sword from doing any damage? How do I manage to render it so harmless much of the time?

I would suggest that I use some rather effective armor to

defend myself against that two-edged sword of God's word. I suspect that you use the same sort of armor.

One way I defend myself is that very often I just don't listen. That's not too difficult to do. All I need to do is think of something else as the words are being read. Like a skilled swordsman I deftly sidestep the thrust of my opponent, and his sword may be sharp, but if he can't hit me with it he can do me no damage. So I hear or even read the words, but they might just as well be in Latin, for they convey no meaning to me because my mind is somewhere else.

A second way I defend myself is that I apply the words to someone else. That is a particularly effective defense for me. I study a text and I have to pay attention to it, for I know that I have to preach on it the next Sunday. But instead of asking the question, What does this say to *me*? I ask the question, How can I apply this to my congregation? What does it say to them? I use questions like these as a shield, so that the sword of the word glances off, away from me, and towards someone else.

Of another thing I can do is to make God's word into some vague generality. God's word says, "Love one another." And I say, "Yes, everyone ought to love everyone." The trouble with that is that everyone ends up being no one. Thus the sharp sword bounces off my armor harmlessly. It is only when I say "I must love Jim" that the word becomes specific and cutting.

Or I defend myself by coming to the word with my own preconceived ideas. I decide what the word means, and it doesn't mean exactly what it says, it means something less, something that I am already doing very nicely. The word says, "Love one another," and I decide that I am doing that very nicely every time I put something in the offering plate. After all, that money helps feed the hungry and clothe the naked. By that little act I very nicely keep the command and have no need to do anything more. My preconceived idea means that the sword bounces harmlessly off my armor. The blow may hurt a bit, I may even be jarred into giving a bit more next Sunday, but it doesn't really cut and expose the intentions of my heart. I continue to seek my own good and go my own way and achieve my own peace of mind. That hasn't changed.

And if all else fails, I can simply refuse the word and turn away from it. If that sword does get through so that I know I am guilty, I can still refuse to submit. I can stand surrounded with my own self-righteousness, bloodied perhaps, but unbowed, and refuse to admit that God is right and I am wrong. I can turn and go my own way, and God will let me go.

The Rich Young Ruler

We meet someone like that in the man we usually call "The Rich Young Ruler." He comes running to Jesus with his question, "What must I do to inherit eternal life?" And Jesus says, "You know the commandments: 'Do not kill, Do not commit adultery, Do not steal, Do not bear false witness, Do not defraud, Honor your father and mother'." And that blow from the sharp sword should have cut deeply, but instead it bounces off the armor of his preconceived ideas, for he has convinced himself that this is exactly what he has done all his life. "All these I have observed from my youth." He has convinced himself that all God meant when he said, "Do not kill" is to forbid murder. He did not realize that this is also a positive command to help our neighbor with all his physical needs.

So the sword thrusts again, "One thing you lack; go, sell what you have and give to the poor. . . ." That thrust is more telling. That lays bare the intentions of the heart. Now he knows that he has not really kept the commandments, not in their positive sense, not in using his possessions to help those in need. But he refuses the command, and he walks away sorrowfully. His armor has been pierced. The sword of the word has drawn blood. But instead of dropping to his knees in surrender, he turns and walks away.

And in turning away he refuses not only the command but the healing. For the word cuts, but it also heals. The word exposes sin, but it also grants forgiveness. The word exposes the intentions of man's heart, but it also exposes the intentions of God's heart. And in turning away he refuses the very thing he came to find—eternal life. Inside the armor of his own self-sufficiency he nurses his wounds, but the healing does not come, for we cannot heal ourselves. "Then who can be saved?" they asked Jesus. And Jesus replied, "With men it is impossible, but not with God; for all things are possible with God."

Threat or Promise

Our text says, "And before him no creature is hidden, but all are open and laid bare to the eyes of him with whom we have to do." Is that a threat or a promise? God's eyes see everything. Nothing is hidden from him. Is that terror or comfort? Does that promise life or death? Are those eyes that see everything the eyes of the Judge, or the eyes of my Father?

The answer to those questions depends on what I do when that sword of the word aims at my heart. Am I willing to throw down my armor in surrender, or will I continue to fight against him? Do I not grow weary of defending myself? Yet, if I surrender, will that sword kill or heal, will I find life or death? The answer can be found in our text for today which speaks of all that God has prepared, that pictures the One "with whom we have to do" as a Great High Priest, able to sympathize with us in our weakness, and ends with the invitation, "Let us then with confidence draw near to the throne of grace, that we may receive mercy and find grace to help in time of need."

JOHN R. THORSTENSEN
Grace Lutheran Church
Fairmont, Minnesota

RUN FOR YOUR LIFE!

Twenty-third Sunday after Pentecost
Hebrews 5:1-10

For every high priest chosen from among men is appointed to act on behalf of men in relation to God (Heb. 5:1).

At about midnight on Saturday there was a knock on the pastor's apartment door. When he opened the door, he saw a lad whom he had befriended.

"May I use your bathroom," asked the boy. "Sure," said the pastor. Later the boy asked for something to eat. "I don't have anything to eat, but here is two dollars. Now you can leave," he said.

The boy hesitated a minute and requested a glass of milk. When the pastor returned from the refrigerator, he could not believe what he saw. There stood the boy, whom he had befriended, with a butcher knife aimed at him saying, "I'm going to get you."

The pastor called for help and the neighbors came. When the boy heard the neighbors coming, he became frightened and ran away.

This true story suggests the ways a person runs for life. The pastor runs for his life as a Christian act of commitment in befriending the boy.

The neighbors enact a Christian commitment in responding to the call of a neighbor in need. The boy, as we do, runs for his life. Or maybe we should suggest, the boy runs from his life.

The Christian fact of life is simple—run *for* your life in Christ or *from* life.

We are on the run. The Bible tells a story in the Book of Hebrews. The Church Fathers, wisely, I believe, placed the Book of Hebrews under the protection of Paul and his letters. Rooted in this book is the concept, Greek in origin, that we run away from the world's imperfections seeking the perfect heaven.

Jesus Christ is greater than Moses, the angels, and Joshua, the Book of Hebrews announces. Heaven's perfection has come to earth in Jesus. Everyone knew that a priest was a bridge between God and man. Jesus the great high priest showed everyone the way to God.

The qualifications for a priest were set forth: "For every high priest chosen from among men is appointed to act on behalf of men in relation to God. . . ."

A priest has sympathy for people and is divinely appointed. Now we understand there is a priest, in the pastor who befriended the boy and a priest in the neighbor who responds to the call for help. There are people who care for the boy running for his life.

For the Christian comes this clear mandate from the Book of Hebrews. Run for your life, all the way—all the way into a close relationship with the high priest, Jesus Christ. Another mandate says to move out in faith. The author of the Book of Hebrews knew the people were weary, on the verge of turning back. The going seems to be more than they were able to endure. In faith, they could continue on and be a neighbor in need.

Explore running for your life, in these two dimensions: drawing near to Jesus, and moving out in faith.

Draw Near to Jesus

The journey is a long one. In another place, the Book of Hebrews is bold to call the journey, a race. A priestly race, catching up to God is the name of this journey. Always reaching beyond yourself suggests, run for your life, draw near to Jesus.

As Jesus chose to run the agonizing race of mission, so is the Christian's life described. In the funeral service, at the grave, we say, "Ashes to ashes, dust to dust." The service reminds us, in death as in life, where we come from and where we are going. Out of the earth, creation, we came, and to the earth we return.

If Jesus the high priest is greater than Joshua, Jesus will do more than Joshua. Remember, Joshua's run for life. Out of the

wilderness came the children of Israel. Drawing near to Jerusalem their destination, they must first conquer Jericho. Jericho
is the proud guardian of the treacherous path that the Good
Samaritan took to Jerusalem. How did Joshua lead the people
to victory? For six days, they marched around the city walls.
You can feel the seventh day climax coming. The seventh day
had to be a good day to celebrate a job well done, as God had
done in creation. On the seventh day, Joshua and the children of
Israel shouted, "On to Jerusalem." The walls fell, and the victory
was God's. On to Jerusalem, run for your life, draw near to the
new Jerusalem, Jesus.

True, as the story is, how does the truth work out as we run
for life now?

Early in the morning the telephone rang. "Pastor, I need to
talk with you." The voice was recognizable and drunken. "Where
are you?" "In the parking lot at the taxicab stand downtown,"
he responded. Arriving at the parking lot, we talked. He was on
the run for life. Finally, he said, "I have nothing to live for, and
nobody will help me." He drew a gun and said, "I'm going to end
it all." "But first," I said, running beyond myself, "you will have
to kill me because I care about you." He held the gun, unsteadily.
Finally he put the gun down and said, "I couldn't kill someone
who cares about me."

Everyone is a priest called by God. How else could you lay
your life on the line and live beyond yourself?

Everyone is called to be a priest, sympathetic to people. Could
you be Christian and not care for people?

Run for your life, draw near to Jesus, because God as you see
God in Jesus is a *verb:* evoke—invite—foster—offer—explore—
witness—celebrate—confront—encourage!

Move Out in Faith

As you run for life, you need faith. You have drawn near to
Jesus. And you need faith as you befriend a boy, or answer the
neighbor's need, or lay it on the line in the parking lot.

Abraham had faith to run where he knew not. Moses, in the
Exodus, had faith to lift his hands out over the sea, so the chil-
dren of Israel on the run from Egypt could escape. The report,
"The Lord drove the sea back."

St. Paul, witness to the Isthmian games in Corinth, reports
Christians run not for a perishable wreath, but an imperishable
prize.

246

You run, in faith to win in Christ: a boy and a butcher knife
. . . a neighbor and a cry for help . . . a man in the parking lot!
You run with faith in Christ. Each day, by God's grace, you
are a priest.

JAMES R. STEPHENSON
Holy Trinity Church
Hickory, North Carolina

IT'S WHO YOU KNOW

Twenty-fourth Sunday after Pentecost
Hebrews 7:23-28

It's a long way from the priesthood of Melchizedek to the
priesthood of all believers, from Abraham to Jesus of Nazareth,
from man to God. That's what this text is all about, bridging the
gap between man and God.

As we read the seventh chapter of Hebrews we are appre-
hended by the feeling of being in an ancient and distant time.
Our desire to draw near to God is heightened by the awareness
that the mysterious Melchizedek in some small ways stimulated
Abraham's desire for access to God. Perhaps we think it would
be nice to have a man like Melchizedek around today—someone
holy to smooth things over with God. Perhaps we yearn for a
simpler life-style reminiscent of another age, when we would have
more time to think of God. Perhaps Melchizedek could do for us
what he did for Abraham, give us a blessing after the battles of
our lives. Yes, we feel it would not hurt to have such a person
at our elbow to usher us into the presence of God. Someone who
knows the ropes. Someone who has connections, because after all
we know, it's not what you know that counts, but who you know.

Let's for a minute take a look at this mysterious figure, Melchizedek, so we can better understand what it means when Jesus
is called a priest forever after the order of Melchizedek. Melchizedek is mentioned only twice in the Old Testament, in Psalm
110:4 and in Genesis 14. Now, according to Genesis 14, Melchizedek was both a king and a priest. He was king of Salem, which
means "peace." This was later identified in Psalm 76:2, with
the town of Jerusalem. He was also a high priest. We are told
that he was priest of God most high. Melchizedek went out to
meet Abraham as Abraham was returning from the defeat of
Chedorlaomer and bestowed upon Abraham a blessing. Abraham,
in turn, gives Melchizedek a tenth of everything he had. If we

examine Melchizedek's name we find that the name itself means "king of righteousness." This, tied together with the name of the town of which he was the king, means he was king of peace. He was Melchizedek, he was king of righteousness. So, the significance of Melchizedek was not only in what he did, but also his name gives evidence of his godly qualities. Nowhere do we find anything said about the birth or death of Melchizedek. This silence about the start and finish of Melchizedek's life is linked together with what Hebrews says, "A priest for ever." So this is the Melchizedek in the order of which Jesus is designated as a priest for ever. King and high priest, righteousness and peace for ever.

Yes, we are aware of the fact it's not what you know, but who you know in this life. If you go to find a job, you might be the most brilliant person in the world, but if you don't know someone who can open the doors, or, more properly, if someone doesn't know you, if there isn't someone who can recommend you, who can open doors for you, you have a difficult time indeed finding a job in your chosen field. It's not what you know, but who you know. The gospel, of course, is based on the assumption, that it's not what you know, but who you know. More properly said, it's not what you know, but who knows you. For we are told that we have a high priest after the order of Melchizedek, a high priest for ever, this one Jesus Christ. He knows us, has claimed us, has chosen us.

Robert Young of "Marcus Welby" and "Father Knows Best" fame has a granddaughter in our preschool. One day I was introduced to Robert Young and we chatted for ten or fifteen minutes about the preschool, about educational philosophy, about his delight with our preschool and the excitement that the children felt, particularly his granddaughter, when they came to preschool everyday. It wasn't long after that that an article on Robert Young appeared in the L.A. *Times*. Somebody was talking about that and I said, "Oh, I know him," and that got everybody's attention. Then I relayed to them the conversation that I had had with Robert Young and conveyed an impression that I certainly was an authority on Robert Young and that I knew him. Well, reflecting on that later I realized what I really meant when I said, "I know him," is that I had met him and had had a few minutes of casual conversation with him. But as far as knowing Robert Young, I don't know him and certainly as far as any relationship goes, he doesn't know me. In fact, I would imagine that he wouldn't even remember me. So many times we say, "I know someone," and really mean that we have met them, but the important thing about knowing is to be known by someone else, so there is a relationship. To be remembered by somebody else means that we know each other. A relationship can never be a one-way street.

So, when we say it's not what you know, but who you know, we are really talking about relationship. What the author of Hebrews is saying is that we are known by Christ and that means we can know him. We can live in relationship to God through him. We know this is not just some sort of intellectual exercise, because in the second chapter of Hebrews, we read these words, "Therefore he had to be made like his brethren in every respect, so that he might become a merciful and faithful high priest in the service of God, to make expiation for the sins of the people. For because he himself has suffered and been tempted, he is able to help those who are tempted" (2:17-18).

This high priest was without sin and yet there is no temptation that is common to humanity that Jesus did not experience. So when he remembers us and when he makes an intercession for us, he knows whereof he speaks. He has endured this for us. Suffering and temptation refer not only to form, but also to content. Jesus was not just God in human form. He was not just an angel in a slot machine, but he was fully God and fully man. The author of Hebrews goes on to say later on in the fifth chapter, that Jesus learned obedience. "Although he was a Son, he learned obedience through what he suffered" (5:8). This high priest is one who is spoken of as creator of heaven and earth and also as one who has suffered temptation. He is fully human and divine. He is not just God disguised as man.

But that is not all that can be said of this high priest. He died once for all and yet his priesthood is forever. "It is altogether fitting," says the author of Hebrews, "that we should have such a high priest, holy, blameless, unstained, separated from sinners, exalted above the heavens." As a result of that, "He is able for all time to save those who draw near to God through him, since he always lives to make intercession for them." So this work of mediation that Christ does as a high priest is always effective. It has been done once for all, but now Christ, who always lives, intercedes for every person who lives in relationship to him. He intercedes for all who know they have been known by God in Christ.

So, when we say it would be nice to have somebody after the order of Melchizedek who could intercede for us and get us in closer touch with God, we need look no farther, because we have such a high priest in Jesus Christ. He died once for all. He daily intercedes for us and his intercession is not some kind of ivory tower intercession, because he was fully man. He can sympathize and empathize with every person because he has been there. He was tempted in all respects as we are.

So here in Jesus Christ, we truly find a king and the high priest. We find righteousness and peace. We find one who in the beginning was with God and without him was not anything created that was created. We find one who came to earth, not simply disguised as man, but was fully the God-man. We find one who lived and died and put death to death. We find one who rose again as God's yes to man and who ascended into heaven and sits at the right hand of God the Father Almighty. We find one who intercedes for us even now.

This is the high priest that we have. This high priest even now intercedes for us. This high priest desires that we grow in grace. This high priest desires that we reach out and touch the lives of others with love and concern just as we have been touched with his love.

Jesus, our high priest, knows us. Jesus, our high priest, erases the distance between us and God. Jesus, our high priest, make a right relationship with God possible for us. Jesus, our high priest, lovingly nurtures our growth.

If you know him, you know that, and you can live by God's grace.

ROGER J. BERG
Newport Harbor Lutheran Church
Newport Beach, California

WHO NEEDS A KING?

Christ the King—Last Sunday after Pentecost
Revelation 1:4b-8

Kingdoms and reigning monarchs fill the pages of world history. The flow of power has swung back and forth, and kingdoms rise and fall. Alexander, Genghis Khan, Napoleon, the Caesars of Rome, and others conquered and ravaged the world seeking power, riches, and a crown.

Uprisings against earthly kings and kingdoms have written their history as well. The words, "revolution" and "republic" have been placed in opposition to empire and kingdom. Many who sailed to America came with their vow that they would never live under another king. Oppressive rulers would be left behind. Freedom and individual worth for every person would reign in a land where all are equal.

Yet, substitutes have been crowned in our lives—success, riches, beauty, fame, heroes—but most of all we crown ourselves in pride.

And strangely, we live better than the kings of the past. Most of us have traveled farther and seen more of the world than Alexander the Great. Modern technology has made our homes more beautiful and more comfortable than king's palaces of old. The loyalty and love of our families and friends would be great treasures in the eyes of kings who lived among intrigue, envy, and dangerous foes.

With such success and living in such wealth and comfort, we ask, "Who needs a king?"

God Says We Need a King

For all the bravado of self-made men who would captain their own ships and be masters of their own fates, most find the seas of life too wild and dangerous. Who can set the course? Who can bring some order and meaning to the aimless wandering where men's plans are tossed to and fro? How can one dock the ship gracefully without losing freedom and all that must surely be ours by right?

The emptiness of going our own way and doing our own thing makes the throne of our own construction less attractive than we dreamed. The goals of prosperity and security are too narrowing for our minds. Lives based on comfort and the impulsive purchase of pleasure are unfulfilling. With all our wants answered, seemingly with little effort, from among extravagantly advertised goods, we still ask, "Is this all there is?"

God's answer to all our seeking and questioning catches us off guard. He turns us around completely by his revelation that we need a king. Who needs a king? We do! And the king God has in mind is Jesus.

No Last Minute Decision

With his infinite wisdom, God has foreseen the chaos of a world where everyone sails under a different flag and upon different currents wherever the winds might blow. It isn't a last minute decision on his part to set our course, to anoint a king above all kings and to establish his kingdom where truth and justice are honored.

When the people of promise saw their hopes destroyed with

the fall of their nation and the ruin of the Temple in Jerusalem, they sought a message from God. God answered.

The Southern Kingdom of Judah had lived for over five centuries under their kings and could look back to the golden days of their own King David. But now, their earthly kings were of no avail. Their nation was overrun and the people were led into captivity in a foreign land to live at the whim of other kings.

But, there were those who would not let the hope of God's promises die in that land. Daniel was given a special talent by God to interpret visions and dreams. And it was through one of those visions that Daniel beheld a picture of God's kingly glory. "I saw in the night visions, and behold, with the clouds of heaven there came one like a son of man, and he came to the Ancient of Days and was presented before him. And to him was given dominion and glory and kingdom, that all peoples, nations, and languages should serve him; his dominion is an everlasting' dominion, which shall not pass away, and his kingdom one that shall not be destroyed" (Dan. 7:13-14).

That vision was kept alive among the people and they looked forward to their return to their own land and they kept the hope of their future king before them constantly.

Jesus Kingship Is Questioned

Jesus was that man born to be king. The Gospels keep us informed of his kingship from the very beginning in our Christmas story. The geneologies of Jesus were demonstrations that he is the Son of David.

The Wise Men came looking for him who is King of the Jews. His triumphal entrance into Jerusalem was a deliberate dramatized claim of his kingship. Before Pilate, Jesus deliberately accepted the title of king. On the cross, the title of king was written over his head in three languages, even though it was done in mockery.

It has always seemed so strange to us, who accept Jesus as Lord and Savior, that there were those who could question his kingship. But, kings had never before been born so lowly nor walked so comfortably among common people.

We can understand Kaiser Wilhelm riding into Jerusalem on a prancing white stallion, but it takes a lifetime of sermons to explain Jesus riding in on a donkey. We understand the lofty thrones of earthly kings and stand in awe of those who sit upon them, but the world still stumbles on the idea that the King of kings should be lifted aloft on a cross with a crown of thorns pressed upon his brow. We are reminded that God's ways are not our ways.

When we confess that Jesus is our King, we seek to serve him. If our lives are lived only with good intentions while our actual serving is only self-serving, we align ourselves with all others in history who have questioned Jesus' right to reign.

If all our seeking for meaning and direction in life is sincere, we permit the Scriptures to direct our eyes and hearts to a gracious God who holds the whole world in his hands. His message to us makes all our frantic thoughts disappear.

Let Christ Be King

He says, "Grace to you and peace." It is a greeting from God who is a redeeming God, a God who comes, and will come to his people. The greeting, "Grace to you and peace" comes from the Holy Spirit who speaks to the church. And the greeting, "Grace to you and peace" comes from Jesus Christ, who is the faithful witness, the firstborn of the dead, and the ruler of the kings of the earth.

As we confess that Jesus is King, it becomes ironic to read the biblical accounts of Pilate's questions to Jesus concerning his kingship. Jesus, the faithful witness answers, "You say that I am a king. For this I was born, and for this I have come into the world, to bear witness to the truth" (John 18:37).

Jesus was sent into the world by God and he identified himself with the will of God. He could speak with knowledge about God and God's truth as only the Son can.

As Pilate held before Jesus the defeat of death, Jesus held fast to his mission of gaining victory over death. Jesus is Lord of the dead as he is Lord of the living. There is nothing in life or in death, in this world or the world to come, of which Jesus is not Lord.

It is also ironic that the devil tried to bargain with Jesus promising him the kingdoms of the world. Jesus stepped aside from such a throne in favor of the cross. It was through the suffering on the cross and the power of the resurrection that he won the victory and became ruler of the kings of the earth.

We meet our King at the cross. His kingdom lifts us from our earthbound fears and obsession with death to a confident faith and eternal life. He is Christ our King, now and forever.

An anonymous poet has paraphrased Scripture to say,

> If death is to enter a city
> and be hailed as a child of the King;

Oh death, where is thy victory?
Oh death, where is thy sting?

Who needs a king? We do! Thanks to God our search is ended.
We know the king. We know Christ the King.

M. FRANKLIN PUDAS
First Lutheran Church
Mitchell, South Dakota

"THANK YOU, GOD" IS NOT THE END OF A
CONVERSATION

A Day of Thanksgiving
1 Timothy 2:1-4

Notice how often saying "thank you" becomes another way of saying "Good-by." The guests are leaving. They say, "Thank you for inviting us." The host and hostess say, "Thanks for coming." You leave a store by thanking the clerk who waited on you. And the clerk thanks you for patronizing the store. "Thank you" has become a graceful way of saying good-by, a polite way to end a conversation.

We are here today to say "thank you" to God. The customs of society, a proclamation from our government and the urging of Scripture all tell us we are to give thanks to God. Are our "thank yous" a way to end a conversation with God, a gracious way to say, "Good-by, God?"

Our text for today, which includes one of those urgings for us to thank God, says no. "Thank you," is not the end of a conversation. Nor is it the beginning. Our gratitude to God today is part of a conversation with him that started long ago and will continue forever.

Petitions and Thanksgivings in the Same Conversation

"First of all, then" Paul says, "I urge that petitions, prayers, requests, and thanksgivings be offered to God for all people; for kings and all others who are in authority." Paul puts a high priority on our conversations with God. In this Letter to Timothy he talks about many parts of our relationship with God, but "first of all" he is concerned about our prayer life.

Paul lists four aspects of our conversations with God: *petitions* —when we ask for our own needs; *prayers*—including our meal and bedtime talks with God; *requests* or intercessions—our prayers for others; and last, our *thanksgiving*.

We could spend a long time studying only the first verse of the text. Each part of our prayer life could be examined as we look at what we talk to God about. But this is Thanksgiving Day. We want to look especially at the fact that Paul urges us to thank God.

However our thanks cannot be separated from the other parts of our talks with God. If you do not ask God for help, you will have little reason to thank him either. Unless you also thank him, your petitions and requests become one-way, selfish conversations. Our thankfulness depends on an understanding of God's grace as it has been given to us in Jesus Christ. We ask God for help, not because we have the right to demand his assistance, and not because we can bargain with him or offer anything in return, but because he loves us and has invited us to ask for his blessings. Unless we see God's answers to our prayers as gifts of his love, our thankfulness becomes only a matter of politeness or an effort to keep the gifts coming. True thankfulness is a willingness to say, "I accept a gift, knowing I don't deserve it and I can't return a gift in kind. But I know it comes from one who loves me and wants me to have the gift."

Thankfulness Leads to a Quiet and Peaceful Life

Paul gives us the reasons he wants us to thank God. One is, to quote from the text, "that we may live a quiet and peaceful life with all reverence toward God and with proper conduct." At first glance it seems like that reason belongs only to the petition and request part of our prayers. It makes sense to pray that we may live a quiet and peaceful life with all reverence toward God and with proper conduct. But being thankful also helps us live a quiet and peaceful life with all reverence toward God and with proper conduct.

Our "Thank You, God," is not the end of a conversation because our appreciation affects the way we live. Our thanksgiving today shows that we are grateful for what we have received up until now. But our thanksgiving is more than that. We are also showing the attitude with which we will use the blessings for which we are grateful.

Your thankfulness helps you lead a quiet and peaceful life. When you are thankful to God, you live at peace with him. You then understand your relationship with your Creator/Savior God. Being thankful to him removes the tensions of obligation to him for his care for you. Thankfulness for his grace and forgiveness removes the shame and embarrassment of sin. A life of thankfulness makes it possible for the original "Odd Couple," a Holy God and a sinful person, to live together in peace.

Being thankful to God also helps you live at peace with other people. Being thankful for what you have keeps you from being jealous of those who have more than you. Your understanding of God's grace as shown in your thanksgiving keeps you from being boastful or arrogant toward those who have less than you. Your thankfulness for the blessings you receive through the lives and efforts of other people helps you understand the need for the great variety of people on this earth. Often we resent the differences we see in others. But our thankfulness removes those fears. It lets us live at peace with one another.

Our thanksgiving also helps us live at peace with ourselves. We are often our own greatest competitors. Often we cannot enjoy the scene from the top of the mountain we have just climbed because we see another mountain. Having a thankful heart helps us live at peace with ourselves. It helps us recognize and enjoy the blessings we do have. Our gratitude to God helps us accept our limitations and difficulties without resentment because we know we have some abilities and we have missed many problems. A woman in a nursing home had a sign over her bed that showed that she understood that thankfulness helped her live at peace with herself. It said, "If you can't be thankful for what you have, at least be thankful for what you've escaped."

Thankfulness Pleases God

The text suggests another reason why our "thank you" to God is not the end of a conversation. It says, "This (that is the life of prayers and thanksgiving) is good and it pleases God our Savior." God likes to be thanked for the blessings he gives. Our thankfulness is a sign that his gifts are being received and that we know where they come from.

Yet our appreciation to God must not merely be a way to keep the gifts coming. We can't treat God like a rich old uncle who gives birthday and Christmas gifts as long as you send a thank you letter within one week after each gift arrives. God is not buying us with his gifts. He already has a claim on us. Notice that the text says our thanks pleases God, our Savior. He has a claim on us because he is God who created us. After our sin disowned his authority over us, he reclaimed us by coming to be our Savior and buying us back.

Our thankfulness is one way of showing that our relationship with God is still alive. From the beginning God has always given his people a way to thank him. When we speak of the Old Testament offerings we most often think of the sacrifice for sin which people made when they killed animals on an altar to symbolize a payment for their guilt. But thank offerings were also an important part of the Old Testament sacrificial system. The people brought part of their animals, grain, wine, and whatever else they produced as burnt offerings to God. Their gifts showed that God had given them more than they needed for their own use. The gifts also showed that they trusted God to continue to bless them. They could burn part of their food, and yet know that they would have something to eat the next day.

Our thankfulness includes not only our words and songs, but also our offerings—our offerings of money, our gifts of time effort and love to others.

It pleases God for us to be thankful. Our appreciation shows we are grateful not only for the gift, but also for the Giver. We don't say "thank you" and run. Rather our thanks is a part of our remaining with him.

God Has a Lot More to Give

Another reason that God does not want us to thank him and run is that he has a lot more to give. The last line of our text says that God our Savior "wants everyone to be saved and to come to know the truth" (TEV). It tells us clearly that God wants all people to be saved. God's plan for salvation in Jesus Christ includes all people. He died for everyone.

But just as we often reject his other gifts, we can also refuse his gift of eternal life. God does not force you to use any of his blessings. He prepares them for you. He offers them to you. He wants you to have them because he loves you. And his love has no limitations. He wants you to have not only the blessings of a life on earth, but he also wants you to have an eternal life with him.

When you say, "Thank you, God," today you are not ending a conversation with God. You are not making a graceful exit. You are acknowledging that God has been involved in your life. He lives with you and blesses you. As you thank him for the blessings that you have received up until this moment, you can also thank him for the blessings of tomorrow, next year and all eternity.

ELDON WEISHEIT
Fountain of Life Lutheran Church
Tucson, Arizona